ISBN 978-0-265-97484-1
PIBN 10918051

COHASSET

TOWN REPORT

2008

of the

BOARD OF SELECTMEN
of the FINANCIAL AFFAIRS

of the

TOWN OF COHASSET

Reports of the School Committee
and the
Reports of Other Town Officers

FOR THE YEAR ENDING
December 31, 2008

Paul Pratt Memorial Library
35 Ripley Road
Cohasset, MA 02025

TOWN OF COHASSET

Incorporated 1770

Population January 2008 --- 7,617

President of the United States of America
George W. Bush

Massachusetts Senators
Edward M. Kennedy
John F. Kerry

Tenth Congressional District
Representative William D. Delahunt

Norfolk and Plymouth Senatorial District
Senator Robert L. Hedlund

Third Plymouth Representational District
Representative Garrett Bradley

Annual Town Meeting
Date Set by Board of Selectmen

Election of Officers
Within 35 days of the Annual Town Meeting

APR -- 2009

IN MEMORIAM

Betty Lou Pearce – February 15, 2008
Election Worker

Arlene E. Orr - March 5, 2008
Assistant Treasurer

Janet L. Figueiredo - March 16, 2008
School Bus Driver

Helen W. King – March 21, 2008
Election Worker

Katherine F. Stanton – May 3, 2008
School Committee
Council on Elder Affairs
Library Volunteer
Volunteer for Joseph Osgood School

Jean J. Thompson – June 3, 2008
School Nurse
Council on Elder Affairs
Election Worker

William T. Litchfield – August 22, 2008
Firefighter

Frank Allan MacDonald – September 8, 2008
School Teacher
Recycling Committee

Mary Jane McArthur – September 21, 2008
School Teacher
Selectmen
Advisory Committee
Conservation Commission
Historical Commission
Cohasset Historical Society
Government Island Study Committee
Director – Cohasset Bicentennial

Peter C. Murray – October 14, 2008
School Teacher

ELECTED OFFICIALS - TOWN OF COHASSET

BOARD OF SELECTMEN - 3 YEAR TERM	TERM EXPIRES
Edwin G. Carr	2009
Ralph Dormitzer	2010
Paul E. Carlson	2010
Frederick Koed	2011
Karen M. Quigley	2011

MODERATOR - 3 YEAR TERM

Daniel S. Evans	2011

TOWN CLERK – 3 YEAR TERM

Marion L. Douglas	2011

ASSESSOR – 3 YEAR TERM

Michael C. Patrolia	2009
Elsa Miller	2010
Mary E. Granville	2011

SCHOOL COMMITTEE - 3 YEAR TERM

Richard F. Flynn	2009
Steven R. Fusco	2010
Lucia Flibotte	2010
Adrienne MacCarthy	2010
Alfred Slanetz	2011

TRUSTEES PAUL PRATT MEMORIAL LIBRARY – 3 YEAR TERM

Agnes McCann	2009
Patience G. Towle	2009
Elizabeth B. Baker	2009
Sarah R. Pease	2010
Barbara Power	2010
Stacey V. Weaver	2010
Sheila Evans	2011
Rodney M. Hobson	2011
Marylou Lawrence	2011

BOARD OF HEALTH - 3 YEAR TERM	TERM EXPIRES
Margaret S. Chapman	2009
Stephen N. Bobo	2010
Robin M. Lawrence	2011

COHASSET HOUSING AUTHORITY – 5 YEAR TERM

Helen C. Nothnagle (appointed by Governor)	
Ann Barrett	2009
Christopher M. Allen	2010
Susan L. Sardina	2011
Ralph Perroncello	2012

PLANNING BOARD – 5 YEAR TERM

Michael R. Westcott	2009
Stuart W. Ivimey	2010
Clark H. Brewer	2011
Alfred S. Moore	2012
Charles A. Samuelson	2013

RECREATION COMMISSION – 5 YEAR TERM

Anthony J. Carbone	2009
Abigail Alves	2010
Lisa L. Lojacono	2011
Lillian Murray Curley	2012
James Richardson	2012
Daniel J. Martin, Sr.	2012
Roseanne M. McMorris	2013

SEWER COMMISSIONERS – 3 YEAR TERM

John W. Beck	2009
Sean Cunning	2010
Wayne Sawchuk	2011

WATER COMMISSIONERS – 3 YEAR TERM

John McNabb	2009
Nathaniel Palmer	2010
Glenn A. Pratt	2011

TOWN OFFICERS APPOINTED BY THE BOARD OF SELECTMEN

Town **Manager/Chief** Procurement Officer
William Griffin

Town Counsel
Paul R. DeRensis

TOWN OFFICERS APPOINTED BY TOWN MANAGER

ADA Coordinator
Robert M. Egan   2011

Animal Control **Officer**
Paul Murphy   2011

Assessor/Appraiser
Mary E. Quill

Building **Inspector/Zoning Officer**
Robert M. Egan   2011

Constable
Maria Plante   2009

D.P.W. Superintendent
Carl A. Sestito

Director of **Finance/Town** Accountant
J. Michael Buckley, Jr.

Elder Affairs **Director**
Linda A. Elworthy

Fire Chief
Robert D. Silvia

Fire Department under Civil Service

Randy Belanger	Firefighter/EMT-P	
Paul T. Bilodeau	Captain/EMT-B	
Daniel J. Cunningham	FirefighterEMT-P	
James F. Curley	Firefighter/EMT-B	
John J. Dockray	Lieutenant/EMT-P	
Kevin D. Donovan	Firefighter/EMT-P	
Kevin J. Durette	Firefighter/EMT-P	
James E. Fiori	Firefighter	(Retired 6/30/08)
Robert F. Forde	Firefighter/EMT-P	
John W. Haley	Firefighter/EMT-P	
James E. Hall	Firefighter/EMT-P	
John M. Hernan	Firefighter/EMT-P	
Jonathan M. Hickey	Firefighter/EMT-P	
Frances X. Mahoney, Jr.	Captain/EMT-B	
Robert R. Martin II	Firefighter/EMT-P	
Laura C. Morrison	Firefighter/EMT-P	
Robert A. Nadeau	Firefighter/EMT-P	(Appointed 5/19/08)
Joseph M. Pergola	Firefighter/EMT-P	(Appointed 9/15/08)
Robert F. Protulis	Lieutenant/EMT-B	
Randall W. Rosano	Firefighter/EMT-B	(Retired 7/1/08)
James P. Runey	Captain	
Daniel N. Smith	Firefighter/EMT-P	
Mark H. Trask	Captain	
Eric Wenzlow	Lieutenant/EMT-B	

Call Firefighters

Kathleen Adams	
William Brooke	Lieutenant
John MacNeill	Lieutenant
Jordan MacNeill	
Steven Maynard	
Thomas McKay	
Joseph Migliaccio	Lieutenant
Bruce Pratt	

Forest Warden
Robert D. Silvia

Harbormaster
Lorren S. Gibbons

Shellfish Deputy
Paul L. Pattison, (Constable)

Chief of Police
James M. Hussey

Lieutenants of Police under Civil Service
Gregory J. Lennon
William P. Quigley

Sergeants of Police under Civil Service
David C. Cogill   (Retired Dec. 31, 2008)
John C. Conte
Shellee L. Peters   (Retired July 2008)
Jefferey R. Treanor   (Promoted Oct. 2008)

Patrolmen under Civil Service
Edward P. Bagley   (Transferred to Quincy July 2008)
Garrett A. Hunt
Patrick Kenney
Lisa M. Matos
James P. McLean
Brian M. Peebles   (Part-Time Permanent Intermittent)
Patrick W. Reardon   (Appointed April 2008)
John H. Small
Regen E. Steverman
Christy J. Tarantino
Daniel Williams   (Appointed July 2008)
Paul M. Wilson
Francis P. Yannuzzi, Jr.

Plumbing and Gas Inspector

Recreation Director
John M. Worley   2008 (Retired 4/30/08)
James E. Carroll, Jr.   2011

Sealer of Weights and Measures   2009
Robert M. Egan

Town Archivist
David H. Wadsworth   2009

Treasurer-Collector
Linda Litchfield

BOARDS, COMMISSIONS, COMMITTEES and REPRESENTATIVES
APPOINTED by the BOARD of SELECTMEN

Cable Advisory Committee
Paul Carlson	2009
Patricia Martin	2009
James Morrison	2009
Michael Zotos	2009

Call Firefighters Committee
Bruce W. Pratt
Robert D. Silvia
Ian R. Fitzpatrick
Richard Bonanno

Cohasset Common Historic District Commission
Gail Parks (District Resident)	2009
Janice Crowley (Realtor)	2009
Sarah H. Gomez, (District Resident)	2010
Victor Lanzillotti	2010
Virginia Norman (Historical Society Rep)	2010
Can Tiryaki	2010
William A. Hurley (District Resident).	2011
Peter J. Wood	2011

Cohasset Cultural Council
Diane Kennedy	2009
D. Alex Adkins	2009
Betts H. Murray	2009
Selene Carlo-Eymer	2010
Sarah Torrey	2010

Community Preservation Committee
Alfred Moore, Planning Board	
James G. Dedes, Conservation Committee	
Vacant, Open Space	
Ralph Dormitzer, Selectmen	
Helen Nothnagle, Senior Housing	
Sarah E. Charron	2009
Margaret Charles	2011
Stuart Ivimey	2011
Jeffrey Waal	2011

11

Conservation Commission

David H. Farrag	2009
Edward Graham	2010
Veneta Roebuck	2010
Douglas Wilson	2010
Sarah E. Charron	2011
Deborah S. Cook	2011
Richard M. Karoff	2011
Jonathan R. Creighton (associate member)	2009
Richard Perkinson (associate member)	2009

Economic Development Committee

Michael R. Milanoski	2009
Timothy J. O'Brien	2009
Timothy Chamberlain	2010
Alain Pinel	2010
Peter L. Brown	2011
Darilynn Evans	2011

Elder Affairs, Council On

Marjorie Murphy	2009	
Joseph Nedrow	2009	
John W. Campbell	2009	
Anna A. Abbruzzese	2010	
Nancy Barrett	2010	(resigned 5/14/08)
James F. Kearney	2010	
Edward T. Mulvey	2010	
Karen Oronte	2010	
June Hubbard	2011	
Dolores A. Roy	2011	

Emergency Management

Arthur H. Lehr, Director
Glenn A. Pratt, Deputy Director

Fence Viewers

Kearin A. Dunn	2011
Glenn A. Pratt	2011

Government Island Advisory Committee

Constance M. Afshar	2009
Hamilton T. Tewksbury	2011

Growth and Development Task Force
Clark H. Brewer	N/A
Richard W. Swanborg, Jr.	N/A
Michael R. Westcott	N/A

Harbor Committee
Lorren S. Gibbons, (ex-officio)	
John F. Bertolami	2009
Adam Donovan, (Commercial Fisherman)	2009
Gail Parks	2009
Charles Peterson	2009
Mark Rattenbury	2009
Harald Gundersen (Yacht Club Designee)	2010
Lillian Murray Curley (Recreation Designee)	2010
Peter J. Wood	2010

Harbor Health Committee
Noel Collins	
Christopher Evans	
Paul Figueirdo	
Paul Pattison	
Karen Quigley	

Harbormaster - Assistant
Robert A. Johnson	2009
Ryan MacDonald	2009
Thomas J. O'Malley	2009

Historical Commission
Rebecca Bates-McArthur	2009
Marilyn M. Morrison	2009
Hamilton T. Tewksbury	2010
David Wadsworth	2010
Nathaniel Palmer	2011

Housing Partnership Committee
Thomas Callahan	2009
Debra Cammer Hines	2009
Stephen Lucitt	2009
Helen (Taffy) Nothnagle	2009
Margaret Charles	2010
James Lagrotteria	2010
Clark Brewer	2011
Mary E. Grayden	2011
James Hamilton	2011

Keeper of the Lockup
John C. Conte   2009

Keeper of the Town Clock
(1) Vacancy

MBTA Representative
Mark D. Brennan   2011

Metropolitan Area Planning Council
Frederick R. Koed   2011

Norfolk County Advisory Board
Frederick R. Koed   2009

Open Space Committee
Sandra Durant   2011
James (Ted) Carroll   2011

Recycling Committee
 F. Allan MacDonald   N/A
John K. McNabb, Jr.   N/A
Sharyn K. Studley   N/A
Jean White   N/A

Registrars of Voters
Marion L. Douglas, Clerk
Margaret R. Charles   2009
Judith Volungis   2010
Edythe Ford   2011

South Shore Recycling Cooperative Committee
Merle S. Brown
Arthur L. Lehr, Jr.   2011

South Shore Regional School District Representative
Kenneth Thayer   2011

Stormwater Management Committee
Stephen Bobo, Board of Health   2008
James Drysdale, Citizen   2008
Sarah Charron, Conservation Comm   2008
James Kinch, Water Resources Protection Comm   2008
Martin Nee, Citizen   2008
Lawry Reid, President Straits Pond Watershed Ass., Non–Voting 2008

14

Town Hall Restoration and Renovation Committee

David Farrag	2009
Werner Diekman	2009
Donna McGee	2009
Lisa Pratt	2009
David Wadsworth	2009

Town History Committee

Harold E. Coughlin	2009
Louis R. Eaton, Jr.	2009
Nancy Garrison	2009
Julia H. Gleason	2009
James W. Hamilton	2009
Margot Cheel	2010
Jacqueline M. Dormitzer	2010
Ann Pompeo	2010
Ernest Grassey	2011

Veteran Services – Director of

Robert Jackson	(Resigned 12/31/08)

Wastewater Committee

John C. Cavanaro
Paul Davis
James G. Dedes
Joseph R. Godzik (Board of Health)
Jeffrey F. Moy
Raymond Kasperowicz
Stephen N. Bobo, (Board of Health)
Vicky C. Neaves

Weir River Estuary Park Committee

Vincent P. Dunn
Richard J. Avery

Zoning Board of Appeals

Benjamin H. Lacy	2009
Barbara M. Power	2010 (resigned July 8, 2008)
Susan Kent	2010 (to fill unexpired term)
Charles Higginson	2010
S. Woodworth Chittick	2011
Peter L. Goedecke	2011
Kathleen Hunter	2011

BOARDS, COMMITTEES, COMMISSIONS, REPRESENTATIVES
APPOINTED by the TROIKA

Advisory Committee

Vivien A. Bobo	2009
Roger Q. Hill	2009
Edward Lappen	2009
Merle S. Brown	2010
Thomas J. Glavin	2010
Patrick Waters	2010
Chartis Langmaid Tebbetts	2011
Thomas Reardon	2001
Samuel Wakeman	2011

Alternative Energy Committee

Sally Ayers	2009
Michael Bliss	2009
Marie Caristi-McDonald	2009
Rodney Hobson	2009
Mary White	2009
Andrew Willard	2009

By-Law Committee

Jacqueline Dormitzer
Louis F. Eaton
Agnes McCann
Marion L. Douglas, CLERK (ex-officio)
Paul R. DeRensis, ESQ. – TOWN COUNSEL (ex-officio)

Capital Budget Committee

Peter DeCapricio	2009
John Keniley III	2009
Mark Baker	2010
David Bergers	2010
Steve Gaumer	2011

Design Review Board

Robert Egan, Building Inspector, ex-officio
Four Vacancies

2008 REPORT OF THE BOARD OF REGISTRARS

The following elections and town meetings were held:

Presidential Primary, February 5, 2008
Annual Town Meeting, March 29, 2008
Annual Town Election, April 5, 2008
State Primary, September 16, 2008
State (Presidential) Election, November 4, 2008
Special Town Meeting, November 17, 2008

The Annual Listing of Persons seventeen years of age and older as per General Laws, Chapter 51, Section 4 was conducted by mail during January. Any citizen of the United States who is a Massachusetts resident and who will be 18 years old on or before a town meeting or Election Day may register to vote. There is no waiting period to be eligible to register to vote, if you move, you may register to vote as soon as you move into your new home. Registration is closed for a brief period before town meeting and election to allow election officials time to prepare the voting lists. If you register during a "closed" period, you will be eligible to vote only in later town meeting or elections. You must be registered twenty days before all primaries and elections, and ten days before a special town meeting.

Respectfully submitted,

Margaret Charles, Chairwoman
Marion Douglas, Clerk
Edythe Ford
Judith P. Volungis

TOWN MANAGER'S
2008 ANNUAL TOWN REPORT

I am pleased to submit the Town Manager's annual town report for the year 2008. Town finances once again were a central issue over the past year. I was pleased to inform the 2008 annual town meeting that a balanced budget was being presented that did not require an override. By doing so, we were able to maintain level services for town departments and the school system without seeking additional tax levy capacity from the taxpayers.

At the 2008 annual town meeting, two important measures were approved to strengthen the long term financial condition of the Town. A new Capital Stabilization Fund was created to provide a consistent source of money for capital improvement projects and equipment, and a Post-Retirement Health Insurance Liability Stabilization Fund was created to allow the town to put aside funds to offset heath insurance premiums to be paid for retired employees.

During the course of 2008, the significant decline in the federal, state and local economy resulted in a mid-year reduction in state aid to the community. It was thus necessary to curb non-essential spending and closely monitor whether any vacant positions needed to be filled.
On a more positive note, through the efforts of our Finance Director Michael Buckley, the town refinanced bonds issued in 1998 for school construction that will save the taxpayers over $245,000 over the next several fiscal years.

During the past year, the Town saw the retirement of long time Recreation Director Jack Worley. Jack was honored at the annual town meeting for his outstanding service to the community and its residents, and he will be sorely missed. I was pleased to announce that local resident Ted Carroll was appointed to replace Jack and I am confident that Ted will also serve his community in an outstanding manner.

On a professional level, I was pleased to announce during the past year that I had been elected to serve on the Board of Directors of the Massachusetts Interlocal Insurance Association Health Benefits Trust and the Property and Casualty Group.

I wish to remind town residents that the town maintains its official web site at www.townofcohasset.org. I encourage town residents to visit our web site to learn more about town government, check to see meetings to be held, download numerous town forms, and keep posted on important developments in town government.

In closing, I wish to sincerely thank the Board of Selectmen for its support and guidance during the past year. I would like to express my thanks to the many town employees who day in and day out provide excellent services to our citizens. I would also like to thank the many volunteers who serve on our many boards, commissions and committees. It is through the combined efforts of our elected officials, town employees and volunteers that we serve the interests of our residents and businesses.

William R. Griffin
Town Manager

2008 REPORT OF THE BOARD OF SELECTMEN

Dear Residents of Cohasset:

During this past year, the Board of Selectman addressed may diverse issues. One of the most important issues is the impact of the downturn in the economy upon the town of Cohasset. With the help of our town manager Bill Griffin and our town Finance Director Mike Buckley, we have developed and implemented a plan that responds to the recession, making tough decisions about funding and spending. Each department has cut back on expenditures, and been forced to do more with less, while continuing to serve the community. Today we present a balanced budget. We thank the hard work of all town employees at this critical time.

To counteract the budget cuts, we asked each town department to apply for and actively pursue every grant opportunity available to the town. We have pursued public-private partnerships where available, including the turf field project and the Town Hall restoration project to allow us to continue to maintain and grow appropriately.

In addition, the Board of Selectman charged various departments and organizations in Cohasset to prepare a summary of "shovel-ready" projects to be considered for funding under President Obama's Federal Stimulus Bill. The town submitted 16 projects totaling 21 million dollars for consideration. The range of these projects was wide and diverse, including desperately needed flooding mitigation and culvert, road, and bridge infrastructure investments. We proposed water and sewer upgrades, renewable and innovative energy opportunities, and school building upgrades.

The federal stimulus bill that passed in February will make possible moneys available for these projects soon. While we do not expect that all of these projects may be funded, the town showcased the resourcefulness of our people, pulling together information and details under tight deadlines to present the projects in a compelling way

This past year, the Board welcomed Karen Quigley. Karen brings to the Board a wide range of talents and interests, raging from a passion for protecting our environment to helping the board stay focused on priorities. Her participation has been a welcome addition to the team.

During this town meeting, residents will be asked to make some very tough decisions about the finances of the town, priorities, and issues that face us every day. The diversity of the members of our town means that there will be disagreements. But, the Board hopes that these disagreements will be tempered with respectful discourse and thorough discussion.

Aside from the issues to be discussed during this Town Meeting, the Board and the members of this Town worked together to address the following:

Presentation of RTF Brochure by Eagle Scout Candidate Graham Sinclair – Eagle Scout Sinclair's project goal was to increase recycling in Town. The brochure provides a step-by-step for how individuals can help to accomplish this goal.

Fees for the Municipal Facility Stickers – The level for fees related to commercial licenses was revisited.

Capital Request for Information Technology Master Plan – We addressed whether the town should fund the preparation of an information technology master plan for all town departments and the school department.

Senior Center Property – The Council on Elder Affairs has been working to locate a parcel of land upon which a future Senior Center could be built.

Committee on Town History – Mr. Jim Hamilton and Mrs. Jacqueline Dormitzer distributed copies of their newest book, "Exploring Historic Cohasset" -- a must read about Cohasset's rich history.

Stormwater Management Committee (SMC) –The Stormwater Management Committee's charge was finalized.

Discussion on Treat's Pond – The debate and resolution about wetland replication and flooding in the area of Treats pond remain a high priority.

Federal Stimulus Package – For several weeks, Chairman Carr and Mr. Griffin worked closely with town groups to develop proposals for consideration for funding under the Federal Stimulus bill.

Affordable Housing Trust Membership – The Housing Partnership Committee recommended membership for the Affordable Housing Trust. They suggested that one member be a Selectman with an additional six members that come from the Housing Partnership Committee. Presently, the partnership is a nine member committee with seven active members.

Open Space Committee – Ms. Deborah Shadd and Mr. Richard Avery joined the Open Space Committee

40B Proposal for 25 Ripley Road – This issue has come before the Board on several occasions and continues to be discussed.

Trust for Public Lands – Morrissey Property – The Open Space Committee reviewed the benefits of the Morrissey property, which is 12 acres of land located behind Town Hall. The Committee is very much in favor of this land being acquired by the Town as they feel it will link together many other protected parcels and offer great trails and recreation. After careful consideration due to financial concerns, the Board chose not to purchase the Morrissey property.

Goal Setting Session – The Board of Selectman scheduled a session for reviewing the goals of the Board in order to ensure accountability and focus.

Liquor Hearing for All Alcoholic Restaurant License for Blue Restaurant, Inc. at 156 King Street – Mr. Kevin D. Kelley, Sr. applied for and received a liquor and restaurant license for the commercial property most recently operated as Pacini's.

Proposed Regional Public Safety Dispatch Center –The towns of Cohasset, Hingham, Hull and Norwell began to meet to discuss the possibility of creating a regional dispatch center for police, fire and emergency services.

Introduction of New Police Lieutenant Jeffrey Treanor – Police Chief James Hussey introduced newly appointed Jeffrey Treanor to the Board and reviewed the Lieutenant's background. Lieutenant Treanor thanked the Board, the Chief, fellow officers from Cohasset, Hingham and Scituate, as well as his wife and children. His daughter then pinned him with the Lieutenant pin.

Special Town Meeting Article Review - Citizen's Petition – Turf Field – Mr. George McGoldrick provided the background of Cohasset Sports Partnership which spearheaded the petition for funding a turf field. The Fall Town meeting voted to proceed with the public-private partnership.

Ron Ford – Cross Country Meets at Wheelwright Park – Mr. Ford came before the Board to indicate that Cohasset now has a cooperative cross-country team with Hull High School. It was his hope to use the park for training purposes on a regular basis, as well as for around four specific dates for meets.

Departmental Review
The Board of Selectman reviewed every department in the town for purpose and budget, and encouraged the use and pursuit of grants to help control costs.

Cohasset Day Update – Mr. Peter Brown and Ms. Darilynn Evans of the Economic Development Committee (EDC) approached the Board with a request for another Cohasset Day following the resounding success of this year's inaugural event. A second event is planned for next year.

In closing, the Board of Selectmen look forward to an upturn in the economy and our continued work to keep Cohasset the beautifully charming, quintessential New England town that we love. The Board thanks the citizens of Cohasset for your participation at town meeting and for your ongoing participation in town activities. It is the people of Cohasset that make this town the special place we call home.

Respectfully submitted on behalf of the entire Board of Selectman, Ralph Dormitzer, Paul Carlson, Karen Quigley, and Fred Koed

Edwin G. (Ted) Carr
Chairman

ANNUAL REPORT
REPORT OF TOWN COUNSEL
2008

This year was a very active and successful year for the Law Department:

1. <u>Advice & Legal Documents</u>. Numerous advisory opinions were rendered throughout the year to various Town officials and Boards relating to a wide variety of issues and subjects. Frequent and ongoing attention was given to reviewing and/or drafting Bylaws, numerous contract documents and agreements, easements, procurement documents, public road documents, Warrants for Town meetings (both special and annual town meetings), compliance with State Ethics Act, Open Meeting Law, public records requests, various Town rules and regulations (including new/revised Storm Water Management regulations and Village District Design Guidelines), subdivision control issues for proposed developments, and other legal documents.

2. <u>Administrative Agency Proceedings</u>. The Town was involved with a number of state or federal administrative agencies, including issues before Department of Environmental Protection, Alcohol Beverage Control Commission, Attorney General of the Commonwealth and the Army Corps of Engineers.

3. <u>Projects</u>. We assisted with issues related to Wind Energy, storm water management and flood control issues, the Community Preservation Act, various road issues, Little Harbor/Atlantic Avenue sewer expansion project issues, the Avalon, Village Business and T.O.D. proposals, the Cook Estate project, Central Cohasset Sewer Treatment Plant Expansion Project issues, licensing issues, the MBTA Greenbush line, 40B Comprehensive Permit issues, various regulatory environmental issues involving Cat dam, Treats Pond, and Jacobs Meadow, affordable housing issues, enforcement procedures for various town agencies, and acquisition of watershed properties to protect the town's water supply.

4. <u>Labor Issues</u>. We assisted the Town in general employee matters and in connection with employee grievances, labor arbitrations and retirement issues. We also provided advice from time to time during the year regarding the interpretation and application of collective bargaining agreements and the processing of grievances. In addition, several non-union personnel issues, including possible disciplinary proceedings, occurred during this year.

5. <u>Litigation</u>. As of December 31, 2008, the number of claims and lawsuits in which the Town is a party total 23 as follows:

- 3 Matters involving the Board of Selectmen/Town Manager:
     <u>Commonwealth of Massachusetts v. Town of Cohasset</u>, Suffolk Superior Court, C.A. No. 38652.
     <u>DeWolfe v. Town of Cohasset</u>, Norfolk Superior Court, C.A. No. 04-01061.
     <u>JER Trust #2, Polly Dean Trustee v. Town of Cohasset</u>, Norfolk Superior Court C.A. No. 2008-00868

- 7 Matters involving the Board of Appeals:
     <u>Chief Justice Cushing Highway Corporation v. Board of Appeals</u>, Mass. Land Court No. 243862.

Ledgewood Estates, Inc. v. Board of Appeals, Mass. Land Court No. 302403.
Morrissey v. Board of Appeals, Mass. Land Court No. 263788.
Kuolas v. Board of Appeals, et al., Land Court No. 334159.
Susan Tehranian v. Ross, Steven A. Trustee of GMR Nominee Trust and Board of
    Appeals; Land Court Misc. No. 344297.
Schramm v. Board of Appeals Peter A. Cundall and Ann C. Stenbeck, Norfolk Superior
    Court C.A. No. 2007-01700.
Schramm v. Board of Appeals, Peter A. Cundall and Ann C. Stenbeck, Norfolk Superior
    Court, C.A. No. 2008-00031.

- 1   Matter involving the Planning Board:
        Campedelli, Noreen v. Cohasset Planning Board, Building Commissioner Egan and
            Lawrence P. Aherne, Jr. and Karen Aherne, Land Court Misc. No. 330226.

- 1   Matter Involving the Board of Health
        Paul R. Buckley and Patricia M. Buckley, Albert P. Buckley and Joan F. Buckley v. Board of
            Health and Wilmarc Charles; Norfolk Superior Court C.A. No. 2008-01289.

- 6   Matters Involving the Police Department

        Local 66, New England Police Benevolent Association and the Town of Cohasset, JLMC-
            0918P.
        Cohasset Police Association-NEPBA, Local 66 and Town of Cohasset, American Arbitration
            Association No. 11 390 01971 08.
        Cohasset Police Association-NEPBA, Local 66 and Town of Cohasset, AAA No. 11 390 01292
            08.
        Cohasset Police Association-NEPBA, Local 66 and Town of Cohasset, AAA No. 11 390 01972
            08.
        Cohasset Police Association-NEPBA, Local 66 and Town of Cohasset.
        Shellee Peters - Application for Accidental Disability Retirement - Norfolk County Retirement
            Board.

- 1   Matter involving the Fire Department
        Local 2804, International Association of Firefighters and Town of Cohasset, JLMC-08-24F

- 4   Claims pending:

        Arthur Roberts v. Town of Cohasset (Police Department).
        Kathleen Crosby and William Bell (Sewer Commission).
        Barrow v. Town of Cohasset.
        Silva v. Town of Cohasset (DPW).

Respectfully submitted,
Paul R. DeRensis
TOWN COUNSEL

METROPOLITAN AREA PLANNING COUNCIL
ANNUAL REPORT
2008

Created by an act of the Legislature in 1963, the Metropolitan Area Planning Council (MAPC) promotes inter-local cooperation and advocates for smart growth by working closely with cities and towns, state and federal agencies, non-profit institutions, and community-based organizations in the 101 cities and towns of Metropolitan Boston. MAPC strives to provide leadership on emerging issues of regional significance by conducting research, building coalitions, advocating for public policies, and acting as a regional forum for action.

MAPC provides technical assistance and specialized services in land use planning, water resources management, transportation, housing, resource protection, economic development, public safety, geographic information systems (GIS), collective purchasing, data analysis and research, legislative and regulatory policy, and the facilitation and support of inter-local partnerships. More information is available at www.mapc.org.

MAPC is governed by 101 municipal government appointees, 21 gubernatorial appointees, and 13 appointees of state and City of Boston agencies. An Executive Committee comprising 25 elected members oversees agency operations. The agency employs approximately 40 professional staff under the leadership of an executive director. Funding for MAPC activities is derived from governmental contracts and foundation grants, and a per-capita assessment on member municipalities.

To better serve the people who live and work in Metro Boston, MAPC has divided the region into eight subregions. Each subregion is overseen by a council of local leaders and stakeholders, and a staff coordinator provides organizational and technical staff support.

Advancing Smart Growth

MAPC is directed by statute to adopt, from time to time, a comprehensive regional plan. Our current plan, **MetroFuture:** Making a Greater Boston Region, was adopted by the Council on December 2, 2008. This initiative, which has engaged over 5,000 individual and organizations throughout the region, will guide Metro Boston's growth and development, as well as the preservation of critical resources, through the year 2030. At the December 2 meeting, Council members and MetroFuture friends and supporters voted to move the project from planning into advocacy and action, and participants helped to set priorities among a series of implementation strategies designed to move MetroFuture into this dynamic next stage. MetroFuture is uniting the efforts of MAPC, partner organizations, and the thousands of "plan-builders" in an effort to alter regional priorities and growth patterns consistent with the new plan.

As a member of the Massachusetts Smart Growth Alliance, MAPC helped to form the Transportation Investment Coalition last year. This year, the group of business, environmental, public interest, and planning organizations changed its name to Our Transportation Future, and has actively advocated for savings, efficiencies, and new revenues to address the state transportation finance deficit.

MAPC has continued its participation on a zoning reform task force chaired by Undersecretary for Economic Development Gregory Bialecki. The **"Land Use Partnership Act,"** developed through the task force, would establish a framework for municipalities to designate growth and preservation areas, and to develop consistency between master plans and zoning. The bill would significantly modernize the state's outdated zoning and subdivision laws, providing a menu of reforms to all municipalities, and additional relief to those who choose to opt into the bill's planning and smart growth requirements. Passing legislation to reform zoning and planning in the Commonwealth will remain a key area of focus at MAPC throughout 2009.

Collaboration for Excellence in Local Government

Subregional councils continued to communicate with MAPC's eight regions and to gather citizen input this year. Most of the subregional coordinators hosted legislative breakfasts this year, where participants could prioritize legislative goals and ideas with their delegation.

Through its Metro Mayors Coalition, MAPC helped 21 communities secure more than $2 million in Shannon Grant funding over the past three years to implement multi-jurisdictional, multi-disciplinary strategies to combat youth violence, gang violence, and substance abuse. Our North Shore Coalition has grown and flourished during 2008, working on issues as diverse as transportation planning, anti-gang programs, and consolidation of services.

Collaboration for Public Safety

MAPC performs fiduciary, planning, and project management duties for the **Northeast Homeland Security Regional Advisory Council (NERAC)**, a network of 85 cities and towns north and west of Boston. In 2008, MAPC helped to develop evacuation and sheltering plan templates across the region, and created three regional caches of emergency response equipment that can be loaned out to municipalities for drill exercises or emergencies.

MAPC completed **Natural Hazard Mitigation Plans** for 46 cities and towns this year, on top of the 29 plans already completed in recent years. Each plan recommends strategies to mitigate the impacts of natural disasters *before* they occur, along with a GIS map series depicting areas subject to various natural hazards.

Collaboration for Municipal Savings

MAPC's Regional Services Consortia administered procurements for more than 50 cities and towns, saving communities up to 20% on purchases such as office supplies, paving services, and road maintenance. In 2008, MAPC performed multiple procurements for five consortia: North Shore, South Shore, Metrowest, Northwest and Merrimack Valley (the last in collaboration with the Merrimack Valley Planning Commission). MAPC also entered the vehicle fuels market in 2008, procuring a contract for several South Shore towns.

Reliable Data, Available to **All**

MAPC, along with the Massachusetts Executive Office of Transportation, continued this year to provide municipalities with **Pictometry Oblique Aerial Imagery Technology** free of charge to cities and towns. The Pictometry Oblique Aerial Imagery Technology allows users to display features such as buildings, land areas and hydrology, which may be viewed from several directions and at different scales.

In April 2008, Pictometry International once again conducted a flyover of the entire state that provides five-way aerial imagery for all public sector agencies statewide. The five-way imagery consists of four oblique views (north, south, east and west) and one straight down view that may be viewed through Pictometry's Electronic Field Study software version 2.7, which is also available at no cost to municipalities.

MAPC also continued expanding the MetroBostonDataCommon.org Web site, which provides on-line mapping and chart-generating tools for users. This year, the Massachusetts School Building Authority contracted with MAPC for analysis and consulting services, including analysis of the impact of new schools on enrollment patterns. The Data Center also began distributing a monthly e-mail newsletter highlighting new datasets and resources for constituents.

MAPC's data center is partnering with the Donahue Institute at the University of Massachusetts to encourage more accurate counts on the **2010** Federal Census. MAPC is helping municipalities prepare for the Census in many ways, including advocating for the formation of Complete Count Committees that can target hard-to-count population groups such as recent immigrants and renters in each city and town.

Getting Around the Region

MAPC continued its popular Regional Bike Parking Program, negotiating discount group purchasing contracts with three leading vendors of bicycle parking equipment. This allows MAPC communities, the MBTA, and the Department of Conservation and Recreation to purchase discounted equipment. The Boston Region MPO, the Executive Office of Transportation, and the Federal Highway Administration have provided generous funding to support 100% reimbursement of the cost of eligible bike parking equipment bought through this program. Communities around the region have used the program to put new racks at schools, libraries, parks, and shopping areas. A total of 788 racks holding 2472 bicycles have been installed at 25 communities throughout the region.

MAPC continued its work on the Regional Pedestrian **Plan,** administering a survey this year to nearly 2,000 people. The plan will identify policies to make walking more convenient, safe and practical.

On Beacon Hill

- **Municipal Health Insurance:**
  MAPC continued encouraging municipalities to join the **Massachusetts Group Insurance Commission (GIC),** which can help communities save millions of dollars each year by taking advantage of lower insurance rates available through the GIC. To date, 27 municipalities have joined the GIC.

- **Shannon Community Safety Initiative:**
  Over the last three years, MAPC's advocacy and grant development services have helped more than two dozen communities to secure funding for interdisciplinary programs that focus on youth violence, drugs, and enforcement against gangs. The program was funded at $13 million in Fiscal 2009.

- **Statewide Population Estimates Program:**
  A $600,000 line item in the 2008 budget provided the State Estimates Program with more resources to prepare for the 2010 Census. This program will help correct the deficiencies of recent population estimates and to prevent similar deficiencies from occurring in 2010. Conservative estimates suggest Massachusetts stands to gain between $2.5 million and $5 million per year in federal funding, or between $7.5 million and $15 million between 2007 and the 2010 Census as a direct result of the program's efforts.

- **Surplus Land:**
  MAPC continues to advocate for passage of a new policy on the disposition of surplus state land. Specifically, we continue to build support for our proposal that encourages smart growth development on surplus land while giving municipalities a meaningful role in the disposition process, a discounted right of first refusal, and financial participation in the proceeds.

- **Community Preservation Act:**
  CPA has been very popular throughout the region, but recently the state matching fund has declined precipitously. Legislation filed by Senator Cynthia Creem (D-Newton) and Representative Stephen Kulik (D-Worthington) would secure adequate funding over the long term for the state's CPA matching fund, and encourage even more communities to join.

- **District Local Technical Assistance**
  The planning assistance offered through the District Local Technical Assistance Fund (DLTA) was funded at $2 million for Fiscal 2009. It enables the state's 13 Regional Planning Agencies, including MAPC, to provide municipalities with technical assistance in two key areas: achieving smart growth land use objectives, and consolidating procurement, services and planning across city and town lines.

South Shore Coalition (SSC)
Braintree, Cohasset, Duxbury, Hanover, Hingham, Holbrook, Hull, Marshfield, Norwell, Pembroke, Rockland, Scituate, Weymouth

The South Shore Coalition comprises representatives or appointees from the Planning Board and Board of Selectmen or City Council from each of the member municipalities. The Coalition is staffed by MAPC and the Chairman is Holbrook Town Administrator Michael Yunits. The Coalition meets monthly to discuss issues of mutual interest and to learn about MAPC activities and products.

The year 2008 began with a highly successful South Shore Forum in January, on the topic of New Parking Strategies for Town and Village Centers. Over 60 residents and municipal officials attended the forum to hear from parking experts and to discuss application of innovative parking concepts on the South Shore. Since the forum, many cities and towns in the subregion have conducted studies or revised their development controls to try out new concepts.

At subsequent meetings in 2008, participants discussed a variety of topics, including the Patrick Administration's Zoning Reform proposals; best practices for streamlined permitting; the regional Suburban Mobility Program; transportation funding priorities; and recommendations for MetroFuture, MAPC's long-range regional plan. Coalition staff also provided occasional technical assistance to city and town planners and facilitated the preparation and submittal of two letters of interest for the region's Suburban Mobility program.

MAPC Annual Report prepared and submitted by Marc D. Draisen, Executive Director, Metropolitan Area Planning Council.

2008 REPORT OF THE TOWN CLERK

As the year 2008 comes to a close, I respectfully submit my seventeenth report as Town Clerk. It has been a very active year. Unexpectedly the Presidential Primary's date changed from March 4, 2008 to February 5, 2008. This was followed by the Annual Town Meeting, March 29, 2008, Annual Town Election, April 5, 2008, State Primary on September 16, 2008, State (Presidential) Election on November 4, 2008 and the Special Town Meeting, November 17, 2008. The AutoMark Voter Assist Terminal is in place to mark the ballot selections of voters who are visually impaired, have a disability, or who are more comfortable using an alternative language.

More of our books are out being preserved and restored with funds we received from the Community Preservation Committee. Among these are the originals of the Document of Incorporation by the Legislature, a 1657 document entitled the Three Score Acres, Early Land Division – 1895, Selectmen Minutes 1882-1900. Many of these documents were hand written and were in desperate need of restoration.

As always, I would like to thank town officials, department heads, town employees, election workers, committees, citizens of Cohasset and to my assistant for their support and assistance during the year.

Respectfully submitted,

Marion L. Douglas
Town Clerk

Presidential Primary – February 5, 2008

Polls opened at 7 a.m. and closed at 8 p.m.
Percent voted – 53.5%
Absentees – Pre. 1 – D – 67, R – 115; Pre. 2 – D - 48, R - 34.

Election officers sworn in by the Town Clerk, Marion Douglas, at 6:45 a.m. were as follows:

Carol St. Pierre	Debra Krupczak
Grace Tuckerman	Jody Doyle
Kathleen Rhodes	Katherine Lincoln
Katherine Whitley	Roger Whitley
Michael Patrolia	James Carroll
Sandra Murray	Patricia Ranney
Abigail Alves	Gail Collins
James Contis	

Democratic Party – 1510

Pres. Pref.	Pre. 1	Pre. 2	Total
John R. Edwards	6	8	14
Hilary Clinton	323	376	699
Joseph R. Biden, Jr.	4	2	6
Christopher J. Dodd	1	0	1
Mike Gravel	0	0	0
Barack Obama	409	367	776
Dennis J. Kucinich	0	2	2
Bill Richardson	2	0	2
No Preference	2	3	5
Write-Ins/Scattering	0	2	2
Blanks	2	1	3
Total	749	761	1510

State Committee Man

	Pre. 1	Pre. 2	Total
Gregory M. Shanahan	440	467	907
Write-Ins/Scattering	4	0	4
Blanks	305	294	599
Total	749	761	1510

State Com Woman	Pre. 1	Pre. 2	Total
Karen F. DeTellis	443	456	899
Write-Ins/Scattering	1	1	2
Blanks	305	304	609
Total	749	761	1510

Democratic Party – Town Committee

Town Committee Group	286	324	610
Agnes McCann	335	388	723
Thomas J. Callahan	355	408	763
Susan Kent	326	364	690
Gail J. Collins	332	376	708
Kevin McCarthy	317	366	683
Edwin H. Tebbetts	357	374	731
Patricia A. Laugelle	341	407	748
Sally L. Sisson	345	378	723
Chartis L. Tebbetts	387	405	792
Peter J. Pescatore	330	359	689
Edwin G. Carr	333	368	701
Judith Chute	320	354	674
Donna J. McGee	348	403	751
Roseanne M. McMorris	370	424	794
David J. McMorris	340	392	732
Margaret R. Charles	357	394	751
Frederick R. Koed	373	441	814
Carol A. Barrett	328	367	695
Ronald Goodwin	390	449	839
Helen A. Lieb	331	357	688
Edward Lappen	347	366	713
Pamela A. Miles	325	353	678
Betsy W. Connolly	344	392	736
Edward J. Connolly	327	386	713
Coleman F. Nee	325	373	698
Write-Ins	7	5	12
Blanks/Scattering	17,625	16,986	34,611
Total	26,501	26,959	53,460

Republican Party – 1260

Pres. Pref.	Pre. 1	Pre. 2	Total
John McCain	317	271	588
Fred Thompson	2	0	2
Tom Tancredo	0	0	0
Duncan Hunter	0	0	0
Mike Huckabee	9	8	17
Mitt Romney	368	259	627
Ron Paul	7	10	17
Rudy Guiliani	0	0	0
No Preference	0	2	2
Write-Ins/Scattering	3	2	5
Blanks	1	1	2
Total	707	553	1260

State Committee Man

	Pre. 1	Pre. 2	Total
John P. Cafferty	449	355	804
Write-Ins/Scattering	3	4	7
Blanks	255	194	449
Total	707	553	1260

State Committee Woman

	Pre. 1	Pre. 2	Total
Paula E. Logan	492	386	878
Write-Ins/Scattering	11	3	14
Blanks	204	164	368
Total	707	553	1260

Republican Party – Town Committee

Town Committee Group	Pre. 1	Pre. 2	Total
Town Committee Group	243	214	457
Lisa A. Creighton	273	234	507
Terese D'Urso	302	252	554
Daniel S. Evans	348	267	615
David Farrag	298	252	550
F. Roy Fitzsimmons	304	279	583
Edythe B. Ford	294	238	532
Thomas A. Fogarty	283	242	525
Martha K. Gjesteby	327	265	592
Juliette D. Guild	345	266	611
Louis S. Harvey	318	273	591
Bruce A. Herzfelder	333	244	577

Town Committee Group (continued)

Stuart Ivimey	296	249	545
Leonora C. Jenkins	327	280	607
Raymond Kasperowicz	317	260	577
Alexander C. Koines	280	231	511
Paula E. Logan	391	299	690
Beth E. Marsden-Gilman	311	240	551
Jean M. Muir	301	256	557
Kevin F. O'Donnell, Sr.	300	281	581
Paul M. Ognibene	267	226	493
Nathaniel G. Palmer	307	242	549
Karen M. Quigley	326	264	590
Kenneth J. Roth	278	243	521
Peter Richardson	273	229	502
Alfred Slanetz	303	239	542
Catherine B. Taylor	265	226	491
Judith P. Volungis	301	251	552
George B. Watts, Jr.	312	241	553
Jamie G. Williams	304	251	555
Edward F. Woods	320	256	576
Grace R. Tuckerman	209	259	468
R. Murray Campbell	340	274	614
Write-Ins	15	5	19
Blanks/Scattering	463	11,240	11,703
Total	10,473	19,568	30,041

Green Rainbow – 3

Pres Pref.	Pre. 1	Pre. 2	Total
Jared Ball	0	0	0
Ralph Nader	0	1	1
Elaine Brown	0	0	0
Kat Swift	0	0	0
Cynthia McKinney	0	1	1
Kent Mesplay	0	0	0
No Preference	0	0	0
Write-Ins/Scattering	0	0	0
Blanks	0	0	0
Total	0	2	2

State Committee Man	Pre. 1	Pre. 2	Total
Write-Ins/Scattering	0	0	0
Blanks	0	0	0
Total	0	0	0

State Committee Woman

Write-Ins/Scattering	0	0	0
Blanks	0	0	0
Total	0	0	0

Town Committee

Write-Ins/Scattering	0	1	1
Blanks	0	0	0
Total	0	1	1

Working Families - 0

Pres Pref.

No Preference	0	0	0
Write-Ins/Scattering	0	0	0
Blanks	0	0	0
Total	0	0	0

State Committee Man

Write-Ins/Scattering	0	0	0
Blanks	0	0	0
Total	0	0	0

State Committee Woman

Write-Ins/Scattering	0	0	0
Blanks	0	0	0
Total	0	0	0

Town Committee

Write-Ins/Scattering	0	0	0
Blanks	0	0	0
Total	0	0	0

Polls closed at 8 p.m. and the results were declared at 9:10 p.m.

A True Record, ATTEST:

Marion L. Douglas, Town Clerk

Article #	Description of Article
1	Accept annual town report. Unanimous
2	Report of committees. Unanimous.
3	Operating budget. Unanimous.
4	Union contracts and other salary adjustments. Indefinitely postponed.
5	Fund Capital Improvements. Unanimous.
6	Community Preservation Committee. Unanimous.
7	Unpaid bills from previous fiscal years. Indefinitely postponed.
8	Supplemental appropriations for FY2008. Adopted.
9	Capital Stabilization Fund. Unanimous.
10	Post retirement health insurance liability stabilization fund. Unanimous.
11	Personnel classification & compensation bylaw. Unanimous.
12	Smoking bylaw amendment. Unanimous.
13	So Shore Recycling Cooperative – agreement. Unanimous.
14	Zoning bylaw – Wind Energy Conversion Facility Bylaw. Unanimous.
15	Zoning bylaw - Permitted uses – Table of use regulations. Unanimous.
16	Zoning bylaw – Amendments to Section 8. Unanimous.
17	Photovoltaic array system – Paul Pratt Memorial Library. Indefinitely postponed.
18	Sewer Betterment. Unanimous.
19	Affordable Housing Trust Bylaw. Adopted.
20	Zoning Bylaw – Inclusionary Zoning. Indefinitely postponed.
21	Harbor Study Funding. Indefinitely postponed.
22	Treat's Pond restoration project funding. Amendment of a proclamation. Proclamation adopted.
23	Repurchase of cemetery Lot funding. Unanimous.
24	Stormwater Management Bylaw. Adopted.
25	Citizens Petition – Operation of leaf blower's bylaw. Defeated.

Annual Town Meeting -- March 29, 2008

At the Annual Town Meeting held on Saturday, March 29, 2008 at the Cohasset High School Sullivan Gymnasium the following articles were contained in the warrant and acted upon as follows.

Checkers sworn in by the Town Clerk, Marion L. Douglas at 8:30 a.m. were Carol St. Pierre, Debra Krupczak, Alison Krupczak, James Carroll, Ellen Warner and Abigail Alves.   Tellers were appointed and sworn in by the Moderator, Daniel Evans.

The Moderator called the meeting to order at 9:25 a.m. and a quorum of 100 was present at that time. The registered voters checked in on the voting list totaled for Precinct 1 – 192 and Precinct 2 – 101 for a grand total of 293.

Members of the meeting called the pledge of allegiance.   A moment of silence was observed for citizens listed in the memoriam of the town report.

Voted unanimously to dispense with the reading of the call of the Meeting and Return of Service having been examined by the Moderator and found to be in order.

Article 1:

Tò act upon the reports of the various Town Officers as printed in the Annual Town Report for 2007.

Moved that the reports of the various Town Officers as printed in the Annual Town Report for 2007 be accepted, and filed with the permanent records of the Town.

Motion adopted unanimously.

Article 2:

To hear the reports of any Committee heretofore chosen and act thereon.

Moved that the article be indefinitely postponed.

Motion adopted unanimously.

Article 3:

To see if the Town will vote to fix salaries and compensation of Elected Officers, and to see what sums the Town will vote to raise and appropriate from available funds or otherwise, for the payment of the salaries and compensation, expenses, equipment and outlays, capital and otherwise, of the several Town Departments, for the ensuing fiscal year.

MOVED that $36,374,463 be appropriated for the Fiscal Year 2009 Annual Town Budget to be allotted as follows: $74,206 for salaries of elected Town Officials consisting of the Town Clerk $63,689; Clerk, Board of Registrars $329.00; Moderator, $1.00; Selectmen, Chairman, $1,500.00; Members (4) at $1,000.00, $4,000.00; Board of Assessors, Chairman, $1,300.00; Members (2); at $1,200.00, $2,400.00; and the remaining $36,300,257 for Personal Services, Expenses and Capital Outlays, interest on Maturing Debt and other charges for various departments as recommended for purposes set forth in Appendix A as attached to these Town Manager's Recommended Motions for the 2008 Annual Town Meeting and Appendix B of the Warrant for the 2008 Annual Town Warrant, a copy of which Appendices are incorporated here by reference, and to meet the appropriation, the following transfers are made:

$3,438,543	from Water Revenue
$1,021,448	from Sewer Revenue
$ 250,000	from Free Cash (Surplus Revenue)
$ 75,000	from Overlay Surplus
$ 60,894	from School Construction Surplus Fund
$ 160,000	from Sewer Stabilization Fund
$ 60,000	from Pension Reserve
$ 11,645	from Waterways Fund
$ 5,000	from Wetlands Fund

And $31,291,933 is raised from taxation and other general revenues of the Town; and further that the Salary Rate and Schedule as printed in the Warrant and shown in Appendix B be adopted.

A **2/3** vote is required. Motion adopted unanimously.

DEPARTMENT	FISCAL 2006 BUDGETED	FISCAL 2007 BUDGETED	FISCAL 2008 BUDGETED	FISCAL 2009 REQUESTED	FISCAL 2009 RECOMM'D
ADMINISTRATION					
Moderator					
Personal Services	573	573	573	573	573
Total	$573	$573	$573	$573	$573
Selectmen					
Personal Services	5,500	5,500	5,500	5,500	5,500
General Expenses	58,800	58,800	64,050	64,050	61,450
Total	$64,300	$64,300	$69,550	$69,550	$66,950
Town Manager					
Personal Services	115,000	120,000	125,000	125,000	125,000
Town Hall Clerical	400,147	420,664	427,031	399,417	389,554
General Expenses	6,550	35,050	39,150	44,900	39,900
Total	$521,697	$575,714	$591,181	$569,317	$554,454
Advisory Committee					
General Expenses	345	345	345	345	345
Reserve Fund	234,000	100,000	100,000	100,000	100,000
Total	$234,345	$100,345	$100,345	$100,345	$100,345
Director of Finance					
Personal Expenses	92,639	96,323	99,396	99,396	99,396
General Expenses	28,968	28,948	46,850	33,193	29,193
Total	$121,607	$125,271	$146,246	$132,589	$128,589
Board of Assessors					
Personal Expenses	65,830	69,355	71,675	72,025	72,025
General Expenses	26,855	27,655	35,355	35,980	33,780
Total	$92,685	$97,010	$107,030	$108,005	$105,805
Treasurer/Collector					
Personal Expenses	60,002	62,550	64,605	64,605	64,605
General Expenses	40,450	41,486	40,985	40,985	38,865
Total	$100,452	$104,036	$105,590	$105,590	$103,470
Legal Services					
Town Counsel Services	190,000	260,420	150,000	150,000	150,000
Total	$190,000	$260,420	$150,000	$150,000	$150,000
Town Clerk					
Personal Services - Elected	57,119	59,863	62,689	65,600	63,689
Personal Services	11,307	18,153	17,687	16,427	16,427
General Expenses	8,735	11,125	10,010	10,338	8,890
Total	$77,161	$89,141	$90,386	$92,365	$89,006

DEPARTMENT	FISCAL 2006 BUDGETED	FISCAL 2007 BUDGETED	FISCAL 2008 BUDGETED	FISCAL 2009 REQUESTED	FISCAL 2009 RECOMM'D
Conservation Commission					
General Expenses	37,400	37,374	31,910	31,910	31,260
Total	$37,400	$37,374	$31,910	$31,910	$31,260
Planning Board					
Personal Services	10,300	0	0	54,542	54,542
General Expenses	4,400	14,450	15,050	15,050	14,750
Total	$14,700	$14,450	$15,050	$69,592	$69,292
Zoning Board of Appeals					
General Expenses	4,385	3,025	2,560	2,560	2,260
Total	$4,385	$3,025	$2,560	$2,560	$2,260
Town Reports					
General Expenses	15,000	15,000	15,000	15,000	13,000
Total	$15,000	$15,000	$15,000	$15,000	$13,000
Parking Clerk					
General Expenses	2,000	1,800	1,200	1,200	1,200
Total	$2,000	$1,800	$1,200	$1,200	$1,200
Unclassified					
Audit of Accounts	8,500	12,000	12,000	12,000	12,000
S.S. Coalition	4,000	4,000	4,000	4,000	4,000
Water Purchase	50,000	30,000	30,000	30,000	30,000
Total	$62,500	$46,000	$46,000	$46,000	$46,000
ADMINISTRATIVE TOTAL	$1,538,805	$1,534,459	$1,472,621	$1,494,596	$1,462,204
PUBLIC SAFETY					
Police Department					
Personal Services	1,740,415	1,682,451	1,724,267	1,835,378	1,734,996
General Expenses	101,450	112,738	108,950	121,500	105,200
Total	$1,841,865	$1,795,189	$1,833,217	$1,956,878	$1,840,196
Fire Department					
Personal Services	1,607,642	1,617,808	1,668,279	1,695,703	1,644,344
General Expenses	147,345	165,295	193,095	203,785	195,710
Hydrant Services	67,414	87,120	17,120	17,120	17,120
Total	$1,822,401	$1,870,223	$1,878,494	$1,916,608	$1,857,174
Building Commissioner					
Personal Services	67,700	71,209	72,778	73,278	71,778
General Expenses	5,400	5,250	5,250	5,250	4,700
Total	$73,100	$76,459	$78,028	$78,528	$76,478
Gas & Plumbing Inspector					
General Expenses	8,000	10,000	10,000	10,000	9,500
Total	$8,000	$10,000	$10,000	$10,000	$9,500

DEPARTMENT	FISCAL 2006 BUDGETED	FISCAL 2007 BUDGETED	FISCAL 2008 BUDGETED	FISCAL 2009 REQUESTED	FISCAL 2009 RECOMM'D
Weights & Measures					
Personal Services	2,600	2,678	2,678	2,678	2,678
General Expenses	450	450	0	450	0
Total	$3,050	$3,128	$2,678	$3,128	$2,678
Wiring Inspector					
General Expenses	17,500	17,500	17,950	19,164	17,550
Total	$17,500	$17,500	$17,950	$19,164	$17,550
Civil Defense					
Salaries & Expenses	5,350	5,350	7,850	7,850	5,350
Total	$5,350	$5,350	$7,850	$7,850	$5,350
Harbormaster					
Personal Services	62,589	61,623	64,435	64,435	64,435
General Expenses	5,100	8,050	9,400	9,400	7,900
Total	$67,689	$69,673	$73,835	$73,835	$72,335
Shellfish					
Personal Services	500	500	500	500	500
Total	$500	$500	$500	$500	$500
PUBLIC SAFETY TOTAL	$3,839,455	$3,848,022	$3,902,552	$4,066,491	$3,881,761
EDUCATION					
Cohasset Schools					
Salaries & Expenses	12,248,612	12,914,714	13,686,400	14,358,893	14,316,397
Total	$12,248,612	$12,914,714	$13,686,400	$14,358,893	$14,316,397
South Shore VocTech					
Vocational Assessment	95,770	105,910	144,752	133,028	133,028
Total	$95,770	$105,910	$144,752	$133,028	$133,028
EDUCATION SERVICES TOTAL	$12,344,382	$13,020,624	$13,831,152	$14,491,921	$14,449,425
PUBLIC WORKS/FACILITIES					
Department of Public Works					
Personal Services	700,327	718,166	736,299	743,812	743,812
General Expenses	161,715	185,395	194,400	204,050	197,590
Other Appropriations	390,036	427,473	425,110	425,110	433,110
Total	$1,252,078	$1,331,034	$1,355,809	$1,372,972	$1,374,512
Snow & Ice					
General Expenses	51,156	51,437	76,000	76,000	76,000
Total	$51,156	$51,437	$76,000	$76,000	$76,000

DEPARTMENT	FISCAL 2006 BUDGETED	FISCAL 2007 BUDGETED	FISCAL 2008 BUDGETED	FISCAL 2009 REQUESTED	FISCAL 2009 RECOMM'D
Street Lighting					
General Expenses	58,000	62,000	62,000	70,000	70,000
Total	$58,000	$62,000	$62,000	$70,000	$70,000
Building Maintenance					
Personal Services	220,791	224,694	230,896	361,739	243,532
General Expenses	273,265	301,718	391,000	373,800	357,300
Total	$494,056	$526,412	$621,896	$735,539	$600,832
PUBLIC WORKS/FACILITIES TOTAL	$1,855,290	$1,970,883	$2,115,705	$2,254,511	$2,121,344
HEALTH & WELFARE					
Board of Health					
Personal Services	123,527	123,102	126,785	126,785	126,785
General Expenses	12,100	8,350	8,350	8,350	6,150
Total	$135,627	$131,452	$135,135	$135,135	$132,935
Elder Affairs					
Personal Services	126,972	138,829	154,578	156,972	154,226
General Expenses	31,160	42,510	39,400	39,400	38,400
Total	$158,132	$181,339	$193,978	$196,372	$192,626
Veterans Services					
Personal Services	1,600	1,600	1,600	1,600	1,600
General Expenses	425	225	100	100	100
Total	$2,025	$1,825	$1,700	$1,700	$1,700
Commission on Disabilities					
General Expenses	100	100	0	0	0
Total	$100	$100	$0	$0	$0
HEALTH & WELFARE TOTAL	$295,884	$314,716	$330,813	$333,207	$327,261
CULTURE & RECREATION					
Library Services					
Personal Services	355,683	361,450	377,776	403,583	384,515
General Expenses	100,211	110,085	108,118	110,304	98,104
Total	$455,894	$471,535	$485,894	$513,887	$482,619
Recreation					
Personal Services	118,425	121,946	127,601	124,905	124,775
General Expenses	6,380	6,380	6,680	6,680	5,905
Total	$124,805	$128,326	$134,281	$131,585	$130,680
Common Historical Commission					
General Expenses	200	100	100	100	100
Total	$200	$100	$100	$100	$100

APPENDIX A
FISCAL 2009 OPERATING BUDGET
SUMMARY

DEPARTMENT	FISCAL 2006 BUDGETED	FISCAL 2007 BUDGETED	FISCAL 2008 BUDGETED	FISCAL 2009 REQUESTED	FISCAL 2009 RECOMM'D
Historical Preservation					
Personal Services	800	800	800	800	800
General Expenses	200	200	100	100	100
Total	$1,000	$1,000	$900	$900	$900
Celebrations					
General Expenses	2,500	5,000	5,000	5,000	5,000
Total	$2,500	$5,000	$5,000	$5,000	$5,000
CULTURAL & REC. TOTAL	$584,399	$605,961	$626,175	$651,472	$619,299
DEBT SERVICE					
Non-Excluded Principle	1,152,935	1,195,005	1,327,727	1,208,413	1,208,413
Non-Excluded Interest	418,085	415,323	425,844	558,132	558,132
Excluded Principle	1,494,160	1,543,826	1,871,830	1,885,920	1,885,920
Excluded Interest	1,722,110	1,388,817	1,171,128	1,114,548	1,114,548
DEBT SERVICE TOTAL	$4,787,290	$4,542,971	$4,796,529	$4,767,013	$4,767,013
BENEFITS & INSURANCE					
Pensions					
County Assessment	983,173	1,105,000	1,126,111	1,123,165	1,123,165
Total	$983,173	$1,105,000	$1,126,111	$1,123,165	$1,123,165
Worker's Compensation					
General Expenses	70,000	80,000	92,000	92,000	92,000
Total	$70,000	$80,000	$92,000	$92,000	$92,000
Unemployment					
General Expenses	35,000	30,109	20,000	20,000	20,000
Total	$35,000	$30,109	$20,000	$20,000	$20,000
Health Insurance					
General Expenses	1,966,000	2,157,500	2,500,000	2,580,000	2,580,000
Total	$1,966,000	$2,157,500	$2,500,000	$2,580,000	$2,580,000
Life Insurance					
General Expenses	8,000	9,000	11,000	9,000	9,000
Total	$8,000	$9,000	$11,000	$9,000	$9,000

DEPARTMENT	FISCAL 2006 BUDGETED	FISCAL 2007 BUDGETED	FISCAL 2008 BUDGETED	FISCAL 2009 REQUESTED	FISCAL 2009 RECOMM'D
Medicare					
General Expenses	190,000	200,000	206,000	226,000	226,000
Total	$190,000	$200,000	$206,000	$226,000	$226,000
Property & Liability Insurance					
General Expenses	202,500	218,000	236,200	236,000	236,000
Total	$202,500	$218,000	$236,200	$236,000	$236,000
BENEFITS & INSURANCE TOTAL	$3,454,673	$3,799,609	$4,191,311	$4,286,165	$4,286,165
ENTERPRISE FUNDS					
Central Cohasset Sewer					
General Expenses	499,166	538,706	624,897	624,467	624,467
Depreciation/Capital	57,292	82,292	144,253	30,000	30,000
Indirect Expenses	52,730	54,312	22,536	32,818	32,818
Debt Service	47,420	58,550	60,137	60,137	60,137
Total	$656,608	$733,860	$851,823	$747,422	$747,422
North Cohasset Sewer					
General Expenses	143,874	155,490	179,210	165,078	165,078
Depreciation/Capital	54,333	52,750	71,362	97,419	97,419
Indirect Expenses	19,500	20,085	20,688	11,529	11,529
Total	$217,707	$228,325	$271,260	$274,026	$274,026
Water Enterprise Fund					
General Expenses	1,269,000	1,188,600	1,207,600	1,236,100	1,236,100
Capital Outlay	0	0	0	0	0
Town Hall Services	31,296	32,000	32,000	32,000	32,000
Debt Service - Principle	708,531	777,159	857,070	1,022,443	1,022,443
Debt Service - Interest	446,331	695,391	898,930	1,148,000	1,148,000
Total	$2,455,158	$2,693,150	$2,995,600	$3,438,543	$3,438,543
ENTERPRISE FUNDS TOTAL	$3,329,473	$3,655,335	$4,118,683	$4,459,991	$4,459,991
GRAND TOTAL	$32,029,651	$33,292,580	$35,385,541	$36,805,367	$36,374,463

APPENDIX B- COMPENSATION & CLASSIFICATION SCHEDULES

Fiscal Year 2009

Grade	Step	1st	2nd	3rd	4th	5th	6th	7th
A	Hourly	10.46	11.05	11.65	12.25	12.84	13.45	14.06
	35 Hrs.	366.10	386.75	407.75	428.75	449.40	470.75	492.10
	40 Hrs.	418.40	442.00	466.00	490.00	513.60	538.00	562.40
B	Hourly	11.30	11.95	12.60	13.24	13.84	14.49	15.15
	35 Hrs.	395.50	418.25	441.00	463.40	484.40	507.15	530.25
	40 Hrs.	452.00	478.00	504.00	529.60	553.60	579.60	606.00
C	Hourly	12.24	12.89	13.57	14.24	14.96	15.69	16.39
	35 Hrs.	428.40	451.15	474.95	498.40	523.60	549.15	573.65
	40 Hrs.	489.60	515.60	542.80	569.60	598.40	627.60	655.60
D	Hourly	13.18	13.96	14.67	15.44	16.20	16.94	17.71
	35 Hrs.	461.30	488.60	513.45	540.40	567.00	592.90	619.85
	40 Hrs.	527.20	558.40	586.80	617.60	648.00	677.60	708.40
E	Hourly	14.22	15.07	15.84	16.66	17.47	18.30	19.12
	35 Hrs.	497.70	527.45	554.40	583.10	611.45	640.50	669.20
	40 Hrs.	568.80	602.80	633.60	666.40	698.80	732.00	764.80
F	Hourly	15.36	16.25	17.10	17.94	18.86	19.75	20.63
	35 Hrs.	537.60	568.75	598.50	627.90	660.10	691.25	722.05
	40 Hrs.	614.40	650.00	684.00	717.60	754.40	790.00	825.20
G	Hourly	16.61	17.53	18.49	19.43	20.37	21.27	22.24
	35 Hrs.	581.35	613.55	647.15	680.05	712.95	744.45	778.40
	40 Hrs.	664.40	701.20	739.60	777.20	814.80	850.80	889.60
H	Hourly	17.92	18.94	19.96	21.00	21.99	23.00	24.04
	35 Hrs.	627.20	662.90	698.60	735.00	769.65	805.00	841.40
	40 Hrs.	716.80	757.60	798.40	840.00	879.60	920.00	961.60
I	Hourly	19.37	20.45	21.56	22.65	23.75	24.85	25.97
	35 Hrs.	677.95	715.75	754.60	792.75	831.25	869.75	908.95
	40 Hrs.	774.80	818.00	862.40	906.00	950.00	994.00	1,038.80
J	Hourly	20.90	22.06	23.26	24.42	25.68	26.86	28.07
	35 Hrs.	731.50	772.10	814.10	854.70	898.80	940.10	982.45
	40 Hrs.	836.00	882.40	930.40	976.80	1,027.20	1,074.40	1,122.80
K	Hourly	22.59	23.83	25.16	26.42	27.70	28.99	30.30
	35 Hrs.	790.65	834.05	880.60	924.70	969.50	1,014.65	1,060.50
	40 Hrs.	903.60	953.20	1,006.40	1,056.80	1,108.00	1,159.60	1,212.00
L	Hourly	24.40	25.80	27.19	28.58	29.95	31.31	32.70
	35 Hrs.	854.00	903.00	951.65	1,000.30	1,048.25	1,095.85	1,144.50
	40 Hrs.	976.00	1,032.00	1,087.60	1,143.20	1,198.00	1,252.40	1,308.00
M	Hourly	26.38	27.82	29.32	30.83	32.33	33.84	35.36
	35 Hrs.	923.30	973.70	1,026.20	1,079.05	1,131.55	1,184.40	1,237.60
	40 Hrs.	1,055.20	1,112.80	1,172.80	1,233.20	1,293.20	1,353.60	1,414.40
N	Hourly	28.44	30.06	31.68	33.26	34.90	36.51	38.16
	35 Hrs.	995.40	1,052.10	1,108.80	1,164.10	1,221.50	1,277.85	1,335.60
	40 Hrs.	1,137.60	1,202.40	1,267.20	1,330.40	1,396.00	1,460.40	1,526.40
O	Hourly	30.74	32.47	34.24	36.00	37.73	39.46	41.23
	35 Hrs.	1,075.90	1,136.45	1,198.40	1,260.00	1,320.55	1,381.10	1,443.05
	40 Hrs.	1,229.60	1,298.80	1,369.60	1,440.00	1,509.20	1,578.40	1,649.20

APPENDIX B - COMPENSATION AND CLASSIFICATION SCHEDULES

	PAY GROUP	POSITIONS AUTHORIZED	HOURS
Schedule 1 - Regular Employees			
Board of Assessors			
Deputy Assessor/Appraiser	Contract	1	40
Assistant Assessor	H	1	35
Administrative Assistant	G	1	35
Building Department			
Building Commissioner/Zoning Officer	Contract	1	40
Clerk	F	1	20
Civilian Dispatch			
Communications Supervisor	H	1	40
Lead Dispatcher	G	1	40
Dispatcher (FT)	F	3	40
Dispatcher (PT)	F	1	24
Dispatcher (PT)	F	1	16
Elder Affairs			
Director	Contract	1	40
Elder Advocate	I	1	28
Volunteer Coordinator	G	1	19
Clerk	G	1	18
Van Driver	F	1	19
Van Driver	F	2	4
Facilities			
Director	Contract	1	40
Maintenance Worker	G	2	40
Custodial Worker	F	1	40
Custodial Worker	F	1	19
Fire Department			
Fire Chief	Contract	1	40
Captain	FS - 13	4	42
Lieutenant	FS - 12	4	42
Firefighter - Paramedic	FS - 11	15	42
Harbor Department			
Harbormaster	Contract		40
Board of Health			
Health Agent	Contract	1	12
Administrator	Contract	1	40

APPENDIX B - COMPENSATION AND CLASSIFICATION SCHEDULES

	PAY GROUP	POSITIONS AUTHORIZED	HOURS
Library			
Chief Librarian	Contract	1	40
Staff Librarian		1	35
Staff Librarian		1	31
Library Assistant		1	37.5
Library Assistant		1	35
Library Technician		1	29
Library Technician		1	22
Library Technician		2	21
Library Technician		2	20
Administrative Assistant		1	9
Planning Board			
Administrator	Contract	1	38
Police Department			
Police Chief	Contract	1	40
Lieutenant	PS - 11	2	37.5
Sergeant	PS - 11	3	37.5
Patrolman	PS - 09	13	37.5
Secretary	G	1	40
Department of Public Works			
Superintendent	Contract	1	40
General Foreman	K	1	40
Working Foreman	I	3	40
Heavy Equipment Operator	G	4	40
Skilled Utility Worker	F	3	40
Tree Climber	F	1	40
Skilled Utility Worker - Cemetery	F	1	40
Clerk	G	1	35
Recreation			
Director	Contract		40
Board of Selectmen			
Administrative Assistant	I	1	40
Secretary/Receptionist	F	1	27
Director of Finance/Town Accountant			
Director of Finance/Town Accountant	Contract	1	40
Assistant Town Accountant	G	1	25
Town Clerk			
Assistant Town Clerk	G		40

APPENDIX B - COMPENSATION AND CLASSIFICATION SCHEDULES

	PAY GROUP	POSITIONS AUTHORIZED	HOURS
Town Manager			
Town Manager	Contract		40
Treasurer/Collector			
Treasurer/Collector	Contract	1	40
Assistant Treasurer/Collector	H	1	40
Assistant to Treasurer	G	1	35

Schedule 1a - Elected Employees

Town Clerk	$63,689
Clerk, Board of Registrars	$329
Moderator	$1
Board of Selectmen:	
Chair	$1,500
Members (4) at $1,000	$4,000
Board of Assessors	
Chair	$1,300
Members (2) at $1,200	$2,400

Schedule 2a - Part Time Positions Annual

Veterans' Agent	$1,600
Member, Board of Registrars	$326
Sealer of Weights and Measurers	$2,600
Town Archivist	$600
Director of Emergency Management	$350
Assistant Director of Emergency Management	$100
Shellfish Constable	$500
Animal Control Officer	$16,808
Keeper of the Town Clock	$100
Keeper of the Town Pump	$100

APPENDIX B - COMPENSATION AND CLASSIFICATION SCHEDULES

	PAY GROUP	POSITIONS AUTHORIZED	HOURS
Schedule 2b - Part Time Positions Hourly			
Assistant Harbor Master	$13		
Casual Labor	$8		
Election Officers	$12		
Election Clerk	$12		
Election Warden	$12		
Summer Patrolman	$14		
Police Matron	$13		
Deputy Building Inspector (H-Min)	$18		
Library Pages	$8		
Recording Secretary	$13		
Schedule 3 - Part Time Positions			
Constable - Per Notice	$20		

Exempt Positions - Per the Fair Labor Standards Act

Deputy Assessor/Appraiser	Health Agent
Building Commissioner	Chief Librarian
Director of Finance/Town Accountant	Police Chief
Director of Facilities	Recreation Director
Elder Affairs Director	Superintendent of Public Works
Fire Chief	Town Manager
Harbormaster	Treasurer/Collector
Health Administrator	Town Planner

APPENDIX C - CAPITAL IMPROVEMENT PLAN FY 2009 TO FY 2012				
	2009	2010	2011	2012
Department/Description	Proposed	Proposed	Proposed	Proposed
FACILITIES MANAGEMENT				
Library				
Library Gutters and Downspouts	$72,500			
Library East Parapet Wall Repair	$11,000			
Library EPDM repairs		$44,000		
Security System (cameras)			$50,000	
Schools				
Trash Truck	$45,000			
Osgood Pavement (new back turn around / walkway)	$50,000			
Osgood Playground Replacement/Repair	$75,000			
Middle High Science Classroom Exhaust Fans	$25,000			
Osgood Kitchen Upgrade		$40,000		
Osgood Emergency Generator		$160,000		
High School Fitness Center Air Conditioning			$22,000	
Alumni Field Bleachers		$85,000		
Alumni Field Turf/Track Replacement				$1,500,000
Town Hall				
Town Hall Chiller Replacement	$45,000			
Town Hall Windows, Electrical, Restroom, Auditorium Upgrades		$60,000		
Town Hall Sill Replacement		$25,000		
Town Hall Security System (camera and burglar)			$30,000	
Town Hall Basement Air Conditioning				$15,000
Town Hall Emergency Generator				$30,000
Police/Fire				
Emergency Generator	$130,000			
Other				
Town Wide BAS (building automation) System	$80,000			
Maintenance Vehicle (if new maintenance staff hired)	$35,000			
Dark Fiber Install (schools, police, library, town hall)	$30,000			
DPW Security System (camera and burglar)			$30,000	
Sub-Total	**$598,500**	**$414,000**	**$132,000**	**$1,545,000**
TOWN MANAGER				
West Corner Culvert Replacement Design	$50,000			
Sub-Total	**$50,000**			
BOARD OF SELECTMEN				
Lightkeepers Sewer Connection Project	$50,000			

	2009 Proposed	2010 Proposed	2011 Proposed	2012 Proposed
APPENDIX C - CAPITAL IMPROVEMENT PLAN				
FY 2009 TO FY 2012				
Department/Description				
Flood Control Projects	$400,000	$2,000,000	$2,000,000	
Sub-Total	$450,000	$2,000,000	$2,000,000	$0
PUBLIC WORKS				
1985 CAT 950 Loader (refurbishment)	$30,000			
Bucket Truck (replacement)	$70,000			
Tractor (replace 1989 Peterbilt)	$120,000			
Mowing Machine	$30,000			
Replace Sander	$10,000			
Cheverolet C-30 (replace 1990)		$45,000		
Loader/Backhoe (replace 1988 Ford)			$90,000	
Replace 1986 Ford Dump Truck				$85,000
Sub-Total	$260,000	$45,000	$90,000	$85,000
INFORMATION TECHNOLOGY				
Equipment Purchase & Replacement	$10,000	$10,000	$10,000	
Sub-Total	$10,000	$10,000	$10,000	$0
SCHOOL DEPARTMENT				
Technology Replacement	$100,000	$100,000	$100,000	$100,000
Transportation Busses / vans	$80,000	$45,000	$80,000	$80,000
Sub-Total	$180,000	$145,000	$180,000	$180,000
LIBRARY				
Replace 15 Public Computers & 2 notebook computers	$28,200		$28,200	
Replace 11 staff computers				$18,700
Replace 6 children's room computers & 5 PAC's		$18,700		
Install Self-Check out Kiosk	$14,000			
Finish Staff Work Room	$5,000			
Replace Carpet	$2,400			
Replace worn Upholstery		$5,000		
Sub-Total	$49,600	$23,700	$28,200	$18,700

APPENDIX C - CAPITAL IMPROVEMENT PLAN
FY 2009 TO FY 2012

Department/Description	2009 Proposed	2010 Proposed	2011 Proposed	2012 Proposed
POLICE DEPARTMENT				
Vehicle Replacement (marked)	$58,000	$58,000	$29,000	$60,000
Vehicle Replacement (marked)				
Sever & Workstation Replacement	$9,000	$5,000	$5,000	$5,000
Vehicle Replacement (unmarked)	$38,000		$20,000	
Special Vehicle (4X4)			$30,000	
Mobile Radios				$50,000
Portable Radios		$90,000		
Dispatch/911 Consoles Replacement	$150,000			
Police Repeater Update/Refurbish		$30,000		
Firearms - Handguns			$12,500	
Firearms - Long Guns			$3,500	
New Police Station		$4,500,000		
Sub-Total	**$255,000**	**$4,683,000**	**$100,000**	**$115,000**
FIRE DEPARTMENT				
Chief's Vehicle Replacement	$35,000			
Ambulance Replacement	$165,000			
Engine Two Replacement	$450,000			
Forest Fire Truck Replacement				$150,000
Air Compressor/Self Contained Breathing App. Filling Station		$50,000		
Special Hazards Equipment Trailer		$25,000		
Jaws of Life - Gas Powered (replacement)	$20,000			
Jaws of Life - Electric Powered (replacement)			$23,000	
Thermal Imaging Camera Replacement (2)		$27,000		
Desktop & Notebook Computr Replacement			$10,000	
Heart Monitor/Defibrillator - 12 Lead (replacement)	$25,000			$28,000
Hose Replacement	$15,000			
Second Fire Station Feasibility Study	$25,000			
Heavy Rescue Tools				
Sub-Total	**$735,000**	**$102,000**	**$33,000**	**$178,000**
GRAND TOTAL	**$2,588,100**	**$7,422,700**	**$2,573,200**	**$2,121,700**

Article 4:   Union Contracts & Other Salary Adjustments

To see if the Town will vote to raise and appropriate borrow pursuant to any applicable statute, and/or transfer from available funds, a sum or sums of money, to be expended by the Town Manager, to fund the FY09 cost items of a collective bargaining agreement between the Town, represented by the Board of Selectmen, and the Fire Department employees represented by Local 2804, Cohasset Permanent Firefighters, Police Department employees represented by the New England Police Benevolent Association, Inc. Local 9000, the Library employees represented by SEIU Local 888, Clerical employees represented by SEIU Local 888, and Public Safety Dispatch employees represented by Teamsters Local Union No. 25in accordance with Chapter 150E of the General laws, and to fund salary adjustments for non-union and employees with individual employment contracts, or take any other action related thereto.

MOVED that the article be indefinitely postponed.

Motion adopted.

Article 5:   Capital Improvements Budget

To see if the Town will vote to raise and appropriate, transfer from available funds or borrow pursuant to any applicable statute, a sum of money to fund various capital improvements, capital projects and/or capital equipment for the various departments, boards, commissions and agencies of the town, or take any other action related thereto.

MOVED that Fifty Thousand Dollars ($50,000) be transferred from Free Cash (Surplus Revenue) to be expended by the Town Manager for purpose of funding engineering design services for the West Corner Culvert Replacement Project.

Motion adopted unanimously.

Article 6:   Community Preservation Committee

To see if the Town will vote to adopt and approve the recommendations of the Community Preservation Committee for Fiscal Year 2009, and to see if the Town will vote to implement such recommendations by appropriating a sum or sums of money from the Community Preservation Fund established pursuant to Chapter 44B of the General Laws, and by authorizing the Board of Selectmen, with the approval of the Community Preservation Committee to acquire, by purchase, gift or eminent domain such real property interests in the name of the Town, or enforceable by the Town, including real property interests in the form of permanent affordable housing restrictions and historical preservation restrictions that will meet the requirements of Chapter 184 of the General Laws, as may be necessary or proper to carry out the foregoing, or to take any action related thereto.2

Recommendation A: Sub Account Allocations

That Fiscal Year 2009 revenues to the Community Preservation Fund be divided to the following sub accounts to be administered by the Community Preservation Committee as follows:

Historical Resources Sub Account	(10%)	$ 50,000
Open Space Sub Account	(10%	$ 50,000
Community Housing Sub Account	(10%)	$ 50,000
Total Budget		$150,000

Recommendation B. Town Hall Restoration

That Three Hundred Thousand Dollars ($300,000) be transferred from the Community Preservation Fund Discretionary Sub Account with the intention that these funds be available in FY 2008 and thereafter, which funds are to be expended by the Town Manager, for the purposes of rehabilitation and preservation to the exterior of the antique portion of Town Hall, including but not limited the restoration of the windows, gutters, downspouts, clapboard chimney, acquisition of storm windows, and other related work. All work must comply with the requirements of the Community Preservation Act (G.L. ch. 44B, section 2 "rehabilitation" or any other applicable law).

Recommendation C. **Stormwater** Management

That Eighty-Eight Thousand Five Hundred Dollars ($88,500) be transferred from the Community Preservation Fund Discretionary Sub Account with the intention that these funds be available in FY 2008 and thereafter, which funds are to be expended by the Town Manager, for the purposes of designing, installing and constructing of Stormwater Best Management Practice controls within the James Brook watershed that are needed to reduce the impacts of stormwater pollution affecting James Brook, Jacobs Meadow, Cohasset Cove and Cohasset Harbor including, but not limited to, ten locations within a quarter mile radius of Jacobs Meadow on Elm Street, Pleasant Street & Cushing Road, Norfolk Road & Cushing Road, South Main Street, North Main Street & Robert Jason Road, Oak Street & Cushing Road, Cove Road, Pond Street & Cushing Road, Ash Street & Cushing Road, Ripley Road, near Pratt Court and other related work. This project is necessary to preserve James, Brook, Jacobs Meadow, Cohasset Cove, and Cohasset Harbor from destruction.

Recommendation D. Housing Perc Tests

That Twenty Thousand Dollars ($20,000) be transferred from the Community Preservation Fund Housing Resources Sub Account with the intention that these funds be available in FY 2008 and thereafter, which funds are to be expended by the Town Manager for the purposes of performing percolation tests and other related engineering work/studies to determine whether land owned by the Town situated off Smith Place and Pleasant Lane is suitable for development.

Recommendation E. Historical Society

That Fifty One Thousand Seven Hundred Dollars ($51,700) be transferred from the Community Preservation Fund Historical Resources Sub Account with the intention that these funds be available in FY 2008 and thereafter, which funds are to be expended by the Town Manager, for the purposes of rehabilitation and restoration of the Cohasset Historical Society's (former) Paul Pratt Memorial Library to rehabilitate the cupola windows, Front door and loggia, and Rotunda glass dome, installation of ultra-violet filtered Plexiglas inserts at each window of the Cohasset historical Society's Wilson House and Cohasset Historical Society's Maritime Museum, and the acquisition and installation of textile storage racks for the purpose of preserving the Cohasset Historical Society's archives including textiles and other artifacts all other related work, provided, however, that the Board of Selectmen be hereby authorized to acquire in return for such sum a historic preservation restriction in compliance with Chapter 184 of the General Laws and the specific work items be performed with the prior approval of the Community Preservation Committee before performing any of the work and/or contracting for services. All work to (former) Paul Pratt Memorial Library, Wilson House and Maritime Museum must comply with the requirements of the Community Preservation Act (G.L. ch. 44B, section 2 "rehabilitation" or any other applicable law).

Recommendation F. Water Department

That Twenty Five Thousand Dollars ($25,000) be transferred from the Community Preservation Fund Open Space Account and One Hundred Fifty Thousand)$150,000) Dollars from the Community Preservation Discretionary Sub Account, for a total of One Hundred Seventy-Five Thousand ($175,000) Dollars, with the intention that these funds be available in FY 2008 and thereafter, which funds are to be expended by the Town Manager to acquire by purchase, gift or eminent domain the following parcel of land found on Assessor's Map Parcel 66-7 (20.43 acres) (described by deed recorded in Norfolk County Registry of Deeds in Book 5244 at Page 104. Said property is to be acquired in fee simple title for watershed, open space and recreation purposes. The parcel is the last of 15 parcels authorized by the Annual Town Meeting March 27, 2004, Article 13. The assemblage of land for open space and watershed protection came to be known as the Brass Kettle Brook Conservation Area. The town is authorized to grant a conservation restriction to the Trustees of Reservations requiring that this land be used only for watershed, open space and recreation purposes.

Recommendation G. Town Clerk

That Ten Thousand Dollars ($10,000) be transferred from the Community Preservation Fund Historical Resources Sub Account and Forty Thousand Dollars ($40,000) transferred from the Community Preservation Fund Discretionary Sub Account for a total of Fifty Thousand Dollars ($50,000) with the intention that these funds be available in FY 2008 and thereafter, which funds are to be expended by the Town Manager, for the purposes of preserving and making various restorative improvements to the Town Clerk's ancient records and vital statistics.

Recommendation H. Harbor Health Committee

That Thirty-Five Thousand Dollars ($35,000) be transferred from the Community Preservation Fund Discretionary Sub Account with the intention that these funds be available in Fiscal 2008 and thereafter, which funds are to be expended by the Town Manager for the purposes of constructing/restoring the culvert running between the Gulf River and Cohasset Harbor and other related costs, which project is necessary to preserve the Cohasset Harbor, Cohasset Cove and the Gulf River from destruction. Notwithstanding the above, the Harbor Health Committee and or the Conservation Commission must, prior to December 31, 2009, demonstrate to the Town Manager's satisfaction, that it has raised all additional money necessary for completing this project. If the Harbor Health Committee and/or the Conservation Commission fail to receive the Town Manager's endorsement that all such funds are in place by that date, then this appropriation shall expire and the money appropriated herein will return to the Community Preservation Fund Discretionary Sub Account.

Recommendation I. American Legion

That Twenty Thousand Dollars ($20,000) be transferred from the Community Preservation Fund Discretionary Sub Account with the intention that these funds be available in Fiscal 2008 and thereafter, which funds are to be expended by the Town Manager for the purposes of installing a fire sprinkler system, and other related work to the American Legion George H. Mealy Post 118, which is a historical built circa 1850 known as the "Guild Building" or "Legion Hall" and which formerly housed the U.S. Customs and Immigration Service for the Port of Cohasset during the 1800's. Notwithstanding the above, the American Legion must, prior to December 31, 2009, demonstrate to the Town Manager's satisfaction, that it has raised all additional money necessary for completing the this project before any work may commence on this project. If the American Legion fails to receive the Town Manager's endorsement that all such funds are in place by that date, then this appropriation shall expire and the money appropriated herein will return to the Community Preservation Fund Discretionary Sub Account. The project will be supervised by the Town Manager. The American Legion must receive the Town Manager's pre-approval before performing any work item and/or entering into any contract(s) for the work. Invoices for all work performed shall be submitted to the Town Manager for his approval and subject to his inspection (or that of his agents) of the work performed. All payment shall be made by the Town directly to the vendor.

Recommendation J. Harbor Study

That Twenty Thousand Dollars ($20,000) be transferred from the Community Preservation Fund Discretionary Sub Account with the intention that these funds be available in Fiscal 2008 and thereafter, which funds are to be expended by the Town Manager, for the purposes paying a portion of the costs for retaining a municipal planner to prepare a concept plan for the future uses of Cohasset Harbor and the land surrounding it. The plan will focus on opportunities for open space, public access to the harbor, community housing, historical preservation, economic viability and include a build out analysis and recommendations for potential zoning changes.

Recommendation **K.** Debt Service **Payment**

That Thirty-Eight Thousand Four Hundred Seventy Nine Dollars ($38,479) be transferred from the Community Preservation Fund Discretionary Sub Account to be expended by the Town Manager for payment of debt service for the project approved under Article 12 (Recommendation E) of the 2004 annual town meeting (open space land acquisition).

Moved to vote the appropriation as recommended by the Community Preservation Committee as set forth In Appendix D of the warrant shown as recommendations A through I, and K. Recommendation J was withdrawn.

Motion adopted unanimously.

Article 7:   **Unpaid Bills from Previous Years**

To see if the Town will vote to raise and appropriate, transfer from available funds, and/or borrow, pursuant to any applicable statute, a sum or sums of money, to be expended by the Town Manager, to pay for unpaid bills from previous fiscal years, or to take any other action related thereto.

MOVED that the article be indefinitely postponed.

Motion adopted unanimously.

Article 8:   **Supplemental Appropriations for Fiscal 2008**

To see if the Town will vote to raise and appropriate, borrow pursuant to any applicable statute and/or transfer from available funds, a sum or sums of money, to be expended by the Town Manager, needed by various departmental budgets and appropriations to complete the fiscal year ending June 30, 2008, or to take any other action related thereto.

MOVED that One Hundred Seventy Five Thousand Dollars ($175,000), be hereby appropriated to the Fiscal 2008 budgetary items set forth below amending the amounts appropriated by the Town pursuant to Article 3 of the 2006 Annual Town Meeting (which appropriations may have been amended at the November 13, 2007 Special Town Meeting), which funds after transfer are to be expended by the Town Manager, to supplement certain departmental budgets and appropriations set forth below to complete the fiscal year ending June 30, 2008, as follows.

Transfer Funds to:

Legal Services Budget	$ 75,000	Legal Services
Planning Board General Expenses	$ 10,000	Zoning Bylaw Recodification
Police Department Salaries	$ 80,000	Overtime
Facilities Maintenance Salaries	$ 10,000	Overtime

TOTAL AMOUNT TRANSFERRED $ 175,000

And to fund this appropriation, One Hundred Seventy Five Thousand Dollars ($175,000) be transferred from Free Cash (Surplus Revenue).

Motion adopted.

Article 9:   Capital Stabilization Fund

To see if the Town will vote to create a Capital Stabilization Fund pursuant to Chapter 40, Section 5B of the General Laws for the purpose of funding various capital improvements, capital projects and/or capital equipment for the various departments, boards, commissions and agencies of the town; and to raise and appropriate, transfer from available funds and/or borrow pursuant to any applicable statute a sum of money to be deposited into said Capital Stabilization Fund, any other action related thereto.

MOVED that a Capital Stabilization Fund be hereby established in the treasury of the town pursuant to Chapter 40, Section 5B of the General Laws beginning July 1, 2008 and continuing thereafter, for the purpose of funding various capital improvements, capital projects and/or capital equipment for the various departments, boards, commissions and agencies of the town; and further that the sum of Two Hundred Fifty Thousand Dollars ($250,000) be hereby appropriated for deposit into the Capital Stabilization Fund; and to meet this appropriation, One Hundred Twenty Five Thousand Dollars ($125,000) be raised and appropriated from taxation and other general revenues of the Town and One Hundred Twenty Five Thousand Dollars ($125,000) be transferred from Free Cash (Surplus Revenue) in the treasury of the town.

A 2/3 vote required. Motion adopted unanimously.

Article 10:   Post-Retirement Health Insurance Liability Stabilization Fund

To see if the Town will vote to create a Post-Retirement Health Insurance Liability Stabilization Fund pursuant to Chapter 40, Section 5B of the General Laws for the purpose of funding health insurance expenses for future retired town employees, and to raise and appropriate, transfer from available funds and/or borrow pursuant to any applicable statute a sum of money to be deposited into said Post-Retirement Health Insurance Liability Stabilization Fund, or take any other action related thereto.

MOVED that a Post-Retirement Health Insurance Liability Stabilization Fund be hereby established in the treasury of the town pursuant to Chapter 40, Section 5B of the General Laws beginning July 1, 2008 and continuing thereafter for the purpose of funding health insurance expenses for future retired town employees, and that the sum of One Hundred Thousand Dollars ($100,000) be hereby appropriated for deposit into the Post-Retirement Health Insurance Liability Stabilization Fund; and to meet this appropriation, the sum of One Hundred Thousand Dollars ($100,000) be transferred from the Health Insurance budget approved for Fiscal 2008 as appropriated under Article 3 of the 2007 Annual Town Meeting.

A **2/3** vote required. Motion adopted **unanimously**.

Article 11: Amendments to Personnel Classification and Compensation Plan Bylaw

To see if the Town will vote to amend Article XI (Personnel Classification and Compensation Plan), Section 6 (Fringe Benefits), said amendments on file in the Office of the Board of Selectmen, or take any other action related thereto.

MOVED that General Bylaws, Article XI, Personnel Classification and Compensation Plan be hereby amended as follows:

Section 6(a) Vacation Leave is hereby amended by deleting the words "Upon completion of ten (10) years of service – four (4) weeks/year" and adding the following at the end of the first paragraph: "From ten (10) years to nineteen (19) years of service – four (4) weeks/year. Upon completion of twenty (20) years of service – five (5) weeks/year.

Section 6 (c) is hereby amended by substituting the words "two (2) days" for the words "one (1) day" in the first sentence.

Motion adopted unanimously.

Article 12:   Amendment to Smoking Bylaw

To see if the Town will vote to amend the General Bylaws, Article VII, Safety and Public Order, Section 33, Smoking Bylaw, as follows, by amending Section 33.(b)v. by inserting in the fifth line after "libraries;" the following: "membership association;"

and by inserting the following new Section 33.(b)v. and renumbering existing Sections 33.(b)v. through xii. accordingly:

v.   Membership Association", a not-for-profit entity that has been established and operates, for a charitable, philanthropic, civic, social, benevolent, educational, religious, athletic, recreation or similar purpose, and is comprised of members who collectively belong to:

(1)   a society, organization or association of a fraternal nature that operates under the lodge system, and having 1 or more affiliated chapters or branches incorporated in any state; or

(2)   a corporation organized under chapter 180 ; or

(3)   an established religious place of worship or instruction in the commonwealth whose real or personal property is exempt from taxation; or

(4)   a veterans' organization incorporated or chartered by the Congress of the United States, or otherwise, having 1 or more affiliated chapters or branches incorporated in any state.

(5)   Except for a religious place of worship or instruction, an entity shall not be a membership association for the purposes of this definition, unless individual membership is required for all members of the association for a period of not less than 90 days. or take any other action related thereto.

MOVED that this article be indefinitely postponed.

Motion adopted unanimously.

Article 13:   South Shore Recycling Cooperative Memorandum of Agreement

To see if the Town will vote to authorize the Board of Selectmen to enter into a five year extension of the Intermunicipal Agreement relative to the South Shore Recycling Cooperative, effective July 1, 2008, or take any other action related thereto.

MOVED that the Town the Board of Selectmen be hereby authorized to enter into a five year extension of the Intermunicipal Agreement relative to the South Shore Recycling Cooperative, effective July 1, 2008. thereto.

Motion adopted unanimously.

Commendation offered by Ralph **Dormitzer for Gary Vanderweil.**

COMMENDATION

WHEREAS, Gary Vanderweil previously served 18 years as a member of the Cohasset Sewer Commission, including 5 years as Chairman; and

WHEREAS, Gary Vanderweil was elected to the Board of Selectmen in 2005 and has served with honor and distinction over the past three years, including the past year as Chairman of the Board; and

WHEREAS, as a member of the Board of Selectmen, **Gary Vanderweil** has brought great wisdom to the many issues that face our community; and

WHEREAS, as Chairman of the Board of Selectman, **Gary Vanderweil** has helped the Board discharge its responsibilities in a very effective and efficient manner; and

WHEREAS, such dedication and service to the Town can not come without great sacrifice to personal matters and family life;

WHEREAS, the Board of Selectmen now recommends this Unanimous Motion for Commendation to **Gary Vanderweil:**

NOW THEREFORE BE IT RESOLVED that the Citizens of Cohasset, assembled at Annual Town Meeting hereby acknowledge and affirm their appreciation to Selectman **Gary Vanderweil** for his many years of dedicated service to the Town of Cohasset.

GIVEN under our hands and the seal of the **TOWN OF COHASSET** on this twenty ninth day of March in the year Two Thousand Eight.

Commendation adopted **unanimously.**

Article 14: Zoning Bylaw Amendment: Wind Energy Conversion Facility Bylaw

To see if the town will vote to amend the zoning bylaws by adding a new Section 19: Town of Cohasset Wind Energy Conversion Facility Bylaw to read as follows:

19.1 Purpose and Intent

It is the express purpose of this bylaw to accommodate large distributed generation, wind energy conversion facilities, hereinafter referred to as a wind turbine(s), in appropriate locations, while minimizing any adverse visual, safety and environmental impacts of the facilities. The bylaw enables the review of wind turbines by the town's Planning Board in keeping with the Town's existing bylaws. This bylaw is intended to be used in conjunction with other regulations adopted by the Town, including historic district regulations, site plan review and other local bylaws designed to encourage appropriate land use, environmental protection, and provision of adequate infrastructure development in Cohasset.

19.2. Definitions

Height: The height of a turbine(s) is measured to the highest point reached by the blades. The height of the tower will be measured to the top of the nacelle.

Nacelle: The frame and housing at the top of the tower that encloses the gearbox and generators and protects them from the weather.

Rotor: The blades and hub of the wind turbine(s) that rotate during turbine operation.

Set Back: The base of the tower to the nearest lot line.

Size: Only wind turbines greater than 500 kilowatts are covered by this Bylaw

Special Permit Granting Authority (SPGA): Board designated by zoning ordinance or bylaw with the authority to issue permits.

Wind energy conversion facility: All equipment, machinery and structures utilized in connection with the conversion of wind to electricity. This includes, but is not limited to, all transmission, storage, collection and supply equipment, substations, transformers, site access, service roads and machinery associated with the use. A wind energy conversion facility may consist of one or more wind turbines.

Wind Turbine Flickering: The blinking effect while the rotor is in motion. Attention will be paid to siting the wind turbine(s) to reduce significant flickering.

Wind Monitoring or Meteorological ("test" or "met ") Towers: Tower used for supporting anemometer, wind vane and other equipment to assess the wind resource at a predetermined height above the ground.

Wind turbine: A device that converts kinetic energy of the wind into rotational energy to turn an electrical generator shaft. A wind turbine typically consists of a rotor, nacelle and supporting tower.

19.3 District Regulations

19.3.1 Use Regulations:

19.3.1 Wind Turbine
The construction of any wind turbine under this Bylaw shall be permitted in all zoning districts, subject to issuance of a Special Permit and provided the proposed use complies with all Dimensional and Special Permit Requirements set forth in Sections 19.3 and 19.4 of this bylaw.

19.3.1.2. Wind Monitoring or Meteorological Towers

Temporary erection of Wind Monitoring or Meteorological Towers shall be permitted in all zoning districts subject to the issuance of a building permit for a temporary structure for not more than eighteen months.

19.3.2 Site Control

The applicant shall submit with the application documentation of the applicant's legal right to install and use the proposed facility at the subject property. Documentation should also include proof of control over the setback areas.

19.3.3 Dimensional Requirements

All wind turbines shall comply with the requirements set forth in this Section 19.3.3.

19.3.3.1 Height

Wind turbines shall have a maximum height of 350-feet, as measured from the Pre-Construction Grade to the highest point reached by the nacelle. The SPGA may allow this height to be exceeded as part of the special permit process if the project proponent can demonstrate that the additional height is needed and that the additional benefits of the higher tower outweigh any adverse impacts. Monopole towers are the preferred type of support for wind turbines.

19.3.3.2 Setback

a)   Each wind energy conversion facility and its associated equipment shall comply with the

building setback provisions of the zoning district in which the facility is located.

b)   In addition, the following setbacks shall be observed:

1.   In order to ensure public safety and to protect the interest of neighboring property owners, the minimum distance from the base of any wind turbine tower to any property line in a residential district, shall be equal to the total height of the turbine to the highest point.

19.4 Special Permit Criteria

The SPGA may grant a Special Permit only if it finds that the proposal complies with the provisions of this bylaw and is consistent with the applicable criteria for granting Special Permits.

19.4.1 General

Proposed wind turbine(s) shall comply with all applicable local, state and federal requirements, including but not limited to all applicable electrical, construction, noise, safety, environmental and communications requirements.

19.4.1.1 Visual Impact

The proponent shall demonstrate through project siting and proposed mitigation that the wind turbine minimizes any impact on the visual character of surrounding neighborhoods and the community; this may include, without limitation, information regarding site selection, turbine design, buffering, lighting and cable layout.

19.4.1.2. Color

Wind turbine(s) shall be painted a non-reflective color.

19.4.1.3. Lighting **and** Signage

Wind turbine(s) shall be lighted only if required by the Federal Aviation Administration (FAA).

The proponent shall provide a copy of the FAA's determination to establish the required marking

and /or lights for the structure.

a) Lighting of equipment structures and any other facilities on site (except lighting) required by the FAA shall be shielded from abutting properties.

b) Signs on the facility shall be limited to:

    1. those needed to identify the property and the owner and warn of any danger; and,

    2. educational signs providing information on the technology and renewable energy usage.

c) All signs shall comply with the requirements of the Town's sign regulations unless relief is

granted by the S.P.G.A.

19.4.2.1 Land **Clearing/Open Space/Rare** Species

Wind turbines shall be designed to minimize land clearing and fragmentation of open space areas and shall avoid permanently protected open space when feasible. Wind turbines should be sited to make use of previously developed areas wherever possible. Wind turbines facilities shall also be located in a manner that does not have significant negative impacts on rare species in the vicinity (particularly avian species, bats, etc.) as may be applicable law.

19.4.2.2. Storm water

Storm water run-off and erosion control shall be managed in a manner consistent with all applicable state and local law.

19.4.2.3 Noise

The wind turbine and associated equipment shall conform with Massachusetts noise regulations (310 CMR 7.10). An analysis prepared by a qualified engineer shall be presented to demonstrate compliance with these noise standards and shall be consistent with Massachusetts Department of Environmental Protection guidance for noise measurement.

19.4.2.4. Shadowing/Flicker

Wind turbines shall be sited in a manner that does not result in significant shadowing or flicker impacts. Applicant must demonstrate that this effect does not have significant adverse impact on adjacent uses through siting.

19.5 Uses by Telecommunications Carriers

Wind turbines may be used to locate telecommunications antennas, subject to applicable law governing such uses and structures, and subject to the following additional requirements:

a) All ground-mounted telecommunications equipment shall be located in either a shelter, within the wind turbine tower or otherwise screened from view year-round(either through effective landscaping or existing natural vegetated buffers);

b) Antennas shall be flush-mounted to be in keeping with the design of the wind turbine tower; and;

c) All cabling associated with the personal wireless facility shall be contained within the tower structure or enclosed within a conduit painted to match the turbine mount.

19.6 Monitoring and Maintenance

19.6.1   After the wind turbine is operational, the applicant shall submit to the SPGA at annual intervals from the date of issuance of the Special Permit, a report detailing operating data for the facility (including but not limited to days of operation, energy production in accordance with the special permit conditions)

19.6.2   The applicant shall maintain the wind energy conversion facility in good condition. Such maintenance shall include, without limitations, painting, structural integrity of the foundation and support structure and security barrier (if applicable), and maintenance of the buffer areas and landscaping if present.

19.6.3   Notice shall be provided to the SPGA of any change in ownership of the facility.

19.7 Abandonment or Discontinuation of Use

19.7.1 Within six months that a wind turbine(s) is scheduled to be discontinued, the applicant will notify the SPGA by certified U.S. mail of the proposed date of abandonment or discontinuance of operations. In the event that an applicant fails to give such notice, the facility shall be considered abandoned or discontinued if the facility is inoperable for 190 days. In the case of a multi-turbine facility, the SPGA shall determine in its decision what proportion of the facility would be inoperable for the facility to be considered abandoned.

19.7.2 Upon abandonment or discontinuation of use, the owner shall physically remove the wind turbine(s) within 90 days from the date of abandonment or discontinuation of use. This period may be extended at the request of the owner and at the discretion of the SPGA." Physically remove" shall include, but not be limited to:

   a) Removal of the wind turbine(s) and tower(s), all machinery, equipment, equipment shelters, security barriers and all appurtenant structures from the subject property.
   b) Proper disposal of all solid or hazardous materials and wastes from the site in accordance with local and state solid waste disposal regulations,

   c)Restoration of the location of the wind turbine(s) to its natural condition, except that any landscaping, grading or below grade foundation may remain in the after-condition.

19.7.3 If an applicant fails to remove a wind turbine in accordance with this section of this bylaw, the Town shall have the authority to enter the subject property and physically remove the facility. The SPGA may in its decision provide a form of surety (i.e. post a bond, letter of credit or establish an escrow account or other) at the SPGA's election to cover costs of removal in the event the town must remove the facility. The amount of such surety shall be equal to 150 percent of the cost of removal of the facility as determined by a qualified engineer. The amount shall include a mechanism for a Cost of Living Adjustment after 10 and 15 years.

19.8 Terms of Special Permit

   A Special Permit issued for any wind turbine(s) facility shall be valid for 25 years unless extended or renewed. At the end of that time period, the wind turbine(s) shall be removed by the applicant.

19.9 Application Procedures

19.9.1 Special Permit Granting Authority **(SPGA)**
   The SPGA for wind energy conversion facilities, also referred to as Wind Turbine(s) is this bylaw shall be the Planning Board.

Or, take any other action related thereto.

MOVED that the town vote to amend the zoning bylaws by adding a new Section 19: Town of Cohasset Wind Energy Conversion Facility Bylaw to read as follows:

19.1 Purpose and Intent

It is the express purpose of this bylaw to accommodate large distributed generation, wind energy conversion facilities, hereinafter referred to as a wind turbine(s), in appropriate locations, while minimizing any adverse visual, safety and environmental impacts of the facilities. The bylaw enables the review of wind turbines by the town's Planning Board in keeping with the Town's existing bylaws. This bylaw is intended to be used in conjunction with other regulations adopted by the Town, including historic district regulations, site plan review and other local bylaws designed to encourage appropriate land use, environmental protection, and provision of adequate infrastructure development in Cohasset.

19.2. Definitions

Height: The height of a turbine(s) is measured to the highest point reached by the blades. The height of the tower will be measured to the top of the nacelle.

Nacelle: The frame and housing at the top of the tower that encloses the gearbox and generators and protects them from the weather.

Rotor: The blades and hub of the wind turbine(s) that rotate during turbine operation.

Set Back: The base of the tower to the nearest lot line.

Size: Only wind turbines greater than 500 kilowatts are covered by this Bylaw

Special Permit Granting Authority (SPGA): Board designated by zoning ordinance or bylaw with the authority to issue permits.

Wind energy conversion facility: All equipment, machinery and structures utilized in connection with the conversion of wind to electricity. This includes, but is not limited to, all transmission, storage, collection and supply equipment, substations, transformers, site access, service roads and machinery associated with the use. A wind energy conversion facility may consist of one or more wind turbines.

Wind Turbine Flickering: The blinking effect while the rotor is in motion. Attention will be paid to siting the wind turbine(s) to reduce significant flickering.

Wind Monitoring or Meteorological ("test" or "met ") Towers: Tower used for supporting anemometer, wind vane and other equipment to assess the wind resource at a predetermined height above the ground.

Wind turbine: A device that converts kinetic energy of the wind into rotational energy to turn an electrical generator shaft. A wind turbine typically consists of a rotor, nacelle and supporting tower.

19.3 District Regulations

19.3.1 Use Regulations:

19.3.1 Wind Turbine
The construction of any wind turbine under this Bylaw shall be permitted in all zoning districts, subject to issuance of a Special Permit and provided the proposed use complies with all Dimensional and Special Permit Requirements set forth in Sections 19.3 and 19.4 of this bylaw.

19.3.1.2. Wind Monitoring or Meteorological Towers
Temporary erection of Wind Monitoring or Meteorological Towers shall be permitted in all zoning districts subject to the issuance of a building permit for a temporary structure for not more than eighteen months.

19.3.2 Site Control
The applicant shall submit with the application documentation of the applicant's legal right to install and use the proposed facility at the subject property. Documentation should also include proof of control over the setback areas.

19.3.3 Dimensional Requirements
All wind turbines shall comply with the requirements set forth in this Section 19.3.3.

19.3.3.1 Height
Wind turbines shall have a maximum height of 350-feet, as measured from the Pre-Construction Grade to the highest point reached by the nacelle. The SPGA may allow this height to be exceeded as part of the special permit process if the project proponent can demonstrate that the additional height is needed and that the additional benefits of the higher tower outweigh any adverse impacts. Monopole towers are the preferred type of support for wind turbines.

19.3.3.2 Setback
a)   Each wind energy conversion facility and its associated equipment shall comply with the
building setback provisions of the zoning district in which the facility is located.

b)   In addition, the following setbacks shall be observed:

1.   In order to ensure public safety and to protect the interest of neighboring property owners,   the minimum distance from the base of any wind turbine tower to any property line in a residential district, shall be equal to the total height of the turbine to the highest point.

19.4 Special Permit Criteria

The SPGA may grant a Special Permit only if it finds that the proposal complies with the provisions of this bylaw and is consistent with the applicable criteria for granting Special Permits.

19.4.1 General

Proposed wind turbine(s) shall comply with all applicable local, state and federal requirements, including but not limited to all applicable electrical, construction, noise, safety, environmental and communications requirements.

19.4.1.1 Visual Impact

The proponent shall demonstrate through project siting and proposed mitigation that the wind turbine minimizes any impact on the visual character of surrounding neighborhoods and the community; this may include, without limitation, information regarding site selection, turbine design, buffering, lighting and cable layout.

19.4.1.2. Color

Wind turbine(s) shall be painted a non-reflective color.

19.4.1.3. Lighting and Signage

Wind turbine(s) shall be lighted only if required by the Federal Aviation Administration (FAA).

The proponent shall provide a copy of the FAA's determination to establish the required marking

and /or lights for the structure.

d) Lighting of equipment structures and any other facilities on site (except lighting) required by the FAA shall be shielded from abutting properties.

e) Signs on the facility shall be limited to:

   1. those needed to identify the property and the owner and warn of any danger; and,

   2. educational signs providing information on the technology and renewable energy usage.

f) All signs shall comply with the requirements of the Town's sign regulations unless relief is
granted by the S.P.G.A.

19.4.2.1 Land Clearing/Open Space/Rare Species

Wind turbines shall be designed to minimize land clearing and fragmentation of open space areas and shall avoid permanently protected open space when feasible. Wind turbines should be sited to make use of previously developed areas wherever possible. Wind turbines facilities shall also be located in a manner that does not have significant negative impacts on rare species in the vicinity (particularly avian species, bats, etc.) as may be applicable law.

19.4.2.2. Storm water
Storm water run-off and erosion control shall be managed in a manner consistent with all applicable state and local law.

19.4.2.3 Noise
The wind turbine and associated equipment shall conform with Massachusetts noise regulations (310 CMR 7.10). An analysis prepared by a qualified engineer shall be presented to demonstrate compliance with these noise standards and shall be consistent with Massachusetts Department of Environmental Protection guidance for noise measurement.

19.4.2.4. Shadowing/Flicker
Wind turbines shall be sited in a manner that does not result in significant shadowing or flicker impacts. Applicant must demonstrate that this effect does not have significant adverse impact on adjacent uses through siting.

19.5 Uses by Telecommunications Carriers
Wind turbines may be used to locate telecommunications antennas, subject to applicable law governing such uses and structures, and subject to the following additional requirements:

d) All ground-mounted telecommunications equipment shall be located in either a shelter, within the wind turbine tower or otherwise screened from view year-round(either through effective landscaping or existing natural vegetated buffers);

e) Antennas shall be flush-mounted to be in keeping with the design of the wind turbine tower; and;

f) All cabling associated with the personal wireless facility shall be contained within the tower structure or enclosed within a conduit painted to match the turbine mount.

19.6 Monitoring and Maintenance

19.6.1 After the wind turbine is operational, the applicant shall submit to the SPGA at annual intervals from the date of issuance of the Special Permit, a report detailing operating data for the facility (including but not limited to days of operation, energy production in accordance with the special permit conditions)

19.6.2 The applicant shall maintain the wind energy conversion facility in good condition. Such maintenance shall include, without limitations, painting, structural integrity of the foundation and support structure and security barrier (if applicable), and maintenance of the buffer areas and landscaping if present.

19.6.3 Notice shall be provided to the SPGA of any change in ownership of the facility.

19.7 Abandonment or Discontinuation of Use

19.7.1   Within six months that a wind turbine(s) is scheduled to be discontinued, the applicant will notify the SPGA by certified U.S. mail of the proposed date of abandonment or discontinuance of operations. In the event that an applicant fails to give such notice, the facility shall be considered abandoned or discontinued if the facility is inoperable for 190 days. In the case of a multi-turbine facility, the SPGA shall determine in its decision what proportion of the facility would be inoperable for the facility to be considered abandoned.

19.7.2   Upon abandonment or discontinuation of use, the owner shall physically remove the wind turbine(s) within 90 days from the date of abandonment or discontinuation of use. This period may be extended at the request of the owner and at the discretion of the SPGA." Physically remove" shall include, but not be limited to:

d) Removal of the wind turbine(s) and tower(s), all machinery, equipment, equipment shelters, security barriers and all appurtenant structures from the subject property.
e) Proper disposal of all solid or hazardous materials and wastes from the site in accordance with local and state solid waste disposal regulations,

f) Restoration of the location of the wind turbine(s) to its natural condition, except that any landscaping, grading or below grade foundation may remain in the after-condition.

19.7.3   If an applicant fails to remove a wind turbine in accordance with this section of this bylaw, the Town shall have the authority to enter the subject property and physically remove the facility. The SPGA may in its decision provide a form of surety (i.e. post a bond, letter of credit or establish an escrow account or other) at the SPGA's election to cover costs of removal in the event the town must remove the facility. The amount of such surety shall be equal to 150 percent of the cost of removal of the facility as determined by a qualified engineer. The amount shall include a mechanism for a Cost of Living Adjustment after 10 and 15 years.

19.8 Terms of Special Permit

A Special Permit issued for any wind turbine(s) facility shall be valid for 25 years unless extended or renewed. At the end of that time period, the wind turbine(s) shall be removed by the applicant.

19.9 Application Procedures

19.9.1 Special Permit Granting Authority **(SPGA)**
The SPGA for wind energy conversion facilities, also referred to as Wind Turbine(s) is this bylaw shall be the Planning Board.

Planning Board recommends passage of this article.

A **2/3's** vote required. Motion adopted **unanimously.**

Article 15:   Zoning Bylaw Amendment – Section 4.2 Permitted Uses – Table of Use Regulations

To see if the Town will vote to amend Section 4.2, "Permitted Uses, Table of Use Regulations", of the Zoning Bylaws to indicate that Wind Energy Conversion Facilities are allowed in all zoning districts by special permit issued by the Planning Board (SPP) by inserting the following after "Helicopter landing area and commercial communication towers" under the heading "Retail & Service:"

	Residential			Non-Residential					Office & Open Space District
USE	R-A	R-B	R-C	DB	WB	HB	TB	LI	OS
Wind energy conversion facility	SPP	SPP	SPP	SPP	SPP	SPP	SPP	SPP	SPP

Or take any other action related thereto.

MOVED that the Town vote to amend Section 4.2, "Permitted Uses, Table of Use Regulations", of the Zoning Bylaws to indicate that Wind Energy Conversion Facilities are allowed in all zoning districts by special permit issued by the Planning Board (SPP) by inserting the following after "Helicopter landing area and commercial communication towers" under the heading "Retail & Service:"

	Residential			Non-Residential					Office & Open Space District
USE	R-A	R-B	R-C	DB	WB	HB	TB	LI	OS
Wind energy conversion facility	SPP	SPP	SPP	SPP	SPP	SPP	SPP	SPP	SPP

Planning Board recommends passage of this article.

A **2/3's** vote required. Motion adopted unanimously.

Commendation offered by Robin Lawrence, member of the Board of Health.

COMMENDATION

WHEREAS, Judy Fitzsimmons has served as Cohasset's Public Health Nurse for the past twenty-two years, fifteen years as a contract employee with the Social Service League and the past seven years as a town employee; and

WHEREAS, Judy Fitzsimmons has now retired from her position as Public Health Nurse after many years of dedicated and professional service; and

WHEREAS, during Judy Fitzsimmons' tenure as Public Health Nurse, she ran the important vaccine distribution program, diligently pursued communicable disease surveillance and epidemiological follow up while always maintaining patient privacy; and

WHEREAS, Judy Fitzsimmons initiated Medicare reimbursement for vaccine administration, making Cohasset one of the first communities in the Commonwealth to receive such reimbursement; and

WHEREAS, as Public Health Nurse, Judy Fitzsimmons has been influential in developing the Pandemic Flu Response Plan and other emergency plans; and

WHEREAS, Judy Fitzsimmons will be sorely missed by her clients to whom she provided outstanding personalized care; and

WHEREAS, the Board of Health now recommends this Unanimous Motion for Commendation to Judy Fitzsimmons:

NOW THEREFORE BE IT RESOLVED that the Citizens of Cohasset, assembled at the Annual Town Meeting hereby acknowledge and affirm their appreciation to Judy Fitzsimmons for her many years of dedicated service to the Town of Cohasset.

GIVEN under our hands and the seal of the TOWN OF COHASSET on this twenty ninth day of March in the year Two Thousand Eight.

Commendation adopted unanimously.

Article 16:   Zoning Bylaw Amendment – Amendment to Section 8

To see if the Town will vote to amend Section 8 of the Zoning Bylaw by:

(a) adding to the end of subsection 8.1 the sentence:

The planning board shall be the special permit granting authority under this section in the VB district and the board of appeals shall be the special permit granting authority under this section in all other districts; and,

(b) replacing the words "board of appeals" where they appear in subsections 8.7, 8.8 and 8.10 with the words "special permit granting authority".

MOVED that the Town vote to amend Section 8 of the Zoning Bylaw by:

(a) adding to the end of subsection 8.1 the sentence:

The planning board shall be the special permit granting authority under this section in the VB district and the board of appeals shall be the special permit granting authority under this section in all other districts; and,

(b) replacing the words "board of appeals" where they appear in subsections 8.7, 8.8 and 8.10 with the words "special permit granting authority".

Planning Board recommends passage of this article.

A **2/3's** vote required. Motion adopted unanimously.

Article 17:   Photovoltaic Array System at Paul Pratt Memorial Library

To see if the Town will vote to raise and appropriate, transfer from available funds or borrow pursuant to any applicable statute a sum of money to be expended by the Town Manager to install a photovoltaic array at the Paul Pratt Memorial Library, or take any other action related thereto.

MOVED that the article be indefinitely postponed.

Motion adopted unanimously.

At this time the Girls Basketball Team was introduced and recognized for winning the State Championship.

Article 18:   Sewer Betterment Abatement

To see if the town will vote to raise and appropriate, transfer from available funds or otherwise provide the sum of $6066.99 for the purpose of returning the sewer betterment assessed and paid for the property located at Map 32 Plot 55, or take any other action relative thereto.

MOVED that Six Thousand Sixty Six Dollars and Ninety Nine Cents ($6,066.99) be appropriated for the purpose of returning the sewer betterment assessed and paid for the property located at Map 32 Plot 55; and to meet this appropriation, the sum of Six Thousand Sixty Six Dollars and Ninety Nine Cents ($6,066.99) be transferred from Free Cash (Surplus Revenue) in the treasury of the town.
Motion **adopted unanimously**.

Commendation offered by Gary Vanderweil for Raymond Kasperowicz.

COMMENDATION

WHEREAS, Raymond Kasperowicz previously served three years as a member of the Advisory Committee; and

WHEREAS, Raymond Kasperowicz previously served three years as a member of the Personnel Committee; and

WHEREAS, Raymond Kasperowicz has served nine years as a member of the Cohasset Sewer Commission, including several years as its Chairman; and

WHEREAS, as a member of the Cohasset Sewer Commission, Raymond Kasperowicz discharge his responsibilities with great wisdom, judgment during a period of time where sewer system expansion was debated; and

WHEREAS, Raymond Kasperowicz applied his financial experience and qualifications to decision-making that was always in the interest of the citizens of Cohasset; and

WHEREAS, such dedication and service to the Town can not come without great sacrifice to personal matters and family life;

WHEREAS, the Board of Selectmen now recommends this Unanimous Motion for Commendation to Raymond Kasperowicz.

NOW THEREFORE BE IT RESOLVED that the Citizens of Cohasset, assembled at Annual Town Meeting hereby acknowledge and affirm their appreciation to Raymond Kasperowicz for his many years of dedicated service to the Town of Cohasset.

GIVEN under our hands and the seal of the TOWN OF COHASSET on this twenty ninth day of March in the year Two Thousand Eight.

Commendation adopted unanimously.

Commendation offered by Sam Wakeman for James Gilman.

WHEREAS, since James H. Gilman has lived in Cohasset, he has had a strong ongoing interest in the public affairs of the Town; and

WHEREAS, James H Gilman was appointed to the Advisory Committee in 2002 and has been a dedicated member for the past six years; and

WHEREAS, such dedication and service to the Town can not come without great sacrifice to personal matters and family life; and

WHEREAS, the Advisory Committee now recommends this Unanimous Motion for Commendation to James H Gilman.

NOW THEREFOR BE IT RESOLVED that the Citizens of Cohasset, assembled at Annual Town Meeting hereby acknowledge and affirm their appreciation to James H Gilman for his many years of service to the Town of Cohasset.

GIVEN under our hands and the seal of the Town of Cohasset on this twenty-ninth day of March in the year Two Thousand Eight.

Commendation adopted unanimously.

Article 19:   Affordable Housing Trust Bylaw

To see if the Town will accept Massachusetts General Laws Chapter 44, Section 55C so as to create an affordable housing trust, and amend the General By-Laws of the Town by adding new Article V, Section 21 as follows, or take any other action relative thereto:

COHASSET AFFORDABLE HOUSING TRUST

SECTION 1

A. There shall be in the Town of Cohasset a Cohasset Affordable Housing Trust Fund (hereinafter referred to as "the trust"). The purpose of the trust is to provide for the creation and preservation of affordable housing in the Town of Cohasset for low- and moderate-income households.

B. There shall be a board of trustees which shall include seven (7) trustees. The trustees shall be appointed by the Board of Selectmen and shall include one (1) member of the Board of Selectmen and are designated as public agents for purposes of the constitution of the Commonwealth. The initial terms of the trustees shall be staggered as one (1) or two (2) year terms. All terms thereafter shall be for two (2) years.

SECTION 2

A. The powers of the board of trustees shall include the following:

1. to accept and receive real property, personal property or money, by gift, grant, contribution, devise or transfer from any person, firm, corporation or other public or private entity, including but not limited to money, grants of funds or other property tendered to the trust in connection with the provisions of the Cohasset Zoning By-Law or General By-laws, or any general or special law or any other source, or money from the Community Preservation Act, G.L. Chapter 44B;

2. to accept and receive municipal, school or other public property, subject to a majority vote of Town Meeting to transfer said property to the trust, for the purposes of the trust;

3. to purchase and retain real or personal property for the purposes of the trust, including without restriction investments that yield a high rate of income or no income, and to hold all or part of the trust property uninvested for such purposes and for such time as the board may deem appropriate;

4. to manage or improve real property;

5. to sell, lease, exchange, transfer or convey any real property for such consideration and on such terms as to credit or otherwise, and to make such contracts and enter into such undertakings relative to trust property as the board deems advisable, notwithstanding the length of any such lease or contract;

6. to execute, acknowledge and deliver deeds, assignments, transfers, pledges, leases, covenants, contracts, promissory notes, releases and other instruments sealed or unsealed, necessary, proper or incident to any transaction in which the board engages for the accomplishment of the purposes of the trust;

7. to employ and pay reasonable compensation to advisors and agents, such as accountants, appraisers and lawyers as the board deems necessary.

8. to apportion receipts and charges between income and principal as the board deems advisable, to amortize premiums and establish sinking funds for such purpose, and to create reserves for depreciation, depletion or otherwise;

9. to carry property for accounting purposes at other than acquisition date values;

10. to borrow money on such terms and conditions and from such sources as the trustees deem advisable, to mortgage and pledge trust assets as collateral, subject to approval by a majority vote of the Board of Selectmen. (Any debt issued by the Trust shall not be deemed to constitute a debt or liability of the Town of Cohasset or a pledge of the faith and credit of the Town, but shall be payable solely from the revenues, funds and/or assets of the Trust. Any debt instrument executed by the Trust shall contain on the face thereof a statement to the effect that the Town of Cohasset is not obligated to pay the same or the interest thereof except from revenues, funds and/or assets of the Trust and that neither the faith and credit nor the taxing power of the Town of Cohasset is pledged to the payment of the principal of or the interest on such debt. The issuance of debt by the Trust shall not directly or indirectly or contingently obligate the Town of Cohasset to levy or to pledge any form of taxation whatever therefore or to make any appropriation for their payment);

11. to make distributions or divisions of principal in kind;

12. to defend, enforce, release, settle or otherwise adjust claims in favor or against the trust, including claims for taxes, and to accept any property, either in total or partial satisfaction of any indebtedness or other obligation, and subject to the provisions of this Article, to continue to hold the same for such period of time as the board may deem appropriate;

13. to extend the time for payment of any obligation to the trust;

14. to provide grants or loans to assist low- or moderate-income homebuyers to purchase or rehabilitate a dwelling unit in the Town of Cohasset;

15. to convey, through sale, lease or transfer, real property purchased under this act, to any for-profit or non-profit developer or any public agency to provide low- or moderate-income housing, subject to an affordable housing restriction under Section 26 or Sections 31-33 of Chapter 184 of the General Laws;

16. Expenditures for the acquisition or disposition of real property shall be subject to approval by a majority vote of the Board of Selectmen; and

17. in each fiscal year, expenditures from the fund shall be in accordance with an allocation plan approved by the Town at the Annual Town Meeting and upon the recommendation of the trustees, for purposes consistent with this by-law. The allocation plan shall be a general plan for the use of funds during the fiscal year to which the plan applies, and may provide for moneys to be held in reserve for expenditure in later years. The plan may be amended at a Town Meeting upon favorable recommendation of the board of trustees.

SECTION 3

A. As a means of providing available assets for the trust, all moneys received by the Town through the following means shall be paid directly into the trust and need not be appropriated or accepted and approved into the trust:

1. cash payments made by developers to the Town for purposes of creating or preserving affordable housing, under any development agreements or development approvals pursuant to the Cohasset Zoning By-Law;

2. gifts, grants, donations, contributions or other cash payments to the trust for the purpose of providing low- or moderate-income housing;

B. General revenues appropriated into the trust become trust property, and to be expended these funds need not be further appropriated;

C. All moneys remaining in the trust at the end of any fiscal year, whether or not expended by the board of trustees within one year of the date they were appropriated into the trust, shall remain trust property;

D. The trust is exempt from G.L. Chapters 59 and 62, and from any other provisions concerning payment of taxes based upon or measured by property or income imposed by the Commonwealth or any political subdivision thereof; and

E. The books and records of the trust shall be reviewed annually by an independent auditor in accordance with accepted accounting practices.

SECTION 4

As used in this act, the term "low or moderate income housing" shall mean "low income housing" or "moderate income housing" as defined in Section 2 of Chapter 44B of the General Laws.

SECTION 5

The Town Treasurer shall be the custodian of the trust's funds. Any income or proceeds received from the investment of funds shall be credited to and become part of the fund.

SECTION 6

A. The trust is a governmental body for purposes of Sections 23A, 23B and 23C of Chapter 39 of the General Laws.

B. The trust is a board of the Town for purposes of Chapter 30B and Section 15A of Chapter 40; but agreements and conveyances between the trust and agencies, boards, commissions, authorities, department and public instrumentalities of the Town shall be exempt from Chapter 30B.

C. The trust is a public employer and the members of the board are public employees for purposes of Chapter 258.

D. The trust shall be deemed a public agency and trustees as special municipal employees for purposes of Chapter 268A.

E. All projects for new construction of affordable housing or conversion of existing units into affordable housing that are proposed to be funded or subsidized by the trust shall be so constructed or converted through the Local Initiative or Local Access Programs as governed by the then-applicable regulations of the Department of Housing and Community Development, or its successor.

F. At any time after the expiration of five years after the date on which this trust is created by the Town, it may be terminated in the same manner as it was created, except that it shall remain in existence to complete any pending undertakings or obligations. During such winding down, the then-membership of the Board of Selectmen shall serve as the trustees. The balance of any funds held by the trust after winding down shall pass to the Town's Community Preservation Fund or some other substitute affordable housing fund created by the Town. Non-monetary assets of the trust shall pass to the Town under the control of the Board of Selectmen under such restrictions as applicable law may require or as may have been prior imposed upon such assets.

MOVED that the Town accept Massachusetts General Laws Chapter 44, Section 55C so as to create an affordable housing trust, and amend the General By-Laws of the Town by adding new Article V, Section 21 as follows:

COHASSET AFFORDABLE HOUSING TRUST

SECTION 1

A. There shall be in the Town of Cohasset a Cohasset Affordable Housing Trust Fund (hereinafter referred to as "the trust"). The purpose of the trust is to provide for the creation and preservation of affordable housing in the Town of Cohasset for low- and moderate-income households.

B. There shall be a board of trustees which shall include seven (7) trustees. The trustees shall be appointed by the Board of Selectmen and shall include one (1) member of the Board of Selectmen and are designated as public agents for purposes of the constitution of the Commonwealth. The initial terms of the trustees shall be staggered as one (1) or two (2) year terms. All terms thereafter shall be for two (2) years.

SECTION 2

A. The powers of the board of trustees shall include the following:

1. to accept and receive real property, personal property or money, by gift, grant, contribution, devise or transfer from any person, firm, corporation or other public or private entity, including but not limited to money, grants of funds or other property tendered to the trust in connection with the provisions of the Cohasset Zoning By-Law or General By-laws, or any general or special law or any other source, or money from the Community Preservation Act, G.L. Chapter 44B;

2. to accept and receive municipal, school or other public property, subject to a majority vote of Town Meeting to transfer said property to the trust, for the purposes of the trust;

3. to purchase and retain real or personal property for the purposes of the trust, including without restriction investments that yield a high rate of income or no income, and to hold all or part of the trust property uninvested for such purposes and for such time as the board may deem appropriate;

4. to manage or improve real property;

5. to sell, lease, exchange, transfer or convey any real property for such consideration and on such terms as to credit or otherwise, and to make such contracts and enter into such undertakings relative to trust property as the board deems advisable, notwithstanding the length of any such lease or contract;

6. to execute, acknowledge and deliver deeds, assignments, transfers, pledges, leases, covenants, contracts, promissory notes, releases and other instruments sealed or unsealed, necessary, proper or incident to any transaction in which the board engages for the accomplishment of the purposes of the trust;

7. to employ and pay reasonable compensation to advisors and agents, such as accountants, appraisers and lawyers as the board deems necessary.

8. to apportion receipts and charges between income and principal as the board deems advisable, to amortize premiums and establish sinking funds for such purpose, and to create reserves for depreciation, depletion or otherwise;

9. to carry property for accounting purposes at other than acquisition date values;

10. to borrow money on such terms and conditions and from such sources as the trustees deem advisable, to mortgage and pledge trust assets as collateral, subject to approval by a majority vote of the Board of Selectmen .(Any debt issued by the Trust shall not be deemed to constitute a debt or liability of the Town of Cohasset or a pledge of the faith and credit of the Town, but shall be payable solely from the revenues, funds and/or assets of the Trust. Any debt instrument executed by the Trust shall contain on the face thereof a statement to the effect that the Town of Cohasset is not obligated to pay the same or the interest thereof except from revenues, funds and/or assets of the Trust and that neither the faith and credit nor the taxing power of the Town of Cohasset is pledged to the payment of the principal of or the interest on such debt. The issuance of debt by the Trust shall not directly or indirectly or contingently obligate the Town of Cohasset to levy or to pledge any form of taxation whatever therefore or to make any appropriation for their payment);
11. to make distributions or divisions of principal in kind;
12. to defend, enforce, release, settle or otherwise adjust claims in favor or against the trust, including claims for taxes, and to accept any property, either in total or partial satisfaction of any indebtedness or other obligation, and subject to the provisions of this Article, to continue to hold the same for such period of time as the board may deem appropriate;
13. to extend the time for payment of any obligation to the trust;
14. to provide grants or loans to assist low- or moderate-income homebuyers to purchase or rehabilitate a dwelling unit in the Town of Cohasset;
15. to convey, through sale, lease or transfer, real property purchased under this act, to any for-profit or non-profit developer or any public agency to provide low- or moderate-income housing, subject to an affordable housing restriction under Section 26 or Sections 31-33 of Chapter 184 of the General Laws;
16. Expenditures for the acquisition or disposition of real property shall be subject to approval by a majority vote of the Board of Selectmen; and
17. in each fiscal year, expenditures from the fund shall be in accordance with an allocation plan approved by the Town at the Annual Town Meeting and upon the recommendation of the trustees, for purposes consistent with this by-law. The allocation plan shall be a general plan for the use of funds during the fiscal year to which the plan applies, and may provide for moneys to be held in reserve for expenditure in later years. The plan may be amended at a Town Meeting upon favorable recommendation of the board of trustees.

SECTION 3

A. As a means of providing available assets for the trust, all moneys received by the Town through the following means shall be paid directly into the trust and need not be appropriated or accepted and approved into the trust:

1 cash payments made by developers to the Town for purposes of creating or preserving affordable housing, under any development agreements or development approvals pursuant to the Cohasset Zoning By-Law;
2 gifts, grants, donations, contributions or other cash payments to the trust for the purpose of providing low- or moderate-income housing;

B. General revenues appropriated into the trust become trust property, and to be expended these funds need not be further appropriated;

C. All moneys remaining in the trust at the end of any fiscal year, whether or not expended by the board of trustees within one year of the date they were appropriated into the trust, shall remain trust property;

D. The trust is exempt from G.L. Chapters 59 and 62, and from any other provisions concerning payment of taxes based upon or measured by property or income imposed by the Commonwealth or any political subdivision thereof; and

E. The books and records of the trust shall be reviewed annually by an independent auditor in accordance with accepted accounting practices.

SECTION 4

As used in this act, the term "low or moderate income housing" shall mean "low income housing" or "moderate income housing" as defined in Section 2 of Chapter 44B of the General Laws.

SECTION 5

The Town Treasurer shall be the custodian of the trust's funds. Any income or proceeds received from the investment of funds shall be credited to and become part of the fund.

SECTION 6

A. The trust is a governmental body for purposes of Sections 23A, 23B and 23C of Chapter 39 of the General Laws.

B. The trust is a board of the Town for purposes of Chapter 30B and Section 15A of Chapter 40; but agreements and conveyances between the trust and agencies, boards, commissions, authorities, department and public instrumentalities of the Town shall be exempt from Chapter 30B.

C. The trust is a public employer and the members of the board are public employees for purposes of Chapter 258.

D. The trust shall be deemed a public agency and trustees as special municipal employees for purposes of Chapter 268A.

E. All projects for new construction of affordable housing or conversion of existing units into affordable housing that are proposed to be funded or subsidized by the trust shall be so constructed or converted through the Local Initiative or Local Access Programs as governed by the then-applicable regulations of the Department of Housing and Community Development, or its successor.

F. At any time after the expiration of five years after the date on which this trust is created by the Town, it may be terminated in the same manner as it was created, except that it shall remain in existence to complete any pending undertakings or obligations. During such winding down, the then-membership of the Board of Selectmen shall serve as the trustees. The balance of any funds held by the trust after winding down shall pass to the Town's Community Preservation Fund or some other substitute affordable housing fund created by the Town. Non-monetary assets of the trust shall pass to the Town under the control of the Board of Selectmen under such restrictions as applicable law may require or as may have been prior imposed upon such assets.

Motion adopted.

Article 20:   Zoning Bylaw Amendment – Inclusionary Zoning

To see if the Town will amend the provisions of the Zoning Bylaw by striking Subsection 14 of Section 4.3 and Section 17.8 and replacing them with the following new Section 20, in order to better encourage and facilitate the development of affordable housing:
SECTION 20 – Inclusionary Zoning

1. Definitions. In addition to the definitions found in Section 2, the following definitions shall apply for purposes of implementation of this Section.

   Affordable unit: housing or housing units constituting Low or Moderate Income Housing as such terms are defined by M.G.L. c 40B, Sections 20 through 23, as amended, or successor law, and its implementing regulations in 760 CMR 30.00 et seq. and 31.00 et seq. or successor regulations.

2. Purpose and Intent

   a. To recognize the affordable housing need in Cohasset;
   b. To require applicants for development projects having a significant impact on the Town to contribute toward this need;
   c. To encourage the expansion and upgrade of the Town's affordable housing in order to provide for a full range of housing choices for households of all families, ages and sizes;
   d. To prevent the displacement of low to moderate income Cohasset residents;
   e. To increase the production of affordable housing units;
   f. To meet the requirements of the Local Initiative Program; and
   g. To qualify housing for inclusion on the Subsidized Housing Inventory.

3. Applicability

   a. The provisions of this Section shall apply to all projects requiring approval as any and all commercial, residential or mixed-use projects requiring Site Plan Review, to single family residential subdivisions on sites having a development potential under current zoning of five or more lots, and to the construction of "multiple unit" developments of five (5) or more dwelling units in accordance with any Section of the Zoning Bylaw, whether on one or more contiguous parcels, and including, but not limited to, any characterization of units, such as "multifamily", "apartments, "condominiums", "cooperatives" and any other development governed by a common scheme, restrictions or covenants, and without regard to how many dwelling units exist per building in the development.

b. The provisions of this Section shall not apply to any project undertaken by the Town for any municipal purposes.

c. The provisions of this Section shall not apply to any project undertaken pursuant to MGL c. 40B.

4. Mandatory Provision of Affordable Units

The Planning Board or Board of Appeals or any other authority giving permission for construction of dwelling units, shall, as a condition of approval of any development referred to in Subsections 3 above, require that the applicant for site plan review, subdivision, special permit or building permit approval comply with the obligation to provide affordable housing pursuant to this Bylaw and more fully described in Subsection 5 below.

5. Provision of Affordable Units

a. Residential-Only Development. To facilitate the provision of affordable housing in an all residential-only development, the number of units that are required to be affordable shall be ten percent (10%) of the number of units that could be developed "as of right" (AOR), rounded up to the nearest whole number. The number of affordable units required shall not subtract from the number of AOR units, but instead shall be added to the AOR units as a density bonus. Thus, a proposal that would have 5 AOR units would include those 5 plus 1 affordable unit. If the number of affordable units plus the AOR units yields a result where the number of affordable units is less than 10% of the total number of units being provided with the density bonus, then an additional affordable unit shall be added to bring overall percentage at or above 10%.

b. Commercial-Only Development. In a commercial development, affordable units are not expected to be provided on-site unless "mixed-use" zoning is available. Nevertheless, such development should also and is compelled to contribute to the need for affordable housing by a fee-in-lieu-of-construction payment, per subsection (e) and Section 11 below. The required number of affordable units shall be calculated as follows: .02 affordable housing units per each 2,000 square feet of floor area in the development.

c. Mixed-Use Development. In the VB and TOD districts, and in any other location where "mixed use" development is permitted, both the calculations of required affordable units set forth in subsections (a) and (b) above shall be made, and the one yielding the larger number of affordable units shall be applied.

In the VB district, if there is a conflict between (i) the density allowed under this subsection (c) (referenced in terms of number of units) and the number of units this Section 5 requires of a development in the VB district and (ii) the density allowed under Section 18(1) (referenced in terms of Floor Area Ratio and allowable apartment sizes) and the number of units such density bonus would yield, the density limits and affordable unit number results of Section 18.1 will control.

d. An applicant may offer, and the Planning Board or Board of Appeals, in concert with the Board of Selectmen, may accept a parcel of land in fee simple, on or off-site, that the Planning Board or Board of Appeals determines are suitable for the construction of affordable housing units. The value of donated land shall be equal to or greater than the value of the construction or set-aside of the affordable units. The Planning Board or Board of Appeals may require, prior to accepting land as satisfaction of the requirements of this Section, that the applicant submit appraisals of the land in question, as well as other data relevant to the determination of equivalent value;

e. In substitution for providing affordable housing units, a cash payment to the Cohasset Housing Trust Fund (or similar affordable housing fund) may be made subject to Subsection 11 below.

f. The applicant may offer, and the Planning Board or Board of Appeals may accept, any combination of the above requirements provided that in no event shall the total number of units or land area provided be less than the equivalent number or value of affordable units required by this Section.

6.   Provisions Applicable to Affordable Housing Units On-and Off-Site

a. Siting of affordable units - All affordable units constructed or rehabilitated under this Section shall be situated within the development so as not to be in less desirable locations than market-rate units in the development and shall, on average, be no less accessible to public amenities, such as open space, as the market-rate units.

b. Minimum design and construction standards for affordable units - Affordable housing units within market rate developments shall be integrated with the rest of the development and shall be compatible in design, appearance, construction and quality of materials with other units, and built in accordance with the following ratios:

Market Rate Unit %	Affordable Housing Unit %
Up to 30%	None required
30% + 1 unit	At least 10%
Up to 50%	At least 30%
Up to 75%	At least 50%
75% + 1 unit	At least 70%
Up to 90%	100%

Fractions of units shall not be counted.

7.   Marketing Plan for Affordable Units

Applicants under this Bylaw shall submit a marketing plan or other method, prepared with the assistance of and approved by, the Cohasset Housing Partnership approved by to the Planning Board or Board of Appeals for approval, which describes how the affordable units will be marketed to potential homebuyers. This plan shall include a description of the lottery or other process to be used for selecting buyers. The marketing plan must describe how the applicant will accommodate local preference requirements, if any, established by the Board of Selectmen, in a manner that complies with the nondiscrimination in tenant or buyer selection guidelines of the Local Initiative Program.

8.   Provision of Affordable Housing Units Off-Site

As an alternative to the requirements of Subsection 5(a), (b) and (c) above, an applicant subject to this Section may develop, construct or otherwise provide affordable units equivalent to those required by Subsection 5 off-site. All requirements of this Section that apply to on-site provision of affordable units, shall apply to provision of off-site affordable units. In addition, the location of the off-site units to be provided shall be approved by the Planning Board or Board of Appeals as an integral element of the review and approval process for the permit requested..

9.   Maximum Incomes and Selling Prices: Initial Sale

a. The developer of the housing units or his/her agent shall verify prior to transferring title or executing a lease that each prospective purchaser or renter of an affordable housing unit created under this Section is a household of low or moderate income, as defined by the Commonwealth's Local Initiative Program (LIP). Toward this end:

(1) the developer shall engage a qualified certifying agent acceptable to the Planning Board or to the Board of Appeals to receive purchase or rental applications, obtain and review documentation concerning sources and amounts of household income, and certify to the Town that all purchasers or renters approved for an affordable unit meet LIP income eligibility requirements (which certifying agent may be the Town's Housing Partnership, Housing Authority or consultant(s) thereto).

(2) The developer is responsible for making arrangements acceptable to the Planning Board or to the Board of Appeals to provide annual certifications to the Town as may be required to place and maintain the affordable units on the Commonwealth's Chapter 40B Subsidized Housing Inventory.

b. The maximum allowable purchase price or maximum allowable rent for affordable units created under this Bylaw shall comply with the regulations and guidelines of the Local Initiative Program (LIP).

10.   Preservation of Affordability; Restrictions on Resale

a. Each affordable unit created in accordance with this Section shall have the following limitations governing its resale. The purpose of these limitations is to preserve the long-term affordability of the unit and to ensure its continued availability to qualified purchasers in the future. The resale controls shall be established through a deed rider or an affordable housing restriction as defined by M.G.L. c.184, Section 31, recorded at the Norfolk County Registry of Deeds or the Land Court, and shall be in force for as long a period as is lawful. The affordable housing use restriction shall meet the requirements of the Local Initiative Program.

b. Resale price -Sales beyond the initial sale to a qualified affordable income purchaser shall include the initial discount rate between the sale price and the unit's appraised value at the time of resale. This percentage shall be recorded as part of the restriction on the property noted in this Subsection 10. For example, if a unit appraised for $300,000 is sold for $225,000 as a result of this Section, it has sold for 75% of its appraised value. If, several years later, the appraised value of the unit at the time of proposed resale is $325,000, the unit may be sold for no more than $243,750, or 75% of the appraised value of $325,000.

c. Right of first refusal to purchase -The purchaser of an affordable housing unit developed as a result of this Section shall agree to execute a deed rider prepared by the Town, granting, among other things, the Town's right of first refusal for a period not less than the maximum period allowable under guidelines set by the Department of Housing and Community Development for Local Initiative Units as defined by the Local Initiative Program, to purchase the property or assignment thereof, in the event that, despite diligent efforts to sell the property, a subsequent qualified purchaser cannot be located.

d. The Planning Board or Board of Appeals shall require, as a condition for subdivision, special permit or building permit approval under this Section, that the deeds to the affordable housing units contain a restriction against renting or leasing said unit during the period for which the housing unit contains a restriction on affordability.

e. The Planning Board or Board of Appeals shall require, as a condition for special permit approval under this Bylaw, that the applicant comply with the mandatory set- asides and accompanying restrictions on affordability, including the execution of the deed rider noted in this Subsection 10. The Zoning Enforcement Officer shall not issue an occupancy permit for any affordable unit until the deed restriction is recorded at the Norfolk County Registry of Deeds or the Land Court.

f. Affordability restrictions as set forth herein shall be in perpetuity.

11.   Fees in Lieu of Affordable Housing Units

As a further alternative to Subsection 5 above, an applicant may contribute a cash payment to the Cohasset Housing Trust Fund (or if none exists to the Cohasset Community Preservation Fund), to be used for the development of affordable housing by the Town or its designees, in lieu of constructing and offering affordable units within the locus of the proposed development or off-site.

a. Calculation of fees-in-lieu of units. The applicant for development subject to this Section may pay a fee in lieu of the construction of affordable units. For each affordable unit not constructed or provided through one or a combination of the methods specified in Subsection 5 above, the fee shall be an amount equal to the difference between the median sale price for new single-family homes built in Cohasset during the preceding three fiscal years, as determined and reported by the Board of Assessors, and the purchase price of a similar home that is affordable to a qualified purchaser. For developments of multi-family condominiums, the Planning Board or Zoning Board of Appeals may substitute the median sale price for new condominiums built in Cohasset during the preceding three fiscal years for the median sale price of new single-family homes.

b. The methodology used to determine an affordable purchase price shall comply with Local Initiative Program guidelines in effect at the time of application for a special permit.

c. The assumptions used to determine an affordable purchase price, including but not limited to minimum down payment, mortgage interest rate, term, closing and other costs shall be consistent with first-time homebuyer mortgage products available from commercial lending institutions located in or serving Cohasset at the time of application for a special permit, all in accordance with the Inclusionary Housing Submission Requirements and Procedures Manual adopted by the Planning Board and filed with the Town Clerk.

d. Upon adoption of this Section by town meeting, the Planning Board shall prepare and adopt an Inclusionary Housing Submission Requirements and Procedures Manual after holding a public hearing on the same. This will be used by Zoning Board of Appeals where it is the permit granting authority. Or take any other action related thereto.

MOVED that the article be indefinitely postponed.

Motion adopted unanimously.

Article 21:   Harbor Study Funding

To see if the Town will vote to raise and appropriate, transfer from available funds, or borrow pursuant to any applicable statute, a sum of money in order to retain a professional consulting/planning firm overseen by the Planning Board acting under its powers and duties of the General Laws of the Commonwealth and the General and Zoning Bylaws of the Town, to assist the Planning Board and Board of Selectmen in the development of bylaws which enhance the vitality of the Waterfront Business District (WB), the Harbor portion of the Downtown Business District (DB), the Harbor portion of the Light Industry District (LI), the Harbor portion of the Official and Open Space District and the all other properties abutting the Harbor around its perimeter, while maintaining its general.

MOVED that the article be indefinitely postponed.

Motion adopted unanimously.

Commendation offered by Frederick Koed, member of the Board of Selectmen for Jack Worley.

COMMENDATION

WHEREAS, Jack Worley was appointed as Recreation Director for the Town of Cohasset in November of 1976; and

WHEREAS, Jack Worley will soon retire after serving the Town of Cohasset for over 31 years in a highly professional, dedicated manner; and

WHEREAS, during Jack Worley's tenure as Recreation Director, he has introduced many recreation programs and activities that have been the source of great fun and education for children and adults of all ages in the Town of Cohasset; and

WHEREAS, Jack Worley in his capacity of Recreation Director has put his heart and soul into his responsibilities, including always working from early morning to late at night and on weekends to serve the needs of this community; and

WHEREAS, during his tenure as Recreation Director, Jack Worley has always served this community with a smile on his face and a good word for everyone; and

WHEREAS, the Board of Selectmen now recommends this Unanimous Motion for Commendation to Jack Worley:

NOW THEREFORE BE IT RESOLVED that the Citizens of Cohasset, assembled at the Annual Town Meeting hereby acknowledge and affirm their appreciation to Jack Worley for his many years of dedicated service to the Town of Cohasset.

GIVEN under our hands and the seal of the TOWN OF COHASSET on this twenty ninth day of March in the year Two Thousand Eight.

Commendation voted unanimously.

Article 22:   Treat's Pond Restoration Project Funding

To see if the Town will vote to raise and appropriate, transfer from available funds, or borrow pursuant to any applicable statute, a sum of money to be expended by the Town Manager in combination with other federal and/or state funds for engineering and design professional services for the designing and permitting, construction supervision and related services in connection with the Treat's Pond ecosystem restoration project, and for the construction of such project and all related construction expenses, including, an independent engineering and environmental assessment, and further to authorize the Board of Selectmen to acquire by purchase, gift or eminent domain such easements or other property interests as may be advisable to carry out this project, or take any other action related thereto.

MOVED that Three Hundred Thousand Dollars ($300,000) be appropriated, with the intention that these funds be available in FY 2008 and, thereafter, to be expended by the Town Manager in combination with other federal and/or state funds for engineering and design professional services for the designing and permitting, construction, supervision and related services in connection with the Treat's Pond ecosystem restoration project, and for the construction of such project and all related construction expenses, including, an independent engineering and environmental assessment, and that to fund this appropriation, the Treasurer, with the approval of the Board of Selectmen, is hereby authorized to borrow Three Hundred Thousand Dollars ($300,000), under and pursuant to Chapter 44, of the General Laws of the Commonwealth, as amended, or any other enabling authority, and to issue bonds or notes of the Town, therefore, and that the Board of Selectmen be authorized to accept, as gifts, grants of deeds, easements or other instruments of transfer of all or portions of Treat's Pond located on the parcels known as Assessor Map 31, Parcel 021F and 021G.

Amendment offered by Ralph **Dormitzer,** member of the Board of Selectmen who recluses himself from deliberations on Article **22** and who is speaking as a private citizen.

Moved that the motion under Article 22 be amended by substituting the following language in its entirety:

That Forty Five Thousand Dollars ($45,000) be appropriated with the intention that these funds be available in FY 2008 and thereafter, which funds are to be expended by the Town Manager in addition to and in combination with any other available Federal and/or State grant funds, as s supplement thereto, for the purpose of funding professional services to conduct an independent review of the United States Army Corps of Engineers Treat's Pond ecosystem restoration project and to meet this appropriation, Forty Five Thousand Dollars ($45,000) be transferred from Free Cash (Surplus Revenue) in the treasury of the town.

Amendment offered by Peter Brown.

That Forty Five Thousand Dollars ($45,000) be appropriated with the intention that these funds be available in FY 2008 and thereafter, which funds are to be expended by the Town Manager in addition to and in combination with any other available Federal and/or State grant funds, as s supplement thereto, for the purpose of funding professional services to conduct an independent review of the United States Army Corps of Engineers Treat's Pond ecosystem restoration project and to meet this appropriation, Forty Five Thousand Dollars ($45,000) be transferred from Free Cash (Surplus Revenue) in the treasury of the town.

The scope of which review shall be determined by a committee appointed by the Board of Selectmen, comprised of a member of the Cohasset Conservation Commission, the special engineering assistant to the Town Manager for special project, and a citizeh of the town with extensive environmental expertise.

Amendment offered by Peter Brown is defeated.

Amendment offered by Ralph **Dormitzer** is defeated.

Amendment offered by Frederick Koed, member of the Board of Selectmen in the form of a proclamation.

PROCLAMATION

Resolved,

1 That the Town of Cohasset recognizes both the serious nature of the environmental health of Treat's Pond and flooding issues in its surrounding area;

2 That the Town of Cohasset wishes to pursue solutions to these problems and does not wish to foreclose the possibility of Federal Funds to support possible solutions;

3 That the Town of Cohasset, however, needs to further study the issues and proposals that have been made to solve them, owing to the relatively little time they have been public;

4 That the Town of Cohasset is undertaking to comprehensively study town wide flooding issues, the report on which is due in 2008.

Therefore, the town requests the Army Corps of Engineers and Congressman Delahunt provide additional time to the town until the fall town meeting to address the issue at Treat's Pond.

Proclamation adopted.

This amendment of a proclamation is **now the main** motion. **Motion adopted.**

Article 23:   Repurchase of **Cemetery** Lots **Funding**

To see if the Town will vote to raise and appropriate, transfer from available funds, or otherwise provide a sum of money to be expended by the Town Manager for the repurchase of cemetery lots at Town cemeteries, or take any other action related thereto.

MOVED that Eleven Thousand Dollars ($11,000), be appropriated to be expended by the Town Manager for the repurchase of cemetery lots at Town cemeteries, and to meet this appropriation, the sum of Eleven Thousand Dollars ($11,000) be transferred from Free Cash (Surplus Revenue) in the treasury of the town.

Motion adopted **unanimously.**

Article 24:   **Stormwater Management Bylaw**

To see if the Town will vote to amend the General Bylaws by adding the following new Article XV, or take any other action related thereto:

COHASSET STORMWATER MANAGEMENT BYLAW

1. Authority
   This Bylaw is adopted under authority granted by the Home Rule Amendment of the Massachusetts Constitution, the Home Rule statutes, and pursuant to the federal Clean Water Act, 33 U. S. C. §§ 1251-1386 (the "Act") and regulations issued pursuant to the Act which are found at 40 CFR 122.34.

2. Purpose
   A. The purpose of this Bylaw is to:
      1. Prevent and reduce existing and future flooding.
      2. Protect water quality.
      3. Increase groundwater recharge.
      4. Reduce erosion and sedimentation.
      5. Promote environmentally sensitive site design practices.
      6. Ensure long-term maintenance of stormwater controls.
      7. Help the Town of Cohasset meet federal requirements under Phase II of the National Pollutant Discharge Elimination System.
      8. Establish the legal authority by which the Town of Cohasset can enforce the provisions of this Bylaw and accompanying regulations.

3. Definitions
   A. The following definitions shall apply in the interpretation and implementation of this Bylaw. The term "alter" shall include, without limitation, the following activities:
      1. Changing of pre-existing drainage characteristics, adding impervious area or changing type of land cover, or changing sedimentation patterns, flow patterns or flood retention characteristics;
      2. Dumping, discharging or filling with any material, or removal of material, which would alter elevations or change drainage patterns or degrade water quality;
      3. Driving of piles, erection, or expansion of buildings or structures of any kind;
      4. Destruction of plant life, including clearing of trees;
      5. Any activities, changes or work which may cause or tend to contribute to pollution of any body of water or groundwater.

4. Regulated Activities
   A. Regulated Activities Requiring a Stormwater Permit. The following activities, developments or redevelopments require the issuance of a full Stormwater Permit by the Conservation Commission (the "Commission") after the filing by the Applicant of a full application and full review by the Commission through a public hearing:
      1. Any activity that will alter 5,000 square feet or more of land.

2. Any construction or development activity on an undeveloped parcel of any size that will increase the impervious surface area, or increase the amount or rate of runoff from the parcel.

3. Any development or redevelopment of Land Uses with Higher Potential Pollutant Loads as defined in the Massachusetts Stormwater Management Policy, which include, for example:
   - auto salvage yards (auto recycler facilities)
   a. auto fueling facilities (gas stations)
   c. exterior fleet storage areas (cars, buses, trucks, public works equipment)
   d. exterior vehicle service, maintenance and equipment cleaning areas
   e. commercial parking lots
   f. road salt storage and loading areas
   g. commercial nurseries
   h. outdoor storage and loading/unloading of hazardous substances
   i. marinas (service, painting and hull maintenance areas)

B. Regulated Activities Requiring Administrative Approval. The following activities, which are smaller than activities requiring a full Stormwater Permit, shall require approval under an Administrative Approval process by the Commission or its Stormwater Agent:
   1. Any activity that will result in a net increase in impervious surface area of more than 500 square feet of land but which will alter less than 5,000 square feet of land.
   2. Any replacement of an existing building with a new building of more than 500 square feet.

C. Regulated Activities Completed in Phases Requiring a Stormwater Permit or Administrative Approval:
   1. Activities that are completed in phases, such as subdivision developments and phased commercial developments which could be reasonably expected to alter more than the thresholds in 4.A and 4.B shall require a Stormwater Permit or Administrative Approval prior to beginning construction, even if the planned alteration is conducted over separate phases and/or by separate owners.

5. **Exempt Activities**
A. This Bylaw shall not apply to the following activities:
   1. Normal use, maintenance and improvement of land in agricultural use.
   2. Maintenance of existing landscaping.
   3. Repair or modification of a building that remains within its existing footprint.
   4. Construction of a fence that will not alter existing terrain or drainage patterns.
   5. Repairs or alterations to any stormwater management facility or practice that poses a threat to public health, safety, or the environment.
   6. Emergency work associated with accidents, spills or releases of oil or hazardous wastes, or natural disasters.
   7. Repair or maintenance of a sewage disposal system when required by the Board of Health for protection of public health, provided the post-repair condition drainage is similar or more effective than the pre-repair condition.
   8. Any work or projects for which all necessary approvals and permits have been issued before the effective date of this Bylaw.

6. Conservation Commission Authority

   A. The Commission shall be responsible for issuing a Stormwater Permit.
   B. The Commission may appoint a Licensed Professional Engineer with expertise in stormwater management as its Stormwater Agent to assist the Commission. This position shall be funded from application and review fees charged to applicants during the Stormwater Permit and Administrative Approval process.
   C. The Commission shall review Stormwater Permit applications, conduct necessary site inspections and investigations, issue final permits, and monitor and enforce permit conditions. For Administrative Approval of projects regulated under Section 4.B of this Stormwater Management Bylaw, the Stormwater Agent may represent the Commission by conducting site inspections as necessary, issuing a decision based on review, and monitoring conditions stated in the Administrative Approval.
   D. The Commission shall establish (1) Application Fees and (2) Review Fees which are sufficient to recover the cost for application review including assistance from the Stormwater Agent. Separate application and review fees shall be established for the Stormwater Permit process and for the Administrative Approval process which requires no public hearing. Said fees and charges shall be established by regulations issued by the Commission.

7. Rules and Regulations
   A. The Commission shall adopt and amend Rules and Regulations related to the submittal requirements and performance standards required to obtain a Stormwater Permit or Administrative Approval conducted pursuant to this Bylaw. Rules and Regulations shall be adopted and amended after a public hearing and public comment period. The public hearing shall be advertised in a newspaper of general local circulation at least seven days before the hearing date.
   B. Other boards, commissions, and departments are encouraged to adopt those Rules and Regulations by reference.
   C. Failure to promulgate such Rules and Regulations shall not have the effect of suspending or invalidating this Bylaw.

8. Performance Standards
   A. The purpose of the Stormwater Permit and Administrative Approval Program shall be to maintain the post-development runoff characteristics (including peak flow, total volume of runoff, and water quality of the runoff) for development and redevelopment projects as equal to or less than the pre-development runoff characteristics.
   B. Performance standards for site design, erosion control, stormwater management, materials, vegetation, and other aspects of developments shall be outlined in the Rules and Regulations. Performance standards shall include (but are not limited to) standards for the following:
      1. Peak discharge rates and runoff volumes (flooding protection and channel protection).
      2. Recharge volume.
      3. Pretreatment and water quality.
      4. Erosion control and property damage.
      5. Vegetation, site design, and site restoration.
      6. Integrity of stream channels, surface water, and aquatic habitats.

7. Application of Low-Impact Development measures to facilitate the maximum possible infiltration of precipitation on-site.
C. Applicants shall meet these performance standards and those of the Massachusetts Stormwater Management Policy (as may be amended), whichever are more stringent.

9. Submittal Requirements
   A. Submittal requirements for a Stormwater Permit, or for Administrative Approval, shall be as required below and as further defined in the Rules and Regulations.
   B. Submittal requirements for a Stormwater Permit shall include (but may not be limited to) the following:
      1. Stormwater management plan stamped by a Professional Engineer certifying post-development runoff characteristics (including peak flow, total volume of runoff, and water quality of the runoff) for development and redevelopment projects as equal to or less than the pre-development runoff characteristics. The plan shall show proposed grading, description of stormwater management system with map of pre- and post-development drainage, existing and proposed vegetation, recharge analysis, hydrologic calculations, and estimated seasonal high groundwater.
      2. Abutters list.
      3. Erosion control plan.
      4. Operations and maintenance plan listing responsible parties, maintenance agreements, maintenance schedule, and estimated annual budget (including anticipated sources of funding) for operations and maintenance.
      5. Record(s) of stormwater easements.
      6. For subdivision applications, a plan showing the building envelope within each house lot and proposed grading, drainage, and stormwater disposal for each lot.
      7. Application and review fees.
   C. Submittal requirements for an Administrative Approval shall include (but may not be limited to) the following:

      1. A stormwater management plan stamped by a Professional Engineer describing the proposed alteration activities and the mitigation measures and best management practices to be employed to manage stormwater generated by the alteration, and certifying post-development runoff characteristics (including peak flow, total volume of runoff, and water quality of the runoff) for development and redevelopment projects as equal to or less than the pre-development runoff characteristics. The following additional submittals may be required, but only if determined necessary by the Commission or their Stormwater Agent to support the engineer's stormwater Management plan and certification: Plan of proposed grading, more detailed description and/or drawings of proposed stormwater management system with map of pre- and post-development drainage, existing and proposed vegetation, recharge analysis, hydrologic calculations, estimated seasonal high groundwater, and erosion control plan.
      2. Abutters list.
      3. Application and review fees.

10. Application Review

A. <u>Pre-Application Meeting</u>. If a Stormwater Permit or Administrative Approval is required under Section 4 of this bylaw, then applicants are strongly encouraged to schedule a pre-application meeting with the Commission and/or its Stormwater Agent to review the proposed development plans at the earliest feasible time.

B. <u>Review and Comment by Town Boards and Departments</u>. Following receipt of a completed application for Stormwater Permit or for Administrative Approval, the Commission shall provide the opportunity for review and comments from the Planning Board, Board of Health, Sewer Commission, Water Commission, Building Inspector and Department of Public Works. Failure by these other Town Boards or Departments to make recommendations within fourteen days of receipt shall be deemed lack of opposition.

C. <u>Stormwater Permit</u>. If a Stormwater Permit application is filed, then the review process shall include a public hearing held by the Commission in conjunction with public hearings held for other aspects of the project when practicable. The Commission shall hold a separate hearing for the stormwater permit application if necessary. If a separate hearing is required, then written notice shall be given, at the expense of the applicant, in a newspaper of general circulation in the Town at least seven (7) working days prior to the hearing; and the Commission shall also give written notice of the hearing to all abutters, as that term may be defined by the Commission, also at least seven (7) working days prior to the hearing. Such notice shall be given in the form and manner that the Commission shall prescribe.

   1. The Commission shall commence the public hearing within twenty-one (21) calendar days from the receipt of a complete application and shall issue its permit, denial or determination in writing within twenty-one (21) calendar days after the close of said public hearing. The Commission shall have the authority to continue any hearing to a date certain announced at the hearing, for reasons stated at the hearing, which may include receipt of additional information offered by the applicant or others, information and plans required of the applicant deemed necessary by the Commission in its discretion, or comments and recommendations of other Town boards and officials.

   2. After review of the Stormwater Permit application, circulation to other boards, and public hearing, the Commission may take one of the following actions within twenty-one days after closing the public hearing:

      a. Approve the application and issue a Stormwater Permit if it finds that the proposed plan will protect water resources and meets the objectives and requirements of this Bylaw.

      b. Approve the application and issue a Stormwater Permit with conditions, modifications, or restrictions as necessary to ensure protection of water resources or to meet the objectives of this Bylaw.

      c. Disapprove the application and deny a permit if it finds the proposed plan will not protect water resources or fails to meet the objectives of this Bylaw; or if it finds that the applicant has not submitted information sufficient for the Commission to make such a determination.

   3. A decision by the Commission shall be final. Appeal should be to a court of competent jurisdiction pursuant to applicable law. The remedies listed in this Bylaw

are not exclusive of other remedies available under applicable federal, state, or local law.

)1 Administrative Approval. The Administrative Approval process shall require notification of abutters, as that term may be defined by the Commission, but will not require a public hearing and may be conducted by the Stormwater Agent acting on behalf of the Commission. After completing a review and after circulating the application to other boards, the Commission or its Stormwater Agent may take one of the following actions within twenty-one (21) calendar days of receiving a complete application:

1. Approve the application if it finds that the proposed plan will protect water resources and meets the objectives and requirements of this Bylaw.
2. Approve the application with conditions, modifications, or restrictions as necessary to ensure protection of water resources or to meet the objectives of this Bylaw.
3. Disapprove the application and require submission of a Stormwater Permit to the Commission.
4. Disapprove the application if it finds the proposed plan will not protect water resources or fails to meet the objectives of this Bylaw; or if it finds that the applicant has not submitted information sufficient for the Commission or its Stormwater Agent to make such a determination.
5. A decision by the Commission or its Stormwater Agent shall be final. A decision by the Stormwater Agent made under this Bylaw shall be reviewable by the Commission if an appeal of the decision is filed with the Town Clerk within twenty days thereof, and if the applicant files with such appeal a complete application for a Stormwater Permit.

11. Site Inspection

Submittal of the Stormwater Permit or Administrative Approval application shall grant the Commission and its agents with permission to enter the site for inspection.

12. Surety

For projects requiring a Stormwater Permit under 4.A, the Commission may require the posting of a surety bond until work is completed.

13. Enforcement

A. The Commission shall enforce this Bylaw with violation notices, administrative orders and enforcement orders, and may pursue all civil and criminal remedies for such violations. Mechanisms and procedures for enforcement shall be detailed in Rules and Regulations adopted by the Commission pursuant to this Bylaw.
B. Any person who violates any provision of this Article, regulations thereunder, or permits issued thereunder, shall be punished by a fine of one hundred ($100) dollars. Each day or portion thereof during which a violation continues shall constitute a separate offense, and each provision of the bylaw, regulations or permit violated shall constitute a separate offense.
C. Non-criminal disposition. As an alternative to criminal prosecution or civil action, the Commission may elect to utilize the non-criminal disposition procedure set forth in M.G.L. Ch. 40, § 21D and Section 1(h) of the Town's General Bylaws. The penalty for violation shall be $100. Each day or part thereof that such violation occurs or continues shall constitute a separate offence.

14. Severability

If any provision, paragraph, sentence, or clause of this Bylaw shall be held invalid for any reason, all other provisions shall continue in full force and effect.

MOVED that the Town amend the General Bylaws by adding the following new Article **XV**:

COHASSET **STORMWATER** MANAGEMENT BYLAW

1. Authority

This Bylaw is adopted under authority granted by the Home Rule Amendment of the Massachusetts Constitution, the Home Rule statutes, and pursuant to the federal Clean Water Act, 33 U. S. C. §§ 1251-1386 (the "Act") and regulations issued pursuant to the Act which are found at 40 CFR 122.34.

2. Purpose

The purpose of this Bylaw is to:

1. Prevent and reduce existing and future flooding.

2. Protect water quality.

3. Increase groundwater recharge.

4. Reduce erosion and sedimentation.

5. Promote environmentally sensitive site design practices.

6. Ensure long-term maintenance of stormwater controls.

7. Help the Town of Cohasset meet federal requirements under Phase II of the National Pollutant Discharge Elimination System.

8. Establish the legal authority by which the Town of Cohasset can enforce the provisions of this Bylaw and accompanying regulations.

3. Definitions

The following definitions shall apply in the interpretation and implementation of this Bylaw. The term "alter" shall include, without limitation, the following activities:

1. Changing of pre-existing drainage characteristics, adding impervious area or changing type of land cover, or changing sedimentation patterns, flow patterns or flood retention characteristics;

2. Dumping, discharging or filling with any material, or removal of material, which would alter elevations or change drainage patterns or degrade water quality;

3. Driving of piles, erection, or expansion of buildings or structures of any kind;

4.   Destruction of plant life, including clearing of trees;

5.   Any activities, changes or work which may cause or tend to contribute to pollution of any body of water or groundwater.

4.   Regulated Activities

A. Regulated Activities Requiring a Stormwater Permit. The following activities, developments or redevelopments require the issuance of a full Stormwater Permit by the Conservation Commission (the "Commission") after the filing by the Applicant of a full application and full review by the Commission through a public hearing:

1.   Any activity that will alter 5,000 square feet or more of land.

2.   Any construction or development activity on an undeveloped parcel of any size that will increase the impervious surface area, or increase the amount or rate of runoff from the parcel.

3.   Any development or redevelopment of Land Uses with Higher Potential Pollutant Loads as defined in the Massachusetts Stormwater Management Policy, which include, for example:

   a.   auto salvage yards (auto recycler facilities)

   b.   auto fueling facilities (gas stations)

   c.   exterior fleet storage areas (cars, buses, trucks, public works equipment)

   d.   exterior vehicle service, maintenance and equipment cleaning areas

   e.   commercial parking lots

   f.   road salt storage and loading areas

   g.   commercial nurseries

   h.   outdoor storage and loading/unloading of hazardous substances

   i.   marinas (service, painting and hull maintenance areas)

B. Regulated Activities Requiring Administrative Approval. The following activities, which are smaller than activities requiring a full Stormwater Permit, shall require approval under an Administrative Approval process by the Commission or its Stormwater Agent:

1.   Any activity that will result in a net increase in impervious surface area of more than 500 square feet of land but which will alter less than 5,000 square feet of land.

2.   Any replacement of an existing building with a new building of more than 500 square feet.

C. Regulated Activities Completed in Phases Requiring a Stormwater Permit or Administrative Approval:

1. Activities that are completed in phases, such as subdivision developments and phased commercial developments which could be reasonably expected to alter more than the thresholds in 4.A and 4.B shall require a Stormwater Permit or Administrative Approval prior to beginning construction, even if the planned alteration is conducted over separate phases and/or by separate owners.

5. Exempt Activities

A. This Bylaw shall not apply to the following activities:

1. Normal use, maintenance and improvement of land in agricultural use.

2. Maintenance of existing landscaping.

3. Repair or modification of a building that remains within its existing footprint.

4. Construction of a fence that will not alter existing terrain or drainage patterns.

5. Repairs or alterations to any stormwater management facility or practice that poses a threat to public health, safety, or the environment.

6. Emergency work associated with accidents, spills or releases of oil or hazardous wastes, or natural disasters.

7. Repair or maintenance of a sewage disposal system when required by the Board of Health for protection of public health, provided the post-repair condition drainage is similar or more effective than the pre-repair condition.

8. Any work or projects for which all necessary approvals and permits have been issued before the effective date of this Bylaw.

6. Conservation Commission Authority

A. The Commission shall be responsible for issuing a Stormwater Permit.

B. The Commission may appoint a Licensed Professional Engineer with expertise in stormwater management as its Stormwater Agent to assist the Commission. This position shall be funded from application and review fees charged to applicants during the Stormwater Permit and Administrative Approval process.

C. The Commission shall review Stormwater Permit applications, conduct necessary site inspections and investigations, issue final permits, and monitor and enforce permit conditions. For Administrative Approval of projects regulated under Section 4.B of this Stormwater Management Bylaw, the Stormwater Agent may represent the Commission by conducting site inspections as necessary, issuing a decision based on review, and monitoring conditions stated in the Administrative Approval.

D. The Commission shall establish (1) Application Fees and (2) Review Fees which are sufficient to recover the cost for application review including assistance from the Stormwater Agent. Separate application and review fees shall be established for the Stormwater Permit process and for the Administrative Approval process which requires no public hearing. Said fees and charges shall be established by regulations issued by the Commission.

7.   Rules and Regulations

A.   The Commission shall adopt and amend Rules and Regulations related to the submittal requirements and performance standards required to obtain a Stormwater Permit or Administrative Approval conducted pursuant to this Bylaw. Rules and Regulations shall be adopted and amended after a public hearing and public comment period. The public hearing shall be advertised in a newspaper of general local circulation at least seven days before the hearing date.

B.   Other boards, commissions, and departments are encouraged to adopt those Rules and Regulations by reference.

C.   Failure to promulgate such Rules and Regulations shall not have the effect of suspending or invalidating this Bylaw.

8.   Performance Standards

A.   The purpose of the Stormwater Permit and Administrative Approval Program shall be to maintain the post-development runoff characteristics (including peak flow, total volume of runoff, and water quality of the runoff) for development and redevelopment projects as equal to or less than the pre-development runoff characteristics.

B.   Performance standards for site design, erosion control, stormwater management, materials, vegetation, and other aspects of developments shall be outlined in the Rules and Regulations. Performance standards shall include (but are not limited to) standards for the following:

1.   Peak discharge rates and runoff volumes (flooding protection and channel protection).

2.   Recharge volume.

3.   Pretreatment and water quality.

4.   Erosion control and property damage.

5.   Vegetation, site design, and site restoration.

6.   Integrity of stream channels, surface water, and aquatic habitats.

7.   Application of Low-Impact Development measures to facilitate the maximum possible infiltration of precipitation on-site.

C.   Applicants shall meet these performance standards and those of the Massachusetts Stormwater Management Policy (as may be amended), whichever are more stringent.

9.   Submittal Requirements

A.   Submittal requirements for a Stormwater Permit, or for Administrative Approval, shall be as required below and as further defined in the Rules and Regulations.

B.   Submittal requirements for a Stormwater Permit shall include (but may not be limited to) the following:

1.   Stormwater management plan stamped by a Professional Engineer certifying post-development runoff characteristics (including peak flow, total volume of runoff, and water quality of the runoff) for development and redevelopment projects as equal to or less than the pre-development runoff characteristics. The plan shall show proposed grading, description of stormwater management system with map of pre- and post-development drainage, existing and proposed vegetation, recharge analysis, hydrologic calculations, and estimated seasonal high groundwater.

2.   Abutters list.

3.   Erosion control plan.

4.   Operations and maintenance plan listing responsible parties, maintenance agreements, maintenance schedule, and estimated annual budget (including anticipated sources of funding) for operations and maintenance.

5.   Record(s) of stormwater easements.

6.   For subdivision applications, a plan showing the building envelope within each house lot and proposed grading, drainage, and stormwater disposal for each lot.

7.   Application and review fees.

C.   Submittal requirements for an Administrative Approval shall include (but may not be limited to) the following:

1.   A stormwater management plan stamped by a Professional Engineer describing the proposed alteration activities and the mitigation measures and best management practices to be employed to manage stormwater generated by the alteration, and certifying post-development runoff characteristics (including peak flow, total volume of runoff, and water quality of the runoff) for development and redevelopment projects as equal to or less than the pre-development runoff characteristics. The following additional submittals may be required, but only if determined necessary by the Commission or their Stormwater Agent to support the engineer's stormwater Management plan and certification: Plan of proposed grading, more detailed description and/or drawings of proposed stormwater management system with map of pre- and post-development drainage, existing and proposed vegetation, recharge analysis, hydrologic calculations, estimated seasonal high groundwater, and erosion control plan.

2. Abutters list.

3. Application and review fees.

10. Application Review

A. Pre-Application Meeting. If a Stormwater Permit or Administrative Approval is required under Section 4 of this bylaw, then applicants are strongly encouraged to schedule a pre-application meeting with the Commission and/or its Stormwater Agent to review the proposed development plans at the earliest feasible time.

B. Review and Comment by Town Boards and Departments. Following receipt of a completed application for Stormwater Permit or for Administrative Approval, the Commission shall provide the opportunity for review and comments from the Planning Board, Board of Health, Sewer Commission, Water Commission, Building Inspector and Department of Public Works. Failure by these other Town Boards or Departments to make recommendations within fourteen days of receipt shall be deemed lack of opposition.

C. Stormwater Permit. If a Stormwater Permit application is filed, then the review process shall include a public hearing held by the Commission in conjunction with public hearings held for other aspects of the project when practicable. The Commission shall hold a separate hearing for the stormwater permit application if necessary. If a separate hearing is required, then written notice shall be given, at the expense of the applicant, in a newspaper of general circulation in the Town at least seven (7) working days prior to the hearing; and the Commission shall also give written notice of the hearing to all abutters, as that term may be defined by the Commission, also at least seven (7) working days prior to the hearing. Such notice shall be given in the form and manner that the Commission shall prescribe.

1. The Commission shall commence the public hearing within twenty-one (21) calendar days from the receipt of a complete application and shall issue its permit, denial or determination in writing within twenty-one (21) calendar days after the close of said public hearing. The Commission shall have the authority to continue any hearing to a date certain announced at the hearing, for reasons stated at the hearing, which may include receipt of additional information offered by the applicant or others, information and plans required of the applicant deemed necessary by the Commission in its discretion, or comments and recommendations of other Town boards and officials.

2. After review of the Stormwater Permit application, circulation to other boards, and public hearing, the Commission may take one of the following actions within twenty-one days after closing the public hearing:

a. Approve the application and issue a Stormwater Permit if it finds that the proposed plan will protect water resources and meets the objectives and requirements of this Bylaw.

b. Approve the application and issue a Stormwater Permit with conditions, modifications, or restrictions as necessary to ensure protection of water resources or to meet the objectives of this Bylaw.

c. Disapprove the application and deny a permit if it finds the proposed plan will not protect water resources or fails to meet the objectives of this Bylaw; or if it finds that the applicant has not submitted information sufficient for the Commission to make such a determination.

3. A decision by the Commission shall be final. Appeal should be to a court of competent jurisdiction pursuant to applicable law. The remedies listed in this Bylaw are not exclusive of other remedies available under applicable federal, state, or local law.

D. Administrative Approval. The Administrative Approval process shall require notification of abutters, as that term may be defined by the Commission, but will not require a public hearing and may be conducted by the Stormwater Agent acting on behalf of the Commission. After completing a review and after circulating the application to other boards, the Commission or its Stormwater Agent may take one of the following actions within twenty-one (21) calendar days of receiving a complete application:

1. Approve the application if it finds that the proposed plan will protect water resources and meets the objectives and requirements of this Bylaw.

2. Approve the application with conditions, modifications, or restrictions as necessary to ensure protection of water resources or to meet the objectives of this Bylaw.

3. Disapprove the application and require submission of a Stormwater Permit application to the Commission.

4. Disapprove the application if it finds the proposed plan will not protect water resources or fails to meet the objectives of this Bylaw; or if it finds that the applicant has not submitted information sufficient for the Commission or its Stormwater Agent to make such a determination.

5. A decision by the Commission or its Stormwater Agent shall be final. A decision by the Stormwater Agent made under this Bylaw shall be reviewable by the Commission if an appeal of the decision is filed with the Town Clerk within twenty days thereof, and if the applicant files with such appeal a complete application for a Stormwater Permit.

11. Site Inspection

Submittal of the Stormwater Permit or Administrative Approval application shall grant the Commission and its agents with permission to enter the site for inspection.

12. Surety

For projects requiring a Stormwater Permit under 4.A, the Commission may require the posting of a surety bond until work is completed.

13. Enforcement

A. The Commission shall enforce this Bylaw with violation notices, administrative orders and enforcement orders, and may pursue all civil and criminal remedies for such violations.

Mechanisms and procedures for enforcement shall be detailed in Rules and Regulations adopted by the Commission pursuant to this Bylaw.

B.   Any person who violates any provision of this Article, regulations thereunder, or permits issued thereunder, shall be punished by a fine of one hundred ($100) dollars. Each day or portion thereof during which a violation continues shall constitute a separate offense, and each provision of the bylaw, regulations or permit violated shall constitute a separate offense.

C.   Non-criminal disposition. As an alternative to criminal prosecution or civil action, the Commission may elect to utilize the non-criminal disposition procedure set forth in M.G.L. Ch. 40, § 21D and Section 1(h) of the Town's General Bylaws. The penalty for violation shall be $100. Each day or part thereof that such violation occurs or continues shall constitute a separate offence.

14.   Severability

If any provision, paragraph, sentence, or clause of this Bylaw shall be held invalid for any reason, all other provisions shall continue in full force and effect.

Motion **ad**opted.

Article 25:   Citizens Petition – Operation of Leaf Blowers Bylaw

Proposed Bylaw: To limit gas and gas-generated electric leaf-blower usage to the following hours: Tuesday-Saturday, 9 am – 5 pm. Violation of this ordinance will result in the assessment of a two hundred fine upon the offending property owner

NAME	ADDRESS	NAME	ADDRESS
Doris Mandeville	25 Oak St.	Walter Ross	159 So. Main St
Kristin Norton	320 No. Main St.	Lorraine Cunningham	11 Oak St.
S. Woodworth Chittick	98 So. Main St.	Davenport Crocker	79 Spring St.
James Porter 1	94 So. Main St.	George MacCleave	9 James Ln.
Robert Sweeney	15 James Ln.	Mary Louise Clark Slotnick	190 So. Main St

MOVED, that the following bylaw be inserted into the General Bylaws of the Town of Cohasset as section 42, "Noise from Leaf Blowers" of Article VII ("Safety and Public Order", as follows:

Section 42, Noise from Leaf Blowers

(a) No property owner shall operate, nor allow others to operate on his or her property, Gas - Powered, and Gas or Diesel - Generated Electric Leaf Blowers, as defined hereinafter, other than during the following hours: weekly, Tuesday - Saturday, 9 a.m. - 5 p.m.
(b) Definitions

'Gas - Powered Leaf Blowers' are defined as portable power equipment that is powered by a self - contained fuel combustion engine and used in any landscape, maintenance, construction, property repair, or property maintenance for the purpose of blowing, dispersing, redistributing dust, dirt, leaves, grass clippings, cuttings and trimmings from trees and shrubs, or other debris.

'Gas or Diesel - Generated Electric Leaf Blowers' are defined as portable power equipment that is powered by any free - standing, exterior generator that converts gas or diesel fuel into electricity, and used in any landscape, maintenance, construction, property repair, or property maintenance for the purpose of blowing, dispersing, or redistributing dust, dirt, leaves, grass clippings, cuttings and trimmings from trees and shrubs, or other debris.

(c) Notice
of the provisions of this bylaw, including penalties for violations of such provisions and the effective date thereof, shall be posted in all stores selling leaf blowers of any kind, and in all businesses selling landscape, maintenance, construction, property repair or maintenance tools or material. Notice of this bylaw shall also be conspicuously displayed at the Town Hall, and at the Cohasset Public Library.

(d) Violations

Each instance in which a property owner operates or allows the operation of a Gas - Powered, or Gas or Diesel - Generated Electric Leaf Blower as defined in this bylaw, upon his or her property shall constitute a separate violation of this ordinance.

(e) Effective date

The provisions of this bylaw shall become effective on and after January 1, 2009.

(f) Enforcement

The provisions of this bylaw shall be enforced by the town of Cohasset police, who may utilize non criminal ticketing for the violation of this bylaw pursuant to Cohasset General Bylaws Article I General Provisions, section 1(h).

(g) Penalties

First offense: warning to the owner and/or operator.

Second and subsequent offenses: $200 penalty, to be levied upon the property owner.

Motion defeated.

It was moved and seconded at 4 p.m. that this meeting stand adjourned to Saturday, April 5, 2008 for the election of town officers.

A True Record, ATTEST:

Marion L. Douglas, Town Clerk

ANNUAL TOWN ELECTION – TOWN OF COHASSET
APRIL 5, 2008

The polls opened at **8 a.m. and** closed at **6 p.m.**
Total Voters --- **873 ;** Per Cent **– 17.**   Absentee Voters - Pre. **1 – 19; Pre. 2 – 18** .
Total of absentees **was 37.**

Election officers sworn in by **the** Town Clerk, Marion L. Douglas **at 7:45 a.m.** were **as follows:**

Carol St. Pierre	Nancy Barrett
Kathleen Rhodes	Roger Whitley
Debra Krupczak	James Contis
Katherine Lincoln	Alison Krupczak
Grace Tuckerman	Katherine Whitley
Michael Patrolia	Jody Doyle
Ellen Warner	

Selectmen for Three Years (2)

	Pre. 1	Pre. 2	Total
Frederick R. Koed	330	318	648
Karen M. Quigley	333	304	637
Write-ins/Scattering	10	12	22
Blanks	217	222	439
Total	890	856	1746

Moderator for Three Years (1)

Daniel S. Evans	375	315	690
Write-ins/Scattering	1	1	2
Blanks	69	112	181
Total	445	428	873

Town Clerk for Three Years (1)

Marion L. Douglas	371	355	726
Write-ins/Scattering	0	1	1
Blanks	74	72	146
Total	445	428	873

School Committee for Three Years (1)

	Pre. 1	Pre. 2	Total
Alfred Slanetz	329	261	590
Write-ins/Scattering	5	10	15
Blanks	111	157	268
Total	445	428	873

Trustees **Paul Pratt Memorial Library** for Three Years **(3)**

Sheila S. Evans	344	297	641
Rodney M. Hobson	343	308	651
MaryLou Lawrence	328	289	617
Write-ins/Scattering	1	1	2
Blanks	319	389	708
Total	1335	1284	2619

Assessor for Three Years **(1)**

Mary E. Granville	325	292	617
Write-ins/Scattering	2	0	2
Blanks	120	135	255
Total	445	428	873

Board of Health for Three Years **(1)**

Robin M. Lawrence	341	308	649
Write-ins/Scattering	2	0	2
Blanks	102	120	222
Total	445	428	873

Planning Board for Five Years **(1)**

Charles A. Samuelson	315	275	590
Write-ins/Scattering	0	1	1
Blanks	130	152	282
Total	445	428	873

Planning Board for **Three Years** to **fill an unexpired** term **(1)**

Clark H. Brewer	317	277	594
Write-ins/Scattering	0	0	0
Blanks	128	151	279
Total	445	428	873

Recreation Commission for Five Years (1)

Roseanne M. McMorris	278	270	548
Write-ins/Scattering	31	24	55
Blanks	<u>136</u>	<u>134</u>	<u>270</u>
Total	445	428	873

Recreation Commission for Two Years to fill an unexpired term (1)

Write-ins			
Abigail Alves	89	72	161
Susan Kent	37	26	63
Blanks	<u>319</u>	<u>330</u>	<u>649</u>
Total	445	428	873

Sewer Commission for Three Years (1)

James A. Dow	202	200	402
Wayne Sawchuk	223	219	442
Write-ins/Scattering	0	1	1
Blanks	<u>465</u>	<u>436</u>	<u>901</u>
Total	890	856	1746

Water Commission for Three Years (1)

Glenn A. Pratt	346	333	679
Write-ins/Scattering	6	1	7
Blanks	<u>93</u>	<u>94</u>	<u>187</u>
Total	445	428	873

The polls closed at 6 p.m. and the results were declared at 7:00 p.m.

A True Record, ATTEST:

Marion L. Douglas
Town Clerk

STATE PRIMARY - SEPTEMBER 16, 2008

Polls opened at 7 a.m. and closed at 8 p.m.
Total Voters -. Democrats – 344; Republicans – 64.
Percent voted – 8.
Absentees – Pre. 1 – D – 7, R – 4; Pre. 2 – D - 13, R - 4.

Election officers sworn in by the Town Clerk, Marion Douglas, at 6:45 a.m. were as follows:

Carol St. Pierre	Debra Krupczak
Grace Tuckerman	Jody Doyle
Nancy Barrett	Kathleen Rhodes
Katherine Lincoln	James Contis
Katherine Whitley	Roger Whitley
Michael Patrolia	

Democratic **Party**

Senator in Congress	Pre. 1	Pre. 2	Total
John F. Kerry	96	115	211
Edward J. O'Reilly	61	69	130
Blanks	2	1	0
Write-ins/Scattering	0	0	0
Total	159	185	344

Representative in Congress			
William D. Delahunt	111	135	246
Blanks	46	49	95
Write-ins/Scattering	2	1	3
Total	159	185	344

110

Councillor (1)	Pre. 1	Pre. 2	Total
Christopher A. Iannella, Jr.	57	69	126
Stephen F. Flynn	49	64	113
Robert L. Toomey, Jr.	10	16	26
Blank	42	36	78
Write-ins/Scattering	1	0	1
Total	159	185	344

Senator in General Court

	Pre. 1	Pre. 2	Total
Blanks	135	160	295
Write-ins/Scattering	24	25	49
Total	159	185	344

Representative in General Court

	Pre. 1	Pre. 2	Total
Garrett J. Bradley	113	153	266
Blanks	45	32	77
Write-ins/Scattering	3	0	3
Total	159	185	344

Register of Probate

	Pre. 1	Pre. 2	Total
Patrick W. McDermott	87	113	200
Blanks	69	72	141
Write-ins/Scattering	3	0	3
Total	159	185	344

County Treasurer

	Pre. 1	Pre. 2	Total
Joseph A. Connolly	94	116	210
Blanks	65	69	134
Write-ins/Scattering	0	0	0
Total	159	185	344

County Commissioner

John M. Gillis	82	108	190
Francis W. O'Brien	73	96	169
Blanks	163	166	329
Write-ins/Scattering	0	0	0
Total	318	370	688

Republican Party	Pre. 1	Pre. 2	Total

Senator in Congress

Jeffrey K. Beatty	27	30	57
Blanks	4	3	7
Write-ins/Scattering	0	0	1
Total	31	33	66

Representative in Congress

Blanks	28	26	54
Write-ins/Scattering	3	7	10
Total	31	33	66

Councillor (1)

Write-ins/Scattering	2	4	6
Blanks	29	29	58
Total	31	33	66

Senator in General Court

Robert L. Hedlund, Jr.	30	33	63
Blanks	1	0	1
Write-ins/Scattering	0	0	0
Total	31	33	66

Representative in General Court

	Pre. 1	Pre. 2	Total
Write-ins/Scattering	3	7	10
Blanks	28	26	54
Total	31	33	66

Register of Probate

	Pre. 1	Pre. 2	Total
Write-ins/Scattering	3	6	9
Blanks	28	27	55
Total	31	33	66

County Treasurer

	Pre. 1	Pre. 2	Total
Write-ins/Scattering	3	8	11
Blanks	28	25	53
Total	31	33	66

County Commissioner

	Pre. 1	Pre. 2	Total
Thomas E. Gorman	27	26	53
Blanks	34	38	72
Write-ins/Scattering	1	2	3
Total	31	33	66

The Green Rainbow Party did not receive any votes or any write-ins.

The Working Families Party did not receive any votes or any write-ins.

The polls closed at 8 p.m. and the results were declared at 8:30 p.m.

A True Copy, Attest:

Marion Douglas, Town Clerk

November 4, 2008 -- State Election

Polls opened at 7 a.m. and closed at 8 p.m. The total number of registered voters was 5381. The total number that actually voted was 4629. The total absentee voters were 526 for Pre. 1 – 269 and for Pre. 2 – 257.

Election officers sworn in by Town Clerk, Marion L. Douglas at 6:45 a.m. were as follows:

Carol St. Pierre	Nancy Barrett
Katherine Lincoln	James Carroll
Kathleen Rhodes	Debra Krupczak
Gail Collins	Sandra Murray
Grace Tuckerman	Patricia Ranney
Jody Doyle	James Carroll
James Contis	Carolyn Contis
Roger Whitley	Katherine Whitley
Susan Loring	Michael Patrolia

Electors of President/Vice President (Vote for **One**)	Pre 1	Pre 2	Total
Baldwin & Castle	0	2	0
Barr & Root	11	10	21
McCain & Palin	1109	1047	2156
McKinney & Clemente	2	2	4
Nader & Gonzalez	9	13	22
Obama & Biden	1221	1162	2383
Scattering (write-ins)	9	12	21
Blanks	8	12	20
Total	2369	2260	4629

Senator in Congress			
John F. Kerry	1257	1203	2460
Jeffrey K. Beatty	1010	950	1960
Robert J. Underwood	35	51	86
Scattering (write-ins)	0	5	5
Blanks	67	51	118
Total	2369	2260	4629

Representative in Congress

William Delahunt	1648	1637	3285
Scattering (write-ins)	40	41	81
Blanks	681	582	1263
Total	2369	2260	4629

Councillor

Christopher A. Ianella, Jr.	1421	1454	2875
Scattering (write-ins)	26	20	46
Blanks	922	786	1708
Total	2369	2260	4629

Senator in General Court

Robert L. Hedlund	1777	1753	3530
Scattering (write-ins)	26	24	50
Blanks	566	483	1049
Total	2369	2260	4629

Representative in General Court

Garrett J. Bradley	1689	1710	3300
Scattering (write-ins)	24	25	49
Blanks	656	525	1181
Total	2369	2260	4629

Register of Probate

Patrick W. McDermott	1417	1423	2840
Scattering (write-ins)	14	22	37
Blanks	927	815	1752
Total	2369	2260	4629

County Treasurer

Joseph A. Connolly	1413	1419	2832
Scattering (write-ins)	16	17	33
Blanks	940	824	1764
Total	2369	2269	4629

County Commissioner

John M. Gillis	810	856	1666
Francis W. O'Brien	668	753	1421
Thomas E. Gorman	862	768	1630
Michael F. Walsh	531	488	1019
Scattering (write-ins)	2	5	7
Blanks	1865	1650	3515
Total	4738	4520	9258

QUESTION 1: LAW PROPOSED BY INITIATIVE PETITION

Do you approve of a law summarized below, on which no vote was taken by the Senate or the House of Representatives before May 6, 2008?

SUMMARY

This proposed law would reduce the state personal income tax rate to 2.65% for all categories of taxable income for the tax year beginning on or after January 1, 2009, and would eliminate the tax for all tax years beginning on or after January 1, 2010.

The personal income tax applies to income received or gain realized by individuals and married couples, by estates of deceased persons, by certain trustees and other fiduciaries, by persons who are partners in and receive income from partnerships, by corporate trusts, and by persons who receive income as shareholders of "S corporations" as defined under federal tax law. The proposed law would not affect the tax due on income or gain realized in a tax year beginning before January 1, 2009.

The proposed law states that if any of its parts were declared invalid, the other parts would stay in effect.

A YES VOTE would reduce the state personal income tax rate to 2.65% for the tax year beginning on January 1, 2009, and would eliminate the tax for all tax years beginning on or after January 1, 2010.

A NO VOTE would make no change in state income tax laws.

YES	953	892	1845
NO	1369	1314	2683
Blanks	47	54	101
Total	2369	2260	4629

QUESTION 2: LAW PROPOSED BY INITIATIVE PETITION

Do you approve of a law summarized below, on which no vote was taken by the Senate or the House of Representatives before May 6, 2008?

SUMMARY

This proposed law would replace the criminal penalties for possession of one ounce or less of marijuana with a new system of civil penalties, to be enforced by issuing citations, and would exclude information regarding this civil offense from the state's criminal record information system. Offenders age 18 or older would be subject to forfeiture of the marijuana plus a civil penalty of $100. Offenders under the age of 18 would be subject to the same forfeiture and, if they complete a drug awareness program within one year of the offense, the same $100 penalty.

Offenders under 18 and their parents or legal guardian would be notified of the offense and the option for the offender to complete a drug awareness program developed by the state Department of Youth Services. Such programs would include ten hours of community service and at least four hours of instruction or group discussion concerning the use and abuse of marijuana and other drugs and emphasizing early detection and prevention of substance abuse.

The penalty for offenders under 18 who fail to complete such a program within one year could be increased to as much as $1,000, unless the offender showed an inability to pay, an inability to participate in such a program, or the unavailability of such a program. Such an offender's parents could also be held liable for the increased penalty. Failure by an offender under 17 to complete such a program could also be a basis for a delinquency proceeding.

The proposed law would define possession of one ounce or less of marijuana as including possession of one ounce or less of tetrahydrocannibinol ("THC"), or having metabolized products of marijuana or THC in one's body.

Under the proposed law, possessing an ounce or less of marijuana could not be grounds for state or local government entities imposing any other penalty, sanction, or disqualification, such as denying student financial aid, public housing, public financial assistance including unemployment benefits, the right to operate a motor vehicle, or the opportunity to serve as a foster or adoptive parent. The proposed law would allow local ordinances or bylaws that prohibit the public use of marijuana, and would not affect existing laws, practices, or policies concerning operating a motor vehicle or taking other actions while under the influence of marijuana, unlawful possession of prescription forms of marijuana, or selling, manufacturing, or trafficking in marijuana.

The money received from the new civil penalties would go to the city or town where the offense occurred.

A YES VOTE would replace the criminal penalties for possession of one ounce or less of marijuana with a new system of civil penalties.
A NO VOTE would make no change in state criminal laws concerning possession of marijuana.

YES	1494	1492	2986
NO	856	727	1572
Blanks	30	41	71
Total	2369	2260	4629

QUESTION 3: LAW PROPOSED BY INITIATIVE PETITION

Do you approve of a law summarized below, on which no vote was taken by the Senate or the House of Representatives before May 6, 2008?

SUMMARY

This proposed law would prohibit any dog racing or racing meeting in Massachusetts where any form of betting or wagering on the speed or ability of dogs occurs.

The State Racing Commission would be prohibited from accepting or approving any application or request for racing dates for dog racing.

Any person violating the proposed law could be required to pay a civil penalty of not less than $20,000 to the Commission. The penalty would be used for the Commission's administrative purposes, subject to appropriation by the state Legislature. All existing parts of the chapter of the state's General Laws concerning dog and horse racing meetings would be interpreted as if they did not refer to dogs.

These changes would take effect January 1, 2010. The proposed law states that if any of its parts were declared invalid, the other parts would stay in effect.

A YES VOTE would prohibit dog races on which betting or wagering occurs, effective January 1, 2010.

A NO VOTE would make no change in the laws governing dog racing.

YES	1396	1206	2602
NO	910	976	1886
Blanks	63	78	141
Total	2369	2260	4629

QUESTION 4: THIS QUESTION IS NOT BINDING

Shall the state representative from this district be instructed to vote in favor of legislation that would support the development of Cape Wind in Nantucket Sound and other possible future onshore and offshore wind power developments in Massachusetts?

YES	1816	1736	3552
NO	353	326	679
Blanks	200	198	398
Total	2369	2260	4629

Polls closed at 8 p.m. and the results were declared at 9:15 p.m.

A True Record, ATTEST:

Marion L. Douglas
Town Clerk

INDEX SPECIAL TOWN MEETING – NOVEMBER 17, 2008

Article #	Description of Article
1	Amendments to Fy09 Budget. Unanimous
2	Union contracts & other salary adjustments. Unanimous
3	Capital improvements budget. Unanimous
4	Community Preservation Committee – Open Space & recreation plan. Unanimous.
5	Release of easements & right of way. Unanimous.
6	Conservation restrictions for open space. Unanimous.
7	Jerusalem Road Wall & Roadway. Unanimous.
8	Town Hall restoration project. Unanimous.
9	Funding for alternative energy options. Unanimous.
10	Zoning bylaw reconciliation. Unanimous.
11	Grant of easement for gas line – parcel 89 on assessor map 27. Unanimous.
12	Jacobs Meadow culvert repair & upgrade. Unanimous.
13	Turf field & track at Clark Chatterton Athletic Complex. Adopted by required 2/3's.

At the Special Town Meeting held on Monday, November 17, 2008 at the Cohasset High School Sullivan Gymnasium the following articles were contained in the warrant and acted upon as follows.

Checkers sworn in by the Town Clerk, Marion L. Douglas at 6:30 p.m. were Carol St. Pierre, Sandra Murray, Abigail Alves, Debra Krupczak and James Carroll. Tellers were appointed and sworn in by the Moderator, Daniel Evans.

The Moderator called the meeting to order at 7:18 p.m. and a quorum of 100 was present at that time. The registered voters checked in on the voting list totaled for Precinct 1 – 174; and Precinct 2 – 104 for a total of 278 voters.

It was voted unanimously to dispense with the reading of the call of the Meeting and Return of Service having been examined by the Moderator and found to be in order. Citizens recited the pledge of allegiance.

ARTICLE 1:   AMENDMENTS TO FISCAL 2009 OPERATING BUDGET

To see what additional action the Town will vote to amend, modify, increase or decrease, or otherwise, to balance the Fiscal Year 2009 Operating Budget as voted in Article 3 of the March 29, 2008 Annual Town Meeting, including proposed revised appropriations and any additional sums the Town will vote to raise and appropriate, borrow pursuant to any applicable statute, or transfer from available funds or otherwise, for the payment of the salaries and compensation, expenses, equipment, and outlays, capital and otherwise, of the several Town departments, for the current fiscal year, or take any other action related thereto.

MOVED that Twenty Thousand Dollars ($20,000) be hereby appropriated to add to and increase the amounts voted pursuant to Article 3 of the March 29, 2008 Annual Town Meeting as adjusted as set forth below, and to fund such appropriation the amount of Twenty Thousand Dollars ($20,000) be raised from taxation and other general revenues of the Town:

Appropriation/Account	Original Appropriation	Proposed Appropriation	Revised Increase
Unemployment General Expenses	$20,000	$40,000	$20,000

And further that the amounts appropriated pursuant to Article 3 of the March 29, 2008 Annual Town Meeting be reduced by the amount of Five Hundred Six Thousand One Hundred Eighty Seven Dollars ($506,187) as a result of the decreases listed below,

Appropriation/Account	Original Appropriation	Proposed Appropriation	Revised (Decrease)
Debt Service – Excluded Principal	$1,885,920	$1,609,820	($276,100)
Debt Service – Excluded Interest	$1,114,548	$ 884,461	($230,087)

Motion adopted **unanimously.**

ARTICLE 2:   UNION CONTRACTS & OTHER SALARY ADJUSTMENTS

To see if the Town will vote to raise and appropriate borrow pursuant to any applicable statute, and/or transfer from available funds, a sum or sums of money, to be expended by the Town Manager, to fund the FY09 cost items of a collective bargaining agreement between the Town, represented by the Board of Selectmen, and the Fire Department employees represented by Local 2804, Cohasset Permanent Firefighters, the Police Department employees represented by the New England Police Benevolent Association, AFL-CIO, the civilian dispatch employees represented by Teamsters Local Union No. 25, the Library employees represented by SEIU Local 888, Clerical employees represented by SEIU Local 888, in accordance with Chapter 150E of the General laws, and to fund salary adjustments for non-union and employees with individual employment contracts, or take any other action related thereto.

MOVED that the sum of Ninety Six Thousand Dollars ($96,000) be appropriated to fund the FY 09 cost items of certain collective bargaining agreements in accordance with Chapter 150E of the General Laws, and to fund salary adjustments for non union employees and employees with individual employment contracts, as follows:

Civilian Dispatchers represented by Teamsters Local Union No. 25 $6,500
Library employees represented by SEIU Local 888 $11,500
Clerical employees represented by SEIU Local 888 $13,000
Salary adjustments for non-union and employees with individual employment contracts as set forth in a schedule on file with the office of the Town Clerk $65,000

And to fund this appropriation, Ninety Six Thousand Dollars ($96,000) be raised from the FY 09 tax levy and other general revenues of the Town.

And further that the sum of One Hundred Four Thousand Dollars ($104,000) be appropriated to the Town Manager's Personal Services budget to add to and increase the amounts voted pursuant to Article 3 of the March 29, 2008 Annual Town Meeting to a new total of $229,000, for the purpose of future funding of currently unresolved collective bargaining agreements for FY09; and to fund this appropriation, One Hundred Four Thousand Dollars ($104,000) be raised from the FY 09 tax levy and other general revenues of the Town.

Motion adopted **unanimously.**

ARTICLE 3: CAPITAL IMPROVEMENTS BUDGET

To see if the Town will vote to raise and appropriate, transfer from available funds, lease or borrow pursuant to any applicable statute, a sum of money to fund various capital improvements, capital projects and/or capital equipment for the various departments, boards, commissions and agencies of the town, or take any other action related thereto.

MOVED

That One Hundred Sixty Thousand ($160,000) Dollars be hereby appropriated, with the intention that these funds be available in FY 09 and beyond, to be expended by the Town Manager for the acquisition of an ambulance and for the Fire Department, and to fund this appropriation, either of two alternative methods may be employed: (i) the Treasurer, with the approval of the Board of Selectmen, is authorized to borrow One Hundred Sixty Thousand ($160,000) Dollars under and pursuant to Chapter 44, Section 7 of the Massachusetts General Laws, as amended, and to issue bonds an notes of the Town, therefore, such borrowing to be a general obligation of the Town, or (ii) the Town Manager, with the approval of the Board of Selectmen is authorized to enter into a lease/purchase agreement for said ambulance for a period not to exceed five years; and

That Thirty Thousand ($30,000) Dollars be hereby appropriated, with the intention that these funds be available in FY09 and beyond, to be expended by the Town Manager for the acquisition of a command vehicle for the Fire Department; and that to fund this appropriation, the Treasurer, with the approval of the Board of Selectmen, is hereby authorized to borrow Thirty Thousand ($30,000) Dollars under and pursuant to Chapter 44, Section 7 of the Massachusetts General Laws, as amended, and to issue bonds and notes of the Town, therefore, such borrowing to be a general obligation of the Town, or (ii) the Town Manager, with the approval of the Board of Selectmen is authorized to enter into a lease/purchase agreement for said command vehicle for a period not to exceed three years; and

That Twenty Nine Thousand ($29,000) Dollars be hereby appropriated, with the intention that these funds be available in FY09 and beyond, to be expended by the Town Manager for the acquisition of a police cruiser for the Police Department; and that to fund this appropriation, the Treasurer, with the approval of the Board of Selectmen, is hereby authorized to borrow Twenty Nine Thousand ($29,000) Dollars under and pursuant to Chapter 44, Section 7 of the Massachusetts General Laws, as amended, and to issue bonds an notes of the Town, therefore, such borrowing to be a general obligation of the Town, or (ii) the Town Manager, with the approval of the Board of Selectmen is authorized to enter into a lease/purchase agreement for said police cruiser for a period not to exceed three years; and

That Twenty Five Thousand ($25,000) Dollars be hereby appropriated, with the intention that these funds be available in FY09 and beyond, to be expended by the Town Manager for the acquisition of a heart monitor/defibrillator for the Fire Department; and that to fund this appropriation, the sum of Twenty Five Thousand ($25,000) Dollars be transferred from the Capital Stabilization Fund; and

That Ten Thousand ($10,000) Dollars be hereby appropriated, with the intention that these funds be available in FY09 and beyond, to be expended by the Town Manager for the acquisition of a Jaws of Life for the Fire Department; and that to fund this appropriation, the sum of Ten Thousand ($10,000) Dollars be transferred from the Capital Stabilization Fund; and

That Ten Thousand ($10,000) Dollars be hereby appropriated, with the intention that these funds be available in FY09 and beyond, to be expended by the Town Manager for the acquisition of public computers for the Library; and that to fund this appropriation, the sum of Ten Thousand ($10,000) Dollars be transferred from the Capital Stabilization Fund.

A **2/3's** vote required.

Motion adopted **unanimously.**

ARTICLE 4:   COMMUNITY PRESERVATION COMMITTEE

To see what action the Town will take with respect to the recommendations of the Community Preservation Committee for Fiscal Year 2009, and to see if the Town will vote to implement any such recommendation by appropriating a sum or sums of money from the Community Preservation Fund established pursuant to Chapter 44B of the General Laws, and from any other source, by raising and appropriating, transferring from available funds, borrowing pursuant to any applicable statute or borrowing pursuant to any applicable statute for this purpose, and further to authorize the Board of Selectmen to acquire by purchase, gift or eminent domain, or alternatively to convey, sell or dispose of, such real property interests as may be required by the Community Preservation Act to implement any such expenditure of community preservation funds, or take any other action related thereto.

MOVED

Recommendation A:

Applicant has withdrawn application for funding of Item A, so no motion will be offered; and
That Twenty-Five Thousand Dollars ($25,000), be hereby appropriated with the intention that these funds be available in FY 2009 and thereafter, which funds are to be expended by the Town Manager, for the purposes of preparing a new and required Open Space and Recreation Plan for the Town of Cohasset, which shall include the retention of qualified consultant(s) and expert(s) necessary for the completion of this task, and to meet this appropriation Twelve Thousand Dollars ($12,000) be transferred from the Community Preservation Fund Open Space Sub Account and Thirteen Thousand Dollars ($13,000) be transferred from the Community Preservation Fund Discretionary Account; and That Fifteen Thousand Dollars ($15,000) be hereby appropriated with the intention that these funds be available in Fiscal 2009 and thereafter, which funds are to be expended by the Town Manager for the purposes of conducting the necessary engineering studies and preparing the engineering drawings for the restoration of the pond located on Cohasset Common, and to meet this appropriation Fifteen Thousand Dollars ($15,000) be transferred from the Community Preservation Fund Historical Resources Sub Account.

Motion adopted unanimously.

ARTICLE 5: RELEASE OF EASEMENTS AND RIGHT OF WAY

To see if the Town will vote to authorize the Board of Selectmen to sell, convey, release or otherwise dispose of all or any portions of the following property and interests formerly held by the Town's Board of Water Commissioners for the purposes of conveying water throughout the Town, subject to Massachusetts G.L. 30B:

the 12-foot wide easement located off Nichols Road, granted by Charles O. Smith and Marjorie M. Smith to the Town pursuant to that certain grant of easement dated May 3, 1955 and recorded at the Norfolk County Registry of Deeds in Book 3365, Page 515, and

the 30-foot wide right of way located off 100 Pleasant Street, acquired by the Town pursuant to that certain instrument of taking dated August 18, 1886 and recorded at the Norfolk County Registry of Deeds in Book 581, Page 360,

MOVED that the Board of Selectmen be authorized to sell, convey, release or otherwise dispose of all or any portions of the following property and interests formerly held by the Town's Board of Water Commissioners for the purposes of conveying water throughout the Town, subject to Massachusetts G. L. 30B: the 12-foot wide easement located off Nichols Road, granted by Charles O. Smith and Marjorie M. Smith to the Town pursuant to that certain grant of easement dated May 3, 1955 and recorded at the Norfolk County Registry of Deeds in Book 3365, Page 515.

A **2/3's** vote required. Motion adopted unanimously.

ARTICLE 6: CONSERVATION RESTRICTIONS FOR OPEN SPACE

To see if the Town will vote to authorize the Board of Selectmen and Board of Water Commissioners to sell, grant or convey or otherwise dispose to the Trustees of Reservations or to a governmental body of the Commonwealth of Massachusetts or a non-profit organization whose mission is to conserve our natural resources a conservation restriction on, easements over and other lesser interests in the parcels listed below and shown on that certain plan entitled "Brass Kettle Brook Conservation Area, Cohasset, Massachusetts," dated September 22, 2008, and on file with the Board of Water Commissioners; to grant and reserve to National Grid (USA), Inc. easements for use of portions of such parcels for the purposes of maintaining poles, wires, conduits and other facilities and improvements necessary for the transmission of electricity and intelligence, as shown on that certain plan entitled "Compiled Plan of Land off King Street, Cohasset, MA," dated October 3, 2007 and on file with the Board of Water Commissioners; and further to petition the General Court for enactment of a Home Rule special act set forth below and to request the Town's representatives to the General Court to introduce a Special Act set forth below, and further to authorize the General Court, with the approval of the Board of Selectmen and the Board of Water Commissioners, to make constructive changes in language as may be necessary or advisable towards perfecting the intent of this legislation in order to secure passage.

AN ACT APPROVING THE TOWN OF COHASSET TO
GRANT, SELL, CONVEY OR OTHERWISE DISPOSE OF CERTAIN INTERESTS IN
LAND SITUATED IN THE TOWN OF COHASSET ACQUIRED FOR CONSERVATION,
OPEN SPACE AND WATER PROTECTION PURPOSES

Section 1. Pursuant to Article XCVII of the Amendments to the Constitution of the Commonwealth of Massachusetts, and notwithstanding the provisions of any general or special law to the contrary, the Town of Cohasset, acting by and through its Board of Selectmen and Board of Water Commissioners, is hereby authorized to grant to the Trustees of Reservations or to a governmental body of the Commonwealth of Massachusetts or a non-profit organization whose mission is to conserve our natural resources, a conservation restriction on, easements over and other lesser interests in the parcels listed below and shown on that certain plan entitled "Brass Kettle Brook Conservation Area, Cohasset, Massachusetts," dated September 22, 2008, and on file with the Board of Water Commissioners or any portions thereof, for conservation, open space and water protection purposes; to grant and reserve to National Grid (USA), Inc. easements for use of portions of such parcels for the purposes of maintaining poles, wires, conduits and other facilities and improvements necessary for the transmission of electricity and intelligence, as shown on that certain plan entitled "Compiled Plan of Land off King Street, Cohasset, MA," dated October 3, 2007 and on file with the Board of Water Commissioners, or to take any other action related thereto.

MAP	PARCEL	LOCATION	MAP	PARCEL	LOCATION
54	19	Off Riverview Drive	60	13	Off King Street
54	24	Off Riverview Drive	65	1	Off King Street
54	27	Off Riverview Drive	65	2	Off King Street
54	25	Off Riverview Drive	65	3	Off King Street
54	33	Off Riverview Drive	65	4	Off King Street
56	12	Off King Street	65	5	Off King Street
56	14	Off Doane Street	65	6	Off King Street
56	15	Off Doane Street	65	6B	Off King Street
56	16	Off Doane Street	65	7	Off King Street
56	16A	Off Doane Street	65	8	Off King Street
56	52	Off Doane Street	65	9	Off King Street
59	11	Off King Street	65	10	Off King Street
59	12	Off King Street	65	18	Off King Street
59	13	Off King Street	65	19	Off King Street
60	1	Off King Street	65	19	Off King Street
60	2	Off King Street	65	35	Off King Street
60	3	Off King Street	66	1	Off King Street
60	4	Off King Street	66	2	Off King Street
60	5	Off King Street	66	3	Off King Street
60	6	Off King Street	66	4	Off King Street
60	7	Off King Street	66	5	Off King Street
60	8	Off King Street	66	6	Off King Street
60	9	Off King Street	66	7	Off King Street
60	10	Off King Street	72	1	Off Howes Lane
60	11	Off King Street	72	2	Off Howes Lane
60	12	Off King Street	72	3	Off Howes Lane

Section 2. This act shall take effect upon its passage.

MOVED that the Board of Selectmen and/or the Board of Water Commissioners be authorized to sell, grant or convey or otherwise dispose to the Trustees of Reservations or to a governmental body of the Commonwealth of Massachusetts or a non-profit organization whose mission is to conserve our natural resources a conservation restriction on, easements over and other lesser interests in the parcels listed below and shown on that certain plan entitled "Brass Kettle Brook Conservation Area, Cohasset, Massachusetts," dated September 22, 2008, and on file with the Board of Water Commissioners; to grant to and reserve for National Grid (USA), Inc. easements for use of portions of such parcels for the purposes of maintaining poles, wires, conduits and other facilities and improvements necessary for the transmission of electricity and intelligence, as shown on that certain plan entitled "Compiled Plan of Land off King Street, Cohasset, MA," dated October 3, 2007 and on file with the Board of Water Commissioners; and further to petition the General Court for enactment of a Home Rule special act set forth below and to request the Town's representatives to the General Court to introduce a Special Act set forth below, and further to authorize the General Court, with the approval of the Board of Selectmen and the Board of Water Commissioners, to make constructive changes in language as may be necessary or advisable towards perfecting the intent of this legislation in order to secure its passage.

AN ACT APPROVING THE TOWN OF COHASSET TO
GRANT, SELL, CONVEY OR OTHERWISE DISPOSE OF CERTAIN INTERESTS IN
LAND SITUATED IN THE TOWN OF COHASSET ACQUIRED FOR CONSERVATION,
OPEN SPACE AND WATER PROTECTION PURPOSES

Section 1.   Pursuant to Article XCVII of the Amendments to the Constitution of the Commonwealth of Massachusetts, and notwithstanding the provisions of any general or special law to the contrary, the Town of Cohasset, acting by and through its Board of Selectmen and Board of Water Commissioners, is hereby authorized to grant to the Trustees of Reservations or to a governmental body of the Commonwealth of Massachusetts or a non-profit organization whose mission is to conserve our natural resources, a conservation restriction on, easements over and other lesser interests in the parcels listed below and shown on that certain plan entitled "Brass Kettle Brook Conservation Area, Cohasset, Massachusetts," dated September 22, 2008, and on file with the Board of Water Commissioners or any portions thereof, for conservation, open space and water protection purposes; to grant and reserve to National Grid (USA), Inc. easements for use of portions of such parcels for the purposes of maintaining poles, wires, conduits and other facilities and improvements necessary for the transmission of electricity and intelligence, as shown on that certain plan entitled "Compiled Plan of Land off King Street, Cohasset, MA," dated October 3, 2007 and on file with the Board of Water Commissioners.

MAP	PARCEL	LOCATION	MAP	PARCEL	LOCATION
54	19	Off Riverview Drive	60	13	Off King Street
54	24	Off Riverview Drive	65	1	Off King Street
54	27	Off Riverview Drive	65	2	Off King Street
54	25	Off Riverview Drive	65	3	Off King Street
54	33	Off Riverview Drive	65	4	Off King Street
56	12	Off King Street	65	5	Off King Street
56	14	Off Doane Street	65	6	Off King Street
56	15	Off Doane Street	65	6B	Off King Street
56	16	Off Doane Street	65	7	Off King Street
56	16A	Off Doane Street	65	8	Off King Street
56	52	Off Doane Street	65	9	Off King Street
59	11	Off King Street	65	10	Off King Street
59	12	Off King Street	65	18	Off King Street
59	13	Off King Street	65	19	Off King Street

MAP	PARCEL	LOCATION	MAP	PARCEL	LOCATION
60	1	Off King Street	65	19	Off King Street
60	2	Off King Street	65	35	Off King Street
60	3	Off King Street	66	1	Off King Street
60	4	Off King Street	66	2	Off King Street
60	5	Off King Street	66	3	Off King Street
60	6	Off King Street	66	4	Off King Street
60	7	Off King Street	66	5	Off King Street
60	8	Off King Street	66	6	Off King Street
60	9	Off King Street	66	7	Off King Street
60	10	Off King Street	72	1	Off Howes Lane
60	11	Off King Street	72	2	Off Howes Lane
60	12	Off King Street	72	3	Off Howes Lane

Section 2. This act shall take effect upon its passage.

A **2/3's** vote required. **Motion adopted unanimously.**

Proclamation offered by Ted Carr, Chairman of the Board of Selectmen for Stephen Bowen.

PROCLAMATION

WHEREAS CAPTAIN STEPHEN G. BOWEN was born and raised in Cohasset and is a 1982 graduate of Cohasset High school where he was a star student and athlete; and

WHEREAS CAPTAIN BOWEN is a graduate of the United States Naval Academy and holds a Degree of Ocean Engineering from the Massachusetts Institute of Technology; and

WHEREAS CAPTAIN BOWEN serves in the United States Navy with a specialty in nuclear submarines, and in May of 2000 became the first Executive Officer of the first of the new VIRGINIA Class submarines; and

WHEREAS CAPTAIN BOWEN was selected by NASA in July of 2000 as the first Submarine Officer to ever serve as a member of the crew of a space shuttle mission; and

WHEREAS CAPTAIN BOWEN is currently a member of the six person crew of the Space Shuttle Endeavor which launched from the Kennedy Space Center on November 14th for a sixteen day mission to help double the living quarters of the International Space Station; and

WHEREAS CAPTAIN BOWEN will be making a total of three spacewalks during the course of the space shuttle mission, during which he will spend close to twenty hours undertaking highly technical work in support of the International Space Station.

NOW THEREFORE BE IT RESOLVED that on behalf of all the citizens of Cohasset, the Board of Selectmen and the November 17, 2008 Cohasset Town Meeting hereby hail the accomplishments and bravery of CAPTAIN STEPHEN G. BOWEN both for his highly decorated service in the United States Navy and as a crew member of the Space Shuttle Endeavor, and call upon the citizens of Cohasset to recognize and honor the incredible service of this Cohasset native son and wish both he and the entire Space Shuttle Crew a safe journey home.

Given under our hands and the seal of the Town of Cohasset on this seventeenth day of November in the year Two Thousand and Eight.

Proclamation adopted unanimously.

ARTICLE 7: REINFORCEMENT TO CURRENT DESIGN STANDARDS OF JERUSALEM ROAD WALL AND ROADWAY

To see if the Town will vote to raise and appropriate, transfer from available funds, and/or borrow, pursuant to any applicable statue, a sum or sums of money, to be expended by the Town Manager, to reinforce and/or otherwise bring up to current design standards the roadway and deficient retaining wall system currently located on the easterly side of Jerusalem Road between Bow Street and Steep Rocks Way, so as to ensure sufficient stability to support the intended vehicle loads, to acquire by purchase, gift, eminent domain, or otherwise, temporary and permanent real estate easements, leases or other interests in private ways and lands for the purpose of implementing said improvements, to determine whether this appropriation shall be raised by borrowing from the Massachusetts Water Pollution Abatement Trust, or to take any action related thereto.

MOVED that Two Hundred Seventy Thousand ($270,000) Dollars be hereby appropriated, with the intention that these funds be available in FY09 and beyond, to be expended by the Town Manager to reinforce and/or otherwise bring up to current design standards the roadway and deficient retaining wall system currently located on the easterly side of Jerusalem Road between Bow Street and Steep Rocks Way; and that to fund this appropriation, the Treasurer, with the approval of the Board of Selectmen, is hereby authorized to borrow Two Hundred Seventy ($270,000) Dollars pursuant to Chapter 44, Section 7 of the Massachusetts General Laws, as amended, and to issue bonds an notes of the Town, therefore, such borrowing to be a general obligation of the Town.

A **2/3's** vote required. **Motion adopted unanimously.**

ARTICLE 8:   TOWN HALL RESTORATION PROJECT

To see if the Town of Cohasset will vote to authorize the Board of Selectmen to accept grants, gifts, tax credits, and monies for the purposes of restoring and renovating the Cohasset Town Hall, or take any other action related thereto.

MOVED that the Board of Selectmen be hereby authorized to accept grants, gifts, tax credits, and monies for the purposes of restoring and renovating the Cohasset Town Hall.

The following resolution would replace the motion.

RESOLUTION

MOVED   that the Board of Selectmen be hereby authorized and encouraged to pursue grants, gifts, tax credits, and monies for the purposes of restoring and renovating the Cohasset Town Hall.

Resolution adopted unanimously.

ARTICLE 9: FUNDING FOR ALTERNATIVE ENERGY COMMITTEE

To see if the Town will vote to raise, appropriate or transfer from a available funds, or borrow pursuant to any applicable statute a sum of money to be expended by the Town Manager with the approval of the Alternative Energy Committee, to continue to engage consulting services to assist the Committee to investigate alternative energy options for the Town, pursue grant funding, promote clean energy alternatives within the community, and related duties, or take any other action related thereto.

MOVED that the sum of Ten Thousand Dollars ($10,000) be appropriated to be expended by the Town Manager with the approval of the Alternative Energy Committee, to engage consulting services to assist the Committee to investigate alternative energy options for the Town, pursue grant funding, promote clean energy alternatives within the community, and related duties; and to fund this appropriation, Ten Thousand Dollars ($10,000) be raised from the FY 09 tax levy and other general revenues of the Town.

Motion adopted.

ARTICLE 10: ZONING BYLAW RECONCILIATION

To see if the Town will vote to amend the Town of Cohasset Zoning Bylaws, as follows:

That Section 7.1 in the column entitled "Number of Parking Spaces Required Per Unit" for Use "L" be amended in line 6 by changing the word "on" to "of" so that said Section 7.1, Use L as amended shall read as follows: "One space per unit unless the apartments are proposed within that portion of a building existing on 1/5/55 or unless a reduced number is specifically authorized within the final action of the special permit granting authority upon a finding that one space per unit is not necessary for public safety and convenience, that the creation of on-site parking spaces is incompatible with approved design guidelines or that adequate provision for parking has otherwise been proposed."

That Section 17.3.2, second sub-section "f" reading as follows: "Any other information required by the Planning Board in the rules and regulations adopted by it with respect to such special permit process." be amended to be re-labeled as sub-section "g".

That Section 17.4.1, sub-section "ᵉ" reading as follows: "Buildings and uses accessory to the above, including, without limitation, parking garages that are accessory to dwelling units and cafeterias." be amended to be re-labeled as sub-section "f".

That Section 17.9.3, be amended in line 1 by changing "Rules are Regulations consistent ..." to read "Rules and Regulations consistent ..." so that Section 17.9.3 as amended shall read as follows: "The Planning Board shall adopt, and from time to time amend, Rules and Regulations consistent with the provisions of this Zoning Bylaw, Chapter 40A of General Laws and other applicable provisions of the General Laws and shall file a copy of said rules and regulations with the Town Clerk. Such rules and regulations shall, subject to provisions of this Section 17, prescribe as minimum the size, contents, form, style and number of plans and specifications, the Town boards or Departments from which the Planning Board will request written reports and the procedure for submission and approval of a Special Permit under the provisions of this section. The Planning Board shall also specify the fees to be paid in connection with application for a TOD Overlay Development, bonding requirements to satisfy conditions of approval, and reporting requirements to satisfy compliance with the affordability restrictions. Other specifications as deemed necessary by the Planning Board shall be included in the Rules and Regulations. Failure to adopt such Rules and Regulations shall not affect the validity of this Section 17."

That Section 19.4.1.3.c, be amended by changing "S.P.G.A." to read "SPGA" as is used throughout the rest of the document, so that Section 19.4.1.3.c as amended shall read as follows: "c) All signs shall comply with the requirements of the Town's sign regulations unless relief is granted by the SPGA."

That Section 19.7.2, line 3, be amended to correct the first quotation mark by changing "Physically remove" to read "Physically remove", so that Section 19.7.2 as amended shall read as follows: " Upon abandonment or discontinuation of use, the owner shall physically remove the wind turbine(s) within 90 days from the date of abandonment or discontinuation of use. This period may be extended at the request of the owner and at the discretion of the SPGA. "Physically remove" shall include, but not be limited to:"

That Section 19.9.1.Special Permit Granting Authority (SPGA), line 1, be amended by changing "Wind Turbine(s) is …" to read "Wind Turbine(s) in …", so that Section 19.9.1.Special Permit Granting Authority (SPGA) as amended shall read as follows: "The SPGA for wind energy conversion facilities, also referred to as Wind Turbine(s) in this bylaw shall be the Planning Board."

MOVED that the Town's Zoning Bylaws be amended as follows:

That Section 7.1 in the column entitled "Number of Parking Spaces Required Per Unit" for Use "L" be amended in line 6 by changing the word "on" to "of" so that said Section 7.1, Use L as amended shall read as follows: "One space per unit unless the apartments are proposed within that portion of a building existing on 1/5/55 or unless a reduced number is specifically authorized within the final action of the special permit granting authority upon a finding that one space per unit is not necessary for public safety and convenience, that the creation of on-site parking spaces is incompatible with approved design guidelines or that adequate provision for parking has otherwise been proposed."

That Section 17.3.2, second sub-section "f" reading as follows: "Any other information required by the Planning Board in the rules and regulations adopted by it with respect to such special permit process." be amended to be re-labeled as sub-section "g".

That Section 17.4.1, sub-section "ᴮ" reading as follows: "Buildings and uses accessory to the above, including, without limitation, parking garages that are accessory to dwelling units and cafeterias." be amended to be re-labeled as sub-section "f".

That Section 17.9.3, be amended in line 1 by changing "Rules are Regulations consistent …" to read "Rules and Regulations consistent …" so that Section 17.9.3 as amended shall read as follows: "The Planning Board shall adopt, and from time to time amend, Rules and Regulations consistent with the provisions of this Zoning Bylaw, Chapter 40A of General Laws and other applicable provisions of the General Laws and shall file a copy of said rules and regulations with the Town Clerk. Such rules and regulations shall, subject to provisions of this Section 17, prescribe as minimum the size, contents, form, style and number of plans and specifications, the Town boards or Departments from which the Planning Board will request written reports and the procedure for submission and approval of a Special Permit under the provisions of this section. The Planning Board shall also specify the fees to be paid in connection with application for a TOD Overlay Development, bonding requirements to satisfy conditions of approval, and reporting requirements to satisfy compliance with the affordability restrictions. Other specifications as deemed necessary by the Planning Board shall be included in the Rules and Regulations. Failure to adopt such Rules and Regulations shall not affect the validity of this Section 17."

That Section 19.4.1.3.c, be amended by changing "S.P.G.A." to read "SPGA" as is used throughout the rest of the document, so that Section 19.4.1.3.c as amended shall read as follows: "c) All signs shall comply with the requirements of the Town's sign regulations unless relief is granted by the SPGA."

That Section 19.7.2, line 3, be amended to correct the first quotation mark by changing "Physically remove" to read "Physically remove", so that Section 19.7.2 as amended shall read as follows: " Upon abandonment or discontinuation of use, the owner shall physically remove the wind turbine(s) within 90 days from the date of abandonment or discontinuation of use. This period may be extended at the request of the owner and at the discretion of the SPGA. "Physically remove" shall include, but not be limited to:"

That Section 19.9.1.Special Permit Granting Authority (SPGA), line 1, be amended by changing "Wind Turbine(s) is ..." to read "Wind Turbine(s) in ...", so that Section 19.9.1.Special Permit Granting Authority (SPGA) as amended shall read as follows: "The SPGA for wind energy conversion facilities, also referred to as Wind Turbine(s) in this bylaw shall be the Planning Board."

Report of Planning Board given by Alfred Moore.

A **2/3's** vote required. Motion adopted unanimously.

ARTICLE 11: GRANT OF EASEMENT FOR GAS LINE

To see if the Town will vote to authorize the Board of Selectmen to grant a permanent easement or lesser title interest in under that portion of Town-owned property, commonly known as Town Hall, identified as Parcel 89 on Assessor Map No. 27 and numbered 41 Highland Avenue, as shown on that certain plan entitled "Easement Drawing, 29 & 41 Highland Avenue, Cohasset, MA," a copy of which plan is on file with the Town Manager's Office, for the purposes of providing gas service to property owned by St. Stephen's Episcopal Church located at 29 Highland Avenue, or to take any other action related thereto.

MOVED that the Board of Selectmen be authorized to grant a permanent easement or lesser title interest in, over, or under that portion of Town-owned property, commonly known as Town Hall, identified as Parcel 89 on Assessor Map No. 27 and numbered 41 Highland Avenue, as shown on that certain plan entitled "Easement Drawing, 29 & 41 Highland Avenue, Cohasset, MA," a copy of which plan is on file with the Town Manager's Office, for the purposes of providing gas service to property owned by St. Stephen's Episcopal Church located at 29 Highland Avenue in Cohasset

A **2/3's** vote required. Motion adopted unanimously.

ARTICLE 12: JACOBS MEADOW CULVERT REPAIR AND UPGRADE

To see if the Town of Cohasset will vote to raise and appropriate, transfer from available funds, or borrow pursuant to any applicable statute a sum of money to be expended by the Town Manager for the purpose of reconstruction and upgrading the open culvert and tide gates at the Jacobs Meadow culvert at the American Legion Post, and that the town be authorized to accept grants, gifts, tax credits, and monies for that intended purpose, to authorize the Board of Selectmen to acquire by purchase, gift or eminent domain permanent easements or lesser title interests in all or any portions of the following parcels located off Summer Street and Elm Street for drainage purposes, or to take any other action related thereto.

Map	Parcel	Location	Map	Parcel	Location
27	5	85 Elm Street	32	24	80 Summer Street
27	4	87 Elm Street	32	23	84 Summer Street
27	2	95 Elm Street	32	22	88 Summer Street
27	1	97 Elm Street			

MOVED that Four Hundred Fifty Thousand ($450,000) Dollars be hereby appropriated, with the intention that these funds be available in FY09 and beyond, to be expended by the Town Manager to reconstruct and upgrade the open culvert and tide gates at the Jacobs Meadow culvert at the American Legion; and that to fund this appropriation, the Treasurer, with the approval of the Board of Selectmen, is hereby authorized to borrow Four Hundred Fifty Thousand ($450,000) Dollars pursuant to Chapter 44, Section 7 of the Massachusetts General Laws, as amended, and to issue bonds and notes of the Town, therefore, such borrowing to be a general obligation of the Town.

A **2/3's** vote required. Motion adopted **unanimously.**

ARTICLE 13: CITIZENS' PETITION – TURF FIELD

To see if the Town will vote to raise and appropriate, transfer from available funds, or borrow pursuant to any applicable statute, a sum of money to be expended by the Town Manager for the creation of new recreational opportunities by the construction of a synthetic turf field and track at the Clark Chatterton Athletic Complex, or take any other action related thereto.

NAME	ADDRESS	NAME	ADDRESS
Ellen Maher	63 Old Pasture Road	Glenn Pratt	482 King Street
Chris Haggerty	10 Sankey Road	George McGoldrick	744 Jerusalem Road
SallyAnn Chatterton	9 Red Gate Lane	Richard Evans	24 Lantern Lane
Wayne Sawchuk	432 Beechwood Street	Ralph Froio	327 Forest Ave.
Joseph Fitzgerald	516 CJC Way.	Gary Vanderweil	500 Jerusalem Road

MOVED that One Million Fifty Thousand Dollars ($1,050,000) Dollars be hereby appropriated, with the intention that these funds be available in FY 09 and beyond, to be expended by the Town Manager to design, permit and construct a synthetic turf field and track at the Clark Chatterton Athletic Complex; and that to fund this appropriation, the Treasurer, with the approval of the Board of Selectmen, is hereby authorized to borrow Five Hundred Thousand Dollars ($500,000) pursuant to Chapter 44, Section 7 of the Massachusetts General Laws, as amended, and to issue bonds and notes of the Town therefore, such borrowing to be a general obligation of the Town; and Five Hundred Fifty Thousand Dollars ($550,000) to come from donations to be received by the Town as gifts, provided however, that no money shall be borrowed under this vote unless the following condition is met: that the Cohasset Sports Partnership will have raised a sum of at least Five Hundred Fifty Thousand Dollars ($550,000), and delivered same to the Town Manager, by December 31, 2010 it being the understanding of the Town that said Five Hundred Fifty Thousand Dollars($550,000) shall be given to the Town by the Cohasset Sports Partnership for this purpose.

A **2/3's** vote required. Motion adopted by the required **2/3's.**

It was moved and seconded that this Special Town Meeting be dissolved at **9:15 p.m.**

A True Record, ATTEST:

Marion L. Douglas
Town Clerk

VITAL STATISTICS - 2008

Record of birth, marriage and death records in the Town of Cohasset for 2008 are as follows:

BIRTHS

The numbers of births recorded were thirty-nine males and twenty-seven females.

MARRIAGES

The total of marriages was thirty-three. Twenty-two of those were solemnized in Cohasset during the current year.

DEATHS

The total number of deaths was eighty-three including residents of Cohasset who died elsewhere and non-residents who died in Cohasset.

PROSPECTIVE JUROR LIST

Pursuant to Massachusetts General Laws, Chapter 234A, Section 15, the Prospective Juror List is available in the Town Clerk's office with the names of those residents who may be summoned for juror service.

This information is available for public inspection during normal office hours.

Respectfully submitted,

Marion L. Douglas
Town Clerk

TOWN ACCOUNTANT

Submitted herewith is my annual report for the fiscal year ended June 30, 2008. This report includes the following:

GENERAL FUND
1. Historical Data
2. Balance Sheet (Combined)
3. Statement of Revenues, Expenditures and Changes in Fund Balance
4. Report of Appropriations and Expenditures
5. Statement of Revenues, Budget vs. Actual
6. Statement of State and County Assessments

SPECIAL REVENUE FUNDS
1. Balance Sheet (Combined)
2. Statement of Revenues, Expenditures and Changes in Fund Balance, Town Special Revenue Funds
3. Statement of Revenues, Expenditures and Changes in Fund Balance, School Special Revenue Funds

SEWER FUNDS – NORTH AND CENTRAL COHASSET
1. Balance Sheet (Combined)
2. Statement of Revenues, Expenditures and Changes in Fund Balance
3. Report of Appropriations and Expenditures

WATER FUND
1. Balance Sheet (Combined)
2. Statement of Revenues, Expenditures and Changes in Retained Earnings
3. Report of Appropriations and Expenditures

CAPITAL PROJECTS FUND
1. Balance Sheet (Combined)
2. Statement of Revenues, Expenditures and Changes in Fund Balance

TRUST FUNDS
1. Balance Sheet (Combined)
2. Statement of Revenues, Expenditures and Changes in Fund Balance

LONG TERM DEBT GROUP OF ACCOUNTS
1. Statement of Long Term Debt
2. Statement of Debt Authorized and Unissued

OTHER REPORTS
1. Schedule of Reserve Fund Transfers
2. Community Preservation Fund

Respectfully Submitted,

J. Michael Buckley

SUMMARY OF HISTORICAL FINANCIAL DATA

	TAX RATE	TOWN VALUATION
2003	11.99	1,602,813,423
2004	11.89	1,730,261,119
2005	10.44	2,086,149,189
2006	10.84	2,173,147,423
2007	10.50	2,324,029,983
2008	10.60	2,403,120,204
2009	10.78	2,455,174,229

	TAX LEVY	OPERATING BUDGET
2003	19,217,733	26,954,203
2004	20,572,805	28,112,193
2005	22,779,398	29,784,963
2006	23,556,917	31,724,742
2007	24,402,315	33,174,703
2008	25,473,074	35,340,212
2009	26,466,778	36,374,463

	AVERAGE SINGLE FAMILY TAX BILL	STATE AID *
2003	6,909	1,491,660
2004	7,396	915,942
2005	7,804	927,721
2006	8,442	910,613
2007	8,664	1,117,164
2008	8,988	1,284,155
2009	9,346	1,423,127

	FREE CASH	STABILIZATION FUND*
2003	937,302	921,309
2004	346,818	492,660
2005	737,226	38,962
2006	1,007,767	42,781
2007	956,971	562,792
2008	359,773	590,953

* Unrestricted Net

ASSETS	#100 GENERAL FUND	#101-#299 SPECIAL REVENUE	#300-#399 CAPITAL PROJECTS	#600-#700 ENTERPRISE FUNDS	#801-#890 TRUSTS AND AGENCY	#970 LONG-TERM ACCOUNT GROUP	TOTALS ALL FUNDS
CASH AND SHORT TERM INVESTMENTS	2,556,522	1,872,098	1,391,120	1,517,374	4,265,441		11,602,555
DEPARTMENTAL RECEIVABLES(Ambulance)	387,840	6,729					394,569
INTERFUND RECEIVABLES (Due From) Trust	108,196	39,949					148,145
INTERFUND RECEIVABLES (Due From) Enterprise		8,565			116,735		125,300
INTERFUND RECEIVABLES (Due From) General Fund					5,685		5,685
DUE FROM COMMONWEALTH OF MASSACHUSETTS		137,680	48,069	349,415			535,164
EXCISE TAX RECEIVABLE	119,117	4,855					123,972
PERSONAL PROPERTY TAX RECEIVABLE	10,603						10,603
REAL ESTATE TAX RECEIVABLE	450,700						450,700
SPECIAL ASSESSMENTS RECEIVABLE	4,776,957						4,776,957
TAX LIENS	206,320						206,320
TAX DEFERRALS	564,428						564,428
USER CHARGES RECEIVABLE				371,879			371,879
UTILITY LIENS ADDED TO TAXES				7,930			7,930
AMOUNT PROVIDED FOR BONDS						50,783,013	50,783,013
AMOUNT PROVIDED FOR NOTES		100,000	1,157,313	25,282,368			26,539,681
AMOUNT PROVIDED AUTHORIZED BONDS						52,629,390	52,629,390
PROVISIONS FOR ABATEMENTS AND EXEMPTIONS	(267,003)						(267,003)
TAX FORECLOSURES	87,317						87,317
TOTAL ASSETS	9,000,997	2,169,876	2,596,502	27,528,966	4,387,861	103,412,403	149,096,606
LIABILITIES							
ACCOUNTS PAYABLE	1,061,152						1,061,152
BONDS PAYABLE						50,783,013	50,783,013
NOTES PAYABLE		100,000	1,157,313	25,282,368			26,539,681
BONDS AUTHORIZED & UNISSUED						52,629,390	52,629,390
DEFERRED REVENUES	6,336,280	11,584					6,347,864
INTERFUND PAYABLES (Due To) General Fund				148,145			148,145
INTERFUND PAYABLES (Due To) Trust	5,685						5,685
INTERFUND PAYABLES (Due To) Agency				116,735			116,735
INTERFUND PAYABLES (Due To) Special Revenue				8,565			8,565
OTHER LIABILITIES	18,042			1,564			19,606
WITHHOLDINGS PAYABLE					389,343		389,343
TOTAL LIABILITIES	7,421,159	111,584	1,157,313	25,407,668	539,052	103,412,403	138,049,179
FUND EQUITY							
RESERVE FOR ENCUMBRANCES-CURRENT YR	496,813						496,813
RESERVE FOR EXPENDITURES	450,000						450,000
RESERVE FOR PETTY CASH & OTHER ASSETS							0
RESERVE FOR EXCLUDED DEBT							0
RESERVE FOR DEPOSITS							0
RESERVE FOR CONSTRUCTION							0
DESIGNATED		1,990,398	1,439,189	1,785,232			5,214,819
UNRESERVED FUND BALANCE-APPROPRIATION DEFICITS							0
UNRESERVED FUND BALANCE	633,025	67,894		336,066	3,848,809		4,885,794
TOTAL FUND EQUITY	1,579,838	2,058,292	1,439,189	2,121,298	3,848,809	0	11,047,426
TOTAL LIABILITIES AND FUND EQUITY	9,000,997	2,169,876	2,596,502	27,528,966	4,387,861	103,412,403	149,096,605
CHECK BALANCE (S/B 0)	0	0	0	0	0	0	1

STATEMENT OF REVENUES, EXPENDITURES
AND CHANGES IN FUND BALANCE
GENERAL FUND
FISCAL YEAR 2008

Revenue:

Property Taxes	25,150,399	
State Aid	2,854,620	
Excise Taxes	1,284,858	
Other Local Receipts	2,441,734	
Total Revenue		31,731,611

Less:

Expenditures:

General Government	1,558,411	
Public Safety	3,957,409	
Schools	13,877,311	
Public Works	2,247,331	
Public Health	133,745	
Human Services	184,621	
Culture & Recreation	632,596	
Debt Service	4,659,982	
Employee Benefits & Insurance	4,027,657	
State and County Assessments	1,079,456	
Total Expenditures		32,358,519

Encumbrances:

Encumbrances	571,813	
Encumbrances-Prior Year	(689,639)	
Total Encumbrances		(117,826)

Other Financing Sources (Uses))

Operating Transfers In	311,480	
Operating Transfers Out	(405,896)	
Overlay Surplus Release	0	
Appropriation Deficits (net)	0	
Miscellaneous Adjustments	1,183	
Total Financing Sources (Uses))		(93,233)

Excess of Revenues Over Expenditures	(602,315)
Unreserved Fund Balance July 1, 2007	1,235,340
Unreserved Fund Balance June 30, 2008	$633,025

		GENERAL FUND REVENUE			
		BUDGET vs. ACTUAL			
		FISCAL YEAR 2008			
					%
		Budget	Actual	Uncollected	Collected
TAX LEVY					
	Real Estate	25,310,920	24,907,341	(403,579)	98.4%
	Personal Property	162,154	161,184	(970)	99.4%
	Tax Liens	-	81,874	81,874	-
	Rollback Tax	-		-	-
	Deferred Tax	-		-	-
	Total Tax Levy	**25,473,074**	**25,150,399**	**(322,675)**	**98.7%**
STATE AID					
	School Chapter 70	1,696,971	1,696,971	-	100.0%
	School Construction	485,000	485,300	300	100.1%
	Additional Assistance	166,099	166,099	-	100.0%
	Lottery	474,221	474,221	-	100.0%
	Veterans' Exemptions	15,063	11,844	(3,219)	78.6%
	Elderly Exemptions	10,040	10,040	-	100.0%
	Charter School Reimb.	10,795	5,094	(5,701)	47.2%
	Miscellaneous	-	5,051	5,051	
	Total State Aid	**2,858,189**	**2,854,620**	**(3,569)**	**99.9%**
LOCAL RECEIPTS					
	Motor Vehicle Excise	1,209,381	1,276,148	66,767	105.5%
	Boat Excise	7,500	8,710	1,210	116.1%
	Betterments - Sewer	485,000	471,394	(13,606)	97.2%
	Betterments - Drainage	15,000	22,622	7,622	-
	Penalty & Interest on Taxes -				
	Committed Interest	56,000	51,219	(4,781)	91.5%
	Property Taxes	45,000	68,093	23,093	151.3%
	Liens	4,000	40,482	36,482	1012.1%
	Excise	5,000	6,189	1,189	123.8%
	Facility Stickers	140,000	145,465	5,465	103.9%
	Trash Bags	120,000	152,692	32,692	127.2%
	Fees -				
	Board Of Selectmen	4,000	3,232	(768)	80.8%
	Town Clerk	6,000	6,285	285	104.8%
	Treasurer/Collector	27,000	17,819	(9,181)	66.0%
	Assessors	2,000	3,933	1,933	196.7%
	ZBA	3,000	4,155	1,155	138.5%
	Planning Board	6,000	19,450	13,450	324.2%
	Conservation Commission	8,000	7,485	(515)	93.6%
	Police Dept	25,000	27,216	2,216	108.9%
	Ambulance	350,000	371,544	21,544	106.2%
	Fire Department Other	6,000	5,988	(12)	99.8%

		GENERAL FUND REVENUE			
		BUDGET vs. ACTUAL			
		FISCAL YEAR 2008			%
		Budget	Actual	Uncollected	Collected
Weights & Measures		3,000	4,300	1,300	143.3%
Recycling		26,000	46,045	20,045	177.1%
Transfer Station Fees		24,000	19,457	(4,543)	81.1%
School		-	12,086	12,086	-
Library Fees		14,000	14,228	228	101.6%
Cemetery Fees		15,000	13,125	(1,875)	87.5%
Recreation Fees		75,000	97,584	22,584	130.1%
Town Rentals		15,000	5,100	(9,900)	34.0%
In Lieu of Tax		-	1,264	1,264	-
Licenses & Permits -					
Board Of Health		28,000	29,086	1,086	103.9%
Building		233,000	230,040	(2,960)	98.7%
Plumbing		9,000	10,608	1,608	117.9%
Gas		5,000	6,356	1,356	127.1%
Electrical		24,000	28,175	4,175	117.4%
Dog		5,000	6,221	1,221	124.4%
Alcoholic Beverage		20,000	21,475	1,475	107.4%
Selectmen Other		5,000	6,126	1,126	122.5%
Selectmen Road Openings		1,000	5,023	4,023	502.3%
Unclassified		-	10,563	10,563	-
Fines & Forfeits -					
Parking		36,000	25,130	(10,870)	69.8%
Court Fines		6,000	5,115	(885)	85.3%
Registry Fines		13,000	8,010	(4,990)	61.6%
Tailings		-	3,945	3,945	-
Conservation		-	6,000	6,000	-
Investment Income		250,000	273,607	23,607	109.4%
Harbor Fees		103,000	127,802	24,802	124.1%
Indirect Costs		60,000		(60,000)	0.0%
Total Local Receipts		3,493,881	3,726,592	232,711	106.7%
GRAND TOTAL		31,825,144	31,731,611	(93,533)	99.7%

GENERAL FUND
APPROPRIATION EXPENDITURE LEDGER
FISCAL YEAR 2008

	PRIOR YEAR CARRY FWD	ATM APPROP-RIATION	STM TRANSFER	RESERVE FUND/ TRANSFERS	RECEIPTS	TOTAL AVAILABLE FUNDS	EXPENDED	ENCUMBERED	AVAILABLE	% EXP
GENERAL FUND-TOWN										
MODERATOR-114										
Personal Services		573.00				573.00	552.00		21.00	96%
BOARD OF SELECTMEN-122										
Elected Officials		5,500.00				5,500.00	5,416.51		83.49	98%
General Expenses		64,050.00				64,050.00	60,105.52	2,041.72	1,902.76	94%
N. Cohasset Water System 3/97 ATM	2,500.00					2,500.00	0.00	2,500.00	0.00	0%
Beechwood Street Culvert 3/97 ATM	19,650.00					19,650.00	19,650.00		0.00	100%
Sidewalk Capital 10/97 STM	23,153.11					23,153.11	23,153.11		0.00	100%
Eleazer Lane 3/98 ATM	1,500.00					1,500.00	0.00	1,500.00	0.00	0%
Little Harbor Study 3/09 STM	2,278.86					2,278.86	0.00	2,278.86	0.00	0%
Town Memorials 11/03 STM	1,258.05					1,258.05	0.00	1,258.05	0.00	0%
Alternative Energy Committee 11/06 STM	20,000.00					20,000.00	12,690.00	7,310.00	0.00	63%
Stormwater Management Committee 11/06 STM	3,626.75					3,626.75	(4,534.50)	8,161.25	0.00	-125%
Village Master Plan 11/06 STM	7,392.60					7,392.60	7,392.60		0.00	100%
West Corner Culvert 03/08 STM			50,000.00			50,000.00	40,260.51	9,739.49	0.00	81%
Encumbrance	1,200.00					1,200.00	1,177.37		22.63	98%
Encumbrance - Web Site	1,200.00					1,200.00	136.37	1,063.63	0.00	11%
TOWN MANAGER-129										
Personal Services		125,000.00				125,000.00	125,000.00		0.00	100%
Clerical Pool		427,031.00				427,031.00	423,973.56	3,057.44	0.00	99%
General Expenses		39,150.00				39,150.00	23,957.27	15,192.73	0.00	61%
Encumbrance	27,841.08	0.00				27,841.08	15,933.76	11,907.32	0.00	57%
ADVISORY COMMITTEE-131										
General Expenses		345.00				345.00	169.00		176.00	49%
RESERVE FUND-133										
Transfers		100,000.00		(99,967.00)		33.00	0.00		33.00	--
DIRECTOR OF FINANCE-135										
Personal Services		99,396.00				99,396.00	99,396.00		0.00	100%
General Expenses		31,850.00	15,000.00			46,850.00	31,352.73	15,174.95	0.00	67%
Capital Plan - 11/06 STM (Equipment)	4,457.92	0.00				4,457.92	4,425.69	0.00	32.23	99%
Encumbrances	25.00	0.00				25.00	25.00		0.00	100%
ASSESSORS-141										
Elected Officials		3,700.00				3,700.00	3,699.96		0.04	100%
Personal Services		67,975.00				67,975.00	67,915.24		59.76	100%
General Expenses		35,355.00				35,355.00	31,283.78	1,800.00	2,271.22	88%
Revaluation 12/05 STM	10,573.91					10,573.91	7,420.00	3,153.91	0.00	70%
Encumbrances	5,456.48	0.00				5,456.48	5,456.48		0.00	100%
TREASURER/COLLECTOR-145										
Personal Services		64,605.00				64,605.00	64,604.25		0.75	100%
General Expenses		40,985.00				40,985.00	40,427.61		557.39	99%
LEGAL-151										
General Expenses		150,000.00	75,060.00	23,460.00		248,460.00	248,459.33		0.67	100%

	PRIOR YEAR CARRY FWD	ATM APPROPRIATION	STM TRANSFER	RESERVE FUND TRANSFERS	RECEIPTS	TOTAL AVAILABLE FUNDS	EXPENDED	ENCUMBERED	AVAILABLE	% EXP
TOWN CLERK-161										
Elected Official		62,689.00				62,689.00	62,689.00		0.00	100%
Personal Services		17,687.00				17,687.00	10,794.12		6,892.88	61%
General Expenses		10,010.00				10,010.00	9,780.47		229.53	98%
CONSERVATION COMMISSION-171										
General Expenses		31,910.00				31,910.00	31,423.81		486.19	98%
PLANNING BOARD-175										
General Expenses		15,050.00	10,000.00			25,050.00	19,177.09	5,857.51	15.40	77%
Encumbrance	3,459.18	0.00				3,459.18	3,459.18		0.00	100%
ZONING BOARD OF APPEALS-176										
General Expenses		2,560.00				2,560.00	633.96		1,926.04	25%
TOWN REPORTS-195										
General Expenses		15,000.00				15,000.00	14,906.29		93.71	99%
PARKING CLERK-197										
General Expenses		1,200.00				1,200.00	1,024.82		175.18	85%
UNCLASSIFIED-199										
Audit of Accounts		12,000.00				12,000.00	12,000.00		0.00	100%
Water Purchase		30,000.00		21,423.00		51,423.00	29,022.77		22,400.23	56%
South Shore Coalition		4,000.00				4,000.00	4,000.00		0.00	100%
TOTAL GENERAL GOVERNMENT	135,572.94	1,457,621.00	150,000.00	(55,084.00)	0.00	1,688,109.94	1,558,410.66	91,996.86	37,702.42	33.07
POLICE DEPARTMENT-210										
Personal Services		1,724,267.00	80,000.00			1,804,267.00	1,797,487.63		6,779.37	100%
General Expenses		108,950.00		11,245.00		120,195.00	120,188.84		6.16	100%
Encumbrances	2,208.23	0.00				2,208.23	1,632.57		575.66	74%
Capital Plan - 11/06 STM (Terminals)	2,793.36	0.00				2,793.36	2,793.36		0.00	100%
FIRE DEPARTMENT-220										
Personal Services		1,668,279.00				1,668,279.00	1,636,049.95	24,550.29	32,229.05	98%
General Expenses		193,095.00				193,095.00	161,896.45		6,648.26	84%
Hydrant Services		17,120.00				17,120.00	14,328.67		2,791.33	84%
Hepatitis Vaccine	1,742.50	0.00				1,742.50	0.00	1,742.50	0.00	0%
Station Generator 3/94 ATM	859.01	0.00				859.01	0.00	859.01	0.00	0%
Engine Two Repairs 10/96 STM	343.71	0.00				343.71	0.00	343.71	0.00	0%
Encumbrances	14,000.00	0.00				14,000.00	12,522.71	1,477.29	0.00	89%
Encumbrances - Hydrants	4,439.00	0.00				4,439.00	2,689.00		1,750.00	61%
Encumbrances - Call Payroll	10,000.00	0.00				10,000.00	10,000.00		0.00	100%
Encumbrances - Training	29,525.57	0.00				29,525.57	5,095.44	24,430.13	0.00	17%
BUILDING INSPECTOR-241										
Personal Services		72,778.00				72,778.00	72,058.25	500.00	219.75	99%
General Expenses		5,250.00				5,250.00	5,250.00		0.00	100%
Encumbrances	100.00	0.00				100.00	0.00		100.00	0%

	PRIOR YEAR CARRY FWD	ATM APPROP- RIATION	STM TRANSFER	RESERVE FUND/ TRANSFERS	RECEIPTS	TOTAL AVAILABLE FUNDS	EXPENDED	ENCUMBERED	AVAILABLE	% EXP
PLUMBING & GAS INSPECTOR-242										
General Expenses		10,000.00				10,000.00	9,460.00		540.00	95%
Encumbrances	1,660.00	0.00				1,660.00	1,660.00		0.00	100%
WEIGHTS & MEASURES-244										
Personal Services		2,678.00				2,678.00	2,599.92	78.00	0.08	97%
WIRE DEPARTMENT-245										
General Expenses		17,950.00				17,950.00	17,911.88		38.12	100%
CIVIL DEFENSE-291										
Payroll & Expenses		7,850.00				7,850.00	7,850.00		0.00	100%
Equipment 12/05 STM	28,995.26	0.00				28,995.26	1,112.00	27,883.26	0.00	4%
HARBORMASTER-395										
Personal Services		64,435.00				64,435.00	63,935.00		500.00	99%
General Expenses		9,400.00				9,400.00	9,400.00		0.00	100%
Capital Plan - 11/06 STM (Boat)	1,590.07	0.00				1,590.07	987.04	603.03	0.00	62%
Capital Plan - 11/06 STM (Docks)	10,000.00	0.00				10,000.00	0.00	10,000.00	0.00	0%
Capital Plan - 11/06 STM (Shack)	10,000.00	0.00				10,000.00	0.00	10,000.00	0.00	0%
SHELLFISH CONSTABLE-296										
Personal Services		500.00				500.00	500.00		0.00	100%
TOTAL PUBLIC SAFETY	118,256.71	3,902,552.00	80,000.00	11,245.00	0.00	4,112,053.71	3,957,408.71	102,467.22	52,177.78	96%
SCHOOL DEPARTMENT-300										
Salaries & Expenses		13,686,400.00				13,686,400.00	13,631,478.23	48,137.35	6,784.42	100%
Encumbrances	103,049.09	0.00				103,049.09	101,081.00	0.00	1,968.09	98%
SCHOOLS-REGIONAL										
South Shore VoTech		115,000.00	29,752.00			144,752.00	144,752.00		0.00	100%
TOTAL OTHER SCHOOLS	103,049.09	13,801,400.00	29,752.00	0.00	0.00	13,934,201.09	13,877,311.23	48,137.35	8,752.51	100%
PUBLIC WORKS-422										
Personal Services		736,299.00		8,814.00		745,113.00	745,112.88		0.12	100%
General Expenses		619,510.00				619,510.00	580,918.79	22,399.92	16,191.29	94%
Cemetery Lot Repurchase 03/08 ATM		0.00	11,000.00			11,000.00	0.00	11,000.00	0.00	0%
Landfill Monitoring 03/07 ATM	44,788.70	0.00				44,788.70	16,840.00	27,948.70	0.00	38%
Dump Truck 03/07 ATM	66,000.00	0.00				66,000.00	64,207.10	1,792.90	0.00	97%
RTF Scale 03/07 ATM	30,000.00	0.00				30,000.00	0.00	30,000.00	0.00	0%
Beechwood Cemetery 10/94 STM	1,977.45	0.00				1,977.45	0.00	1,977.45	0.00	0%
Private Ways 10/98 STM	4,558.35	0.00				4,558.35	4,092.45	465.90	0.00	99%
Encumbrances	10,768.27	0.00				10,768.27	1,476.45	9,291.82	0.00	14%

	PRIOR YEAR CARRY FWD	ATM APPROP-RIATION	STM TRANSFER	RESERVE FUND/ TRANSFERS	RECEIPTS	TOTAL AVAILABLE FUNDS	EXPENDED	ENCUMBERED	AVAILABLE	% EXP
SNOW REMOVAL-423										
General Expenses		76,000.00		74,862.00		150,862.00	150,861.11		0.89	100%
STREET LIGHTING-424										
General Expenses		62,000.00		7,801.00		69,801.00	69,800.95		0.05	100%
MAINTENANCE DIVISION-426										
Personal Services		235,896.00	10,000.00			245,896.00	245,896.00		0.00	100%
General Expenses		386,000.00				386,000.00	324,414.59	61,500.11	385.30	84%
High School Windows 03/07 ATM	54,000.00	0.00	(40,000.00)			14,000.00	14,000.00		0.00	100%
High School Track 03/07 ATM	5,000.00	0.00				5,000.00	5,000.00		0.00	100%
Capital Plan - 11/06 STM (Police Roof)	5,011.00	0.00				5,011.00	5,011.00		0.00	100%
Encumbrances	20,000.00	0.00				20,000.00	20,000.00		0.00	100%
TOTAL PUBLIC WORKS	242,103.77	2,115,705.00	(19,000.00)	91,477.00	0.00	2,430,285.77	2,247,331.32	166,376.80	16,577.65	12.16
BOARD OF HEALTH-510										
Personal Services		126,785.00				126,785.00	125,394.62		1,390.38	99%
General Expenses		8,350.00				8,350.00	8,350.00		0.00	100%
TOTAL PUBLIC HEALTH	0.00	135,135.00	0.00	0.00	0.00	135,135.00	133,744.62	0.00	1,390.38	99%
COUNCIL ON AGING-541										
Personal Services		154,578.00				154,578.00	149,334.92		5,243.08	97%
General Expenses		39,400.00				39,400.00	33,552.52		5,847.48	85%
Capital Outlay (Vans) 12/04 STM	1,673.72	0.00				1,673.72	0.00	1,673.72	0.00	0%
VETERANS' SERVICES-543										
Personal Services		1,600.00				1,600.00	1,466.63		133.37	92%
General Expenses		100.00				100.00	0.00		100.00	0%
Encumbrance	266.66	0.00				266.66	266.66		0.00	100%
Veterans' Photographs 11/95 STM	544.83	0.00				544.83	0.00	544.83	0.00	0%
TOTAL HUMAN SERVICES	2,485.21	195,678.00	0.00	0.00	0.00	198,163.21	184,620.73	2,218.55	11,323.93	93%
LIBRARY-610										
Personal Services		377,199.00				377,199.00	377,178.93		20.07	100%
General Expenses		108,118.00				108,118.00	108,118.00		0.00	100%
Capital Plan - 11/06 STM (Roof)	3,500.00	0.00				3,500.00	0.00	3,500.00	0.00	0%
RECREATION COMMISSION-630										
Personal Services		127,601.00		7,126.00		134,727.00	134,726.01		0.99	100%
General Expenses		6,680.00				6,680.00	6,680.00		0.00	100%
COMMON HISTORICAL COMM.-691										
General Expenses		100.00				100.00	0.00		100.00	0%
HISTORICAL PRESERVATION-691										
Personal Services		800.00				800.00	800.00		0.00	100%
General Expenses		100.00				100.00	93.43		6.57	93%

GENERAL FUND
APPROPRIATION EXPENDITURE LEDGER
FISCAL YEAR 2008

	PRIOR YEAR CARRY FWD	ATM APPROP-RIATION	STM TRANSFER	RESERVE FUND/ TRANSFERS	RECEIPTS	TOTAL AVAILABLE FUNDS	EXPENDED	ENCUMBERED	AVAILABLE	% EXP
CELEBRATIONS-692										
General Expenses		5,000.00				5,000.00	5,000.00		0.00	100%
TOTAL CULTURE & RECREATION	3,500.00	625,598.00	0.00	7,136.00	0.00	636,234.00	632,596.37	3,500.00	127.63	6.93
DEBT SERVICE-PRINCIPAL-710										
General Expenses		1,327,727.00				1,327,727.00	1,242,592.66		85,134.34	94%
DEBT SERVICE-INTEREST-720										
General Expenses		425,844.00				425,844.00	374,348.75		51,495.25	88%
DEBT SERVICE-EX. PRINCIPAL-750										
General Expenses		1,871,830.00				1,871,830.00	1,871,830.00		0.00	100%
DEBT SERVICE-EX. INTEREST-760										
General Expenses		1,171,128.00				1,171,128.00	1,088,539.14	81,076.42	1,512.44	93%
Encumbrances	82,671.78	0.00				82,671.78	82,671.78		0.00	100%
TOTAL DEBT SERVICE	82,671.78	4,796,529.00	0.00	0.00	0.00	4,879,200.78	4,659,982.33	81,076.42	138,142.03	96%
PENSIONS-911										
Norfolk County System		1,126,111.00				1,126,111.00	1,126,111.00		0.00	100%
WORKERS COMPENSATION-912										
General Expenses		92,000.00				92,000.00	86,754.19		5,245.81	94%
UNEMPLOYMENT-913										
General Expenses		20,000.00		16,740.00		36,740.00	36,739.89		0.11	100%
INSURANCE-EMPLOYEE HEALTH-914										
General Expenses		2,500,000.00	(100,000.00)	(85,753.00)		2,314,247.00	2,313,400.23		846.77	100%
INSURANCE-EMPLOYEE LIFE-915										
General Expenses		11,000.00				11,000.00	7,243.72		3,756.28	66%
MEDICARE-916										
General Expenses		206,000.00		14,249.00		220,249.00	220,248.44		0.56	100%
INSURANCE-PROP & LIABILITY-945										
General Expense		236,200.00				236,200.00	235,159.87	1,040.13	0.00	100%
Encumbrances	2,000.00	0.00				2,000.00	2,000.00		0.00	100%
TOTAL BENEFITS & INSURANCE	2,000.00	4,191,311.00	(100,000.00)	(54,764.00)	0.00	4,038,547.00	4,027,657.34	1,040.13	9,849.53	100%
General Fund Town Totals	689,639.50	31,221,529.00	140,752.00	0.00	0.00	32,051,920.50	31,279,063.31	496,813.33	276,043.86	98%

STATE AND COUNTY ASSESSMENTS
BUDGET VS. ACTUAL
FISCAL YEAR 2008

ASSESSMENT	ESTIMATED CHARGES	ACTUAL CHARGES
County Tax	94,621	94,621
Retired Teachers Health Insurance	730,256	730,256
Mosquito Control Project	29,857	29,831
Air Pollution Control	3,171	3,171
Metro Area Planning Council	2,091	2,091
Registry Non Renewals	3,680	5,400
Mass Bay Transit Authority	145,404	145,404
Special Education	0	
Charter Schools	79,954	68,682
Totals	$1,089,034	$1,079,456

ENTERPRISE FUNDS
STATEMENT OF REVENUE, EXPENDITURES AND CHANGES IN FUND BALANCE
FISCAL YEAR 2008

	Central Sewer	Straits Sewer	Water	Totals
User Charges	714,901	288,191	2,743,222	3,746,314
User Charges-Hingham			322,119	322,119
Connection Fees	108,743		8,520	117,263
Fees & Services	0		33,609	33,609
Penalties & Interest	543	1,861	33,571	35,975
State Aid	17,669			17,669
Total Revenue	841,856	290,052	3,141,041	4,272,949
General Expenses	737,495	153,003	1,093,073	1,983,571
Encumbrances	0	0	18,929	18,929
Depreciation Expense	0	71,364	0	71,364
Debt Service	56,474	0	1,911,676	1,968,150
Indirect Costs	22,536	20,688	33,290	76,514
Total Expenditures	816,505	245,055	3,056,968	4,118,528
Excess of Revenue Over Expenditures	25,351	44,997	84,073	154,421
Retained Earnings July 1, 2007	34,799	65,426	81,420	181,645
Retained Earnings June 30, 2008	60,150	110,423	165,493	336,066

COMMUNITY PRESERVATION FUND
STATEMENT OF REVENUES, EXPENDITURES AND CHANGES IN FUND BALANCE

Revenue:*

Surcharge Revenue 2008	325,734	
Surcharge Revenue 2007	2,793	
Surcharge Revenue 2006	226	
Penalties & Interest	747	
Investment Income	17,292	
State Distribution	317,103	

Total Revenue		663,895
Expenditures	1,063,281	
Encumbrances - Prior Year	(704,175)	
Encumbrances	371,075	

Total Expenditures & Encumbrances		(730,181)

Excess of Revenue Over Expenditures		(66,286)
Undesignated Fund Balance July 1, 2007		134,181
Less: Prior Year Accrual		0
Undesignated Fund Balance June 30, 2008		67,895
		================

*Cash Basis

150

Project	Amount of Issue	Date of Issue	Term	Interest Rate	07/01/07 Outstanding Balance	Principal Additions	Principal Payment	State Assistance	Principal Paydowns	06/30/08 Outstanding Balance	FY08 Interest Payment
x Levy Obligations Issued -											
agerty Property (Refi)	495,911	10/01/04	7 yrs.	2.00-3.25	163,785		30,521			133,264	4,3
hletic Fields Supplement (Refi)	34,453	10/01/04	6 yrs.	2.00-3.00	26,674		7,120			19,554	6
hletic Fields (Refi)	232,367	10/01/04	5 yrs.	2.00-2.87	170,064		58,007			112,057	3,8
blic Works Garage (Refi)		10/01/04	7 yrs.	2.00-3.25	284,479		49,352			235,127	7,6
wer I & I (Refi)	26,145	10/01/04	12 yrs.	2.00-3.60	25,408		3,961			21,447	7
ndfill Capping (Refi)	700,531	10/01/04	12 yrs.	2.00-3.60	681,455		78,792			602,663	20,6
ew Elementary School	10,140,000	10/15/98	19 yrs.	3.90-5.75	7,055,000	2,776,000	495,000	3,974,952	2,585,048	2,776,000	309,9
blic Works Garage Water Main	60,000	10/15/98	10 yrs.	3.90-5.75	12,000	14,700	6,000		6,000	14,700	1,0
blic Works Garage Supplement	230,000	10/15/98	18 yrs.	3.90-5.75	124,000	115,100	13,000		111,000	115,100	5,3
arbor Dredging	75,000	10/15/98	12 yrs.	3.90-5.75	24,000	18,700	6,000		18,000	18,700	9
chool Technology	100,000	10/15/98	9 yrs.	3.90-5.75	10,000		10,000			0	3
wer I & I MWPAT 96-37	188,649	10/06/99	20 yrs.		132,117		6,599	2,208		123,310	1,7
ew Elementary School Completion 2	244,500	12/01/99	15 yrs.	3.75-5.25	120,000		15,000			105,000	5,5
ood Control	260,000	12/01/99	15 yrs.	3.75-5.25	120,000		15,000			105,000	5,5
arbor Moorings	90,000	12/01/99	9 yrs.	3.75-5.25	20,000		10,000			10,000	7
e Trucks	360,000	12/01/00	8 yrs.	4.30-6.00	90,000		45,000			45,000	2,9
arbor Improvements	109,500	12/01/00	9 yrs.	4.30-6.00	30,000		10,000			20,000	1,1
wer I & I	80,000	01/15/02	15 yrs.	2.25-4.60	30,000		10,000			20,000	1,0
agerty Property	255,000	01/15/02	10 yrs.	2.25-4.10	105,000		25,000			80,000	3,7
emetery Construction	750,000	01/15/02	9 yrs.	2.25-4.10	300,000		75,000			225,000	10,5
chool Planning	156,000	06/15/04	20 yrs.	3.00-5.00	125,000		10,000			115,000	5,42
chool Construction	16,720,000	06/15/04	20 yrs.	3.00-5.00	15,050,000		890,000			14,160,000	679,41
tle League Fields	184,600	06/15/04	13 yrs.	3.00-5.00	135,000		15,000			120,000	5,5
partmental Equipment	793,000	06/15/04	10 yrs.	3.00-4.00	470,000		105,000			365,000	18,2
rary	650,000	06/15/04	17 yrs.	3.00-5.00	570,000		40,000			530,000	20,93
lice & Fire Station	950,000	06/15/04	14 yrs.	3.00-5.00	790,000		80,000			710,000	27,52
ntral Sewer Plant	98,288	06/14/04	20 yrs.	3.00-5.00	80,000		5,000			75,000	3,58
mmond Ave Drainage	190,000	06/15/04	3 yrs.	3.00-3.50	180,000		10,000			170,000	7,04
wtonville	54,000	08/11/05	19 yrs.	3.50-4.75	50,000		4,000			46,000	1,92
mes Brook Flooding	96,400	08/11/05	19 yrs.	3.50-4.75	90,000		5,000			85,000	3,52
wtonville Drainage	100,000	08/11/05	18 yrs.	3.50-4.75	90,000		10,000			80,000	3,42
rary Roof	25,000	08/11/05	4 yrs.	3.50-4.75	15,000		5,000			10,000	46
partmental Equipment	373,000	08/11/05		3.50-4.75	255,000		110,000			145,000	7,68
le Harbor Engineering	100,000	08/11/05	3 yrs	3.50-4.75	65,000		35,000			30,000	1,88
g Street Land	400,000	08/11/05	17 yrs.	3.50-4.75	375,000		25,000			350,000	14,5
st Corner Culvert	25,000	08/11/05	3 yrs.	3.50-4.75	15,000		10,000			5,000	4
TOTALS - TAX LEVY FUNDED					27,878,982	2,924,500	2,328,352	3,977,160	2,720,048	21,777,922	1,190,14

DEBT STATEMENT
FISCAL YEAR 2008

Project	Amount of Issue	Date of Issue	Term	Interest Rate	07/01/07 Outstanding Balance	Principal Additions	Principal Payment	State Assistance	Principal Paydowns	06/30/08 Outstanding Balance	FY08 Interest Payment
apter 90 (SAN)					618,993	2,237,986	2,756,979			100,000	29,806
bor Seawall (SAN)					466,750	71,007	537,757			0	
ED (SAN)					310,000	670,000	930,000			50,000	
allite Sewer Plant Study	Sewer				100,000	100,000	100,000			100,000	4,482
e Harbor Sewer	Sewer				300,000	300,000	300,000			300,000	8,975
e Harbor Sewer - SRF	Sewer				0	3,396,243				3,396,243	
p Run & Rust Way	Sewer				100,000	100,000	100,000			100,000	4,488
ver I & I	Sewer				40,000	200,000	40,000			200,000	
k Property	General				300,000	184,310	300,000			184,310	6,386
es Lane Easement	General				64,200	57,000	64,200			57,000	1,367
bor Seawall	General				600,000	600,010	600,000			600,010	5,336
chwood Sidewalk	General				10,000	100,000	10,000			100,000	
nage	General				100,000	100,000	100,000			100,000	
nage - SRF	General				0	65,993				65,993	
er System	Water				4,000,000	3,910,000	4,000,000			3,910,000	129,411
er System	Water				2,000,000	1,915,000	2,000,000			1,915,000	74,170
er System	Water				7,700,000	7,700,000	7,700,000			7,700,000	237,659
er System	Water				0	2,515,000	0			2,515,000	-
er System	Water				0	1,000,000	0			1,000,000	-
er System - SRF	Water				0	4,146,125	0			4,146,125	-
TOTALS - TEMPORARY NOTES					16,709,943	29,368,674	19,538,936	0	0	26,539,681	502,089

ect	Auth. Date	Auth. Amount									
"A Wetlands	11/05/01	1,200,000									
"A Wells	11/05/01	250,000									
er System Improvements	11/05/01	23,752									
er System Improvements	03/30/02	28,248									
er Planning	03/30/02	81,000									
atscape	11/18/02	800,000									
k Property	11/17/03	4,500,000									
er System Improvements	03/27/04	21,682,190									
es Lane Easement	03/27/04	64,200									
wall Repairs	12/06/04	600,000									
er System Improvements	12/06/04	2,000,000									
Harbor Sewer	04/02/05	12,000,000									
er System Improvements	04/02/05	4,000,000									
o Run Sewer	04/02/05	1,200,000									
er Planning	04/02/05	100,000									
chwood Street Sidewalk	12/05/05	100,000									
er I & I	11/13/06	1,000,000									
Harbor Sewer	03/31/07	2,000,000									
nage	03/31/07	1,000,000									
Authorized & Unissued		$52,629,390									

OUNTS AUTHORIZED AND UNISSUED

		Balance July 1	Donations & Receipts	Withdrawals	Investment Income	Transfers	Due From/ (To)	Balance June 30
PARKS AND PLAYGROUNDS								
Billings Park Fund	001	2,126.91			(184.98)			1,941.93
Billings Common Fund	002	1,874.95			(163.10)			1,711.85
H.W. Wadleigh Park Fund	003	9,947.89			(865.32)			9,082.57
Wheelwright Park Fund	004	17,249.05			(1,500.40)			15,748.65
Edith M. Bates Fund	005	12,099.64			(1,052.48)			11,047.16
CEMETERIES								
Perpetual Care-Woodside Cemetery	006	208,082.12	2,652 00	13,396.66	(17,099.51)		500.00	180,737.95
Perpetual Care-Woodside Cemetery	006	52,503.59			(6,928.48)			45,575.11
Perpetual Care-Beechwood Cemetery	007	17,430.93	4,000.00		(2,060.66)			19,370.27
Beechwood Cemetery Association	008	6,836.51			(594.70)			6,241.81
Estate of Harry E. Wilbur (Woodside)	009	11,721.31			(1,019.56)			10,701.75
C. L. Bell Memorial Fund (Greengate)	010	51,663.08			(4,493.84)			47,169.24
Isadora B Newey Fund	011	41,468.08			(3,607.06)			37,861.02
Cedar Street Cemetery	012	5,432.75			(472.54)			4,960.21
SCHOOLS								
Ripley Fund	020	9,490.09			(825.48)			8,664.61
James W. Nichols Scholarship Fund	022	3,766.54		150.00	(311.09)			3,305.45
Major William Arthur Scholarship Fund	024	9,671.06		300.00	(823.67)			8,547.39
Alice and Walter Shuebruk Scholarship Fun	023	148,911.45		3,500.00	(12,593.08)			132,818.37
William Ripley Jr., Athletic Fund	025	23,721.37			(2,063.40)			21,657.97
John F. Creamer Scholarship Fund	027	1,713.54			(149.04)			1,564.50
Margaret M Hardy Scholarship Fund	021	293,302.40		14,000.00	(24,267.54)			255,034.86
Helen & Malcolm Stevens Scholarship Fund	026	225,622.04	1,000.00	5,000.00	(19,469.57)			202,152.47
Noel Ripley Scholarship	042	67,322.89	100.00	250.00	(5,760.85)			61,412.04
Langham Scholarship	029	15,852.05	1,000.00	850.00	(1,438.17)			14,563.88
Staunton Scholarship	041	1,696.39			(147.54)			1,548.85
CHS Alumni Scholarship	045	3,659.87		3,729.72	69.85		3,729.72	3,729.72
Gritzan Scholarship	060	21,300.60	575.00	2,000.00	(1,814.32)			18,061.28
Class of 1958 Scholarship	045	0.00	4,950.00	850.00	15.09			4,115.09
VOLUNTARY CHECKOFF FUNDS								
Scholarship Fund	102	3,337.91			(290.33)		5.02	3,052.60
Education Fund	104	4,679.87	718.89		(504.91)		65.00	4,958.85
Senior Fund	106	397.74	780.09		(140.78)		210.00	1,247.05
OTHER								
Stabilization Fund	031	44,322.74			699.15			45,021.89
Stabilization Fund	031	518,468.82			27,462.74			545,931.56
Stabilization Fund-Sewer	031	505,974.86		17,500 00	26,892.93			515,367.79
Stabilization Fund-OPEB	035		100,000 00		817.74			100,817.74
Conservation Fund	030	39,596.18			624.60		(40,000 00)	220.78
Beechwood Improvement Association	032	11,717.42		625.00	209.14			11,301.56
Beechwood Ball Park Fund	040	24,915.08		25,417.25	502.17			0.00
Pension Reserve Fund	038	442,483.74		80,000.00	20,755.43		(60,000.00)	323,239.17
Pension Reserve Fund	038	114,266.08			1,802.51			116,068.59
Town Pump Maintenance	033	2,421.58			38.19			2,459.77
Reed Corner Trust Fund	034	168.73			2.67			171.40
Cultural Council Fund	043	5,135.83		3,475 00	216.13		975.00	2,851.96
Captains' Walk Fund	044	9,744.16			153.74			9,897.90
Hagerty Trust	046	932.80			14.73		(947 53)	0.00
Elder Affairs Trust Rockland	850	-8,874.18			0.00	8,874.18		0.00
Elder Affairs Trust Hingham	850	33,896.22			1,214.09	(8,874.18)		26,236.13
Elder Affairs Trust Pilgrim South Shore	036	0.00	5,000 00		1.75			5,001.75
PAUL PRATT MEMORIAL LIBRARY								
Alliance Bernstein Global Real Estate	037	0.00	50,000.00		(5,460.19)			44,539.81
Dodge & Cox International Fund	037	39,248.07			(5,165.44)	4,035 00		38,117.63
T. Rowe Price Emerging Markets Fund	037	23,585.74			1,020.45			24,606.19
T Rowe Price New Era Fund	037	26,383.12			8,566.35			34,949.47
Loomis Sayles Global Bond Fund	037	0.00			412.66	5,000 00		5,412.66
Vanguard Money Market Fund	037	934.87		115 00	152.01			971.88
Vanguard International Growth Fund	037	25,869.29			(1,915.83)			23,953.46
Vanguard Star Fund	037	419,567.83	34,363 00		(28,740.21)		(46,997 35)	378,193.27
Vanguard Star Fund (Building Fund)	037	169,319.83			(7,839.41)			161,480.42
Vanguard Wellesley Fund	037	431,195.83		125,000.00	(3,784.39)	(9,000 00)		293,411.44
TRUST FUND TOTALS		$4,154,157.26	$205,138 98	$296,158 63	($71,903.75)	$35 00	($142,460 14)	$3,848,808 72

154

SCHEDULE OF RESERVE FUND TRANSFERS
FISCAL YEAR 2008

Appropriation	07/01/07	Annual Town Meeting	100,000
Police	06/30/08	Vehicle Maintenance	(3,055)
DPW	06/30/08	Snow & Ice	(74,862)
Street Lights	06/30/08	Electricity	(7,801)
Medicare Tax	06/30/08	Assessment	(14,249)
		Total Transfers	(99,967)
		Surplus - (To Free Cash)	$33

	Beginning Balance	Receipts	Expenses	Ending Balance
	-1,355	317,212	314,510	1,347
	64,067	131,173	126,973	68,267
	11,385	0	1,200	10,185
	2,232			2,232
	4,657	40,366	40,630	4,393
	95,630	152,510	162,651	85,489
	3,764	16,475	17,940	2,298
	110,058	77,909	5,838	182,129
	20,324	162,493	157,459	25,358
	122,635	203,417	194,814	131,238
	39,838	104,323	125,395	18,766
	6,159	26,389	21,777	10,771
	2,868	9,150	8,648	3,370
	1,922			1,922
	13,111	17,219	13,434	16,895
	2,460	3,529	2,803	3,186
rant	415	15,293	17,973	-2,265
	424	470	894	0
	6,332	285,433	291,765	0
	1,125		1,125	0
	314	9,719	10,033	0
	7,026	4,812	11,060	778
	0	904	904	0
	0	20,094	19,521	573
	1,181	288,080	286,635	2,626
	1,393	3,245	4,632	6
	310,121	354,970	310,734	354,356
	0	7,373	7,373	0
	0	2,108	890	1,218
	93,376		6,339	87,037
	0	56,788	56,788	0
	$921,462	$2,311,454	$2,220,740	$1,012,176

STATEMENT OF REVENUES, EXPENDITURES AND CHANGES IN FUND BALANCE
TOWN SPECIAL REVENUE

	Beginning Balance	Receipts	Expenses	Transfers	Ending Balance
Revolving Funds -					
Lighthouse Keepers Gift Fund	738	510			1,248
Adopt a Street Gift Fund	0	500	142		358
Beechwood Ball Park Fund	0	70,004	61,225		8,779
Cat Dam Gift Fund	0	25,138	25,138		0
Mary Babaian Fund	4,690				4,690
Selectmen Gifts	2,294	6,059	5,521		2,833
Drug & Alcohol Gift Fund	4,121				4,121
Little Harbor Insurance	0	8,565	8,565		0
Selectmen Insurance	1,781	2,251	4,032		0
Linden Drive Gift Fund	242				242
Waterways Fund	38,128	8,828		-11,645	35,310
Sale of Cemetery Lots Fund	0	40,000		-40,000	0
Bond Premiums	49,965	59,949	100,251		9,663
Conservation Deposits	18,533	41,346	37,823		22,056
Conservation Bonds	23,000				23,000
Wetlands Fund	12,260	11,890	0	-10,000	14,150
Planning Deposits	53,513	53,765	55,153		52,125
Zoning Board Deposits	3,639				3,639
Police Insurance	7,790		8,987		-1,197
Police Gift Fund	525				525
Police Bicycle Gift Fund	288				288
Fire Gift Fund	2,061				2,061
Fire Defibrillator Gift Fund	7,138	2,112	3,070		6,180
Harbor Insurance Fund	232	-232			0
Harbor Gift Fund	3,000		3,000		0
DPW Insurance Fund	3,500	3,943	7,443		0
DPW Gift Fund	1,130				1,130
Health Gift Fund	6,014	1,599	3,833		3,781
Health Deposits	0	1,590	1,590		0
Elder Affairs MAP Gifts	962				962
Elder Affairs Gifts	12,460	15,074	9,307		18,226
Elder Affairs Outreach Gifts	2,456		276		2,180
Elder Affairs Coblentz Gifts	2,587		1,221		1,366
Disabilities Fine Fund	6,820	1,000	3,664		4,156
Library Gift Fund	16,071	5,838	4,384		17,525
Library Trust Income Fund	-22,187	55,209	23,461		9,561
Library Music Circus Gift Fund	10,000	10,000			20,000
Recreation Revolving	66,839	31,310	28,791		69,357
Captains Walk Fund	1,680	495	581		1,594
Historical Book Fund	23,141	1,192			24,333
Revolving Totals	$365,411	$457,935	$397,457	-$61,645	$364,244

STATEMENT OF REVENUES, EXPENDITURES AND CHANGES IN FUND BALANCE
TOWN SPECIAL REVENUE

	Beginning Balance	Receipts	Expenses	Transfers	Ending Balance
Grants -					
Downtown Master Plan Grant	0	25,000	25,000		0
Non Point Pollution Grant	13,850		12,835		1,016
TOD Grant	0	116,320	116,320		0
Downtown Parking Lot Grant	0	110,000	1,220		108,780
BMP Grant	0	15,963	15,963		0
Polling Hours Grant	2,241	608			2,849
Planning Grants	4,349				4,349
Child Passenger Safety Grant	-707	707			0
Law Enforcement Fund	29,065		3,108		25,957
Vest Program Grant	5,601	2,355			7,956
Community Policing Grant	9,989	11,299	13,496		7,793
Police Block Grant	36				36
Police Equipment Grant	3,000				3,000
Police Traffic Safety Grant	663	-207			456
Police SETB Grant	5,000				5,000
Fire Safety Grant	1,318				1,318
Fire Ambulance Grant	2,000				2,000
Fire Equipment Grant	6,050		1,798		4,252
Fire SAFE Grant	6,933	7,513	281		14,165
Fire Equipment Grant	3				3
Fire Emergency Prepare Grant	146				146
Harbor Pumpout Grant	14,934	8,500	17,739		5,695
DPW Recycling Grant	4,848				4,848
Emergency Preparedness Grant	0	7,250	2,711		4,539
Medicare Reimbursements	24,288	15,160	6,198		33,250
Elder Affairs Caregiver Grant	66	2,252	1,616		702
Elder Affairs Formula Grant	0	9,171	9,171		0
Elder Affairs Outreach Grant	1,237		80		1,157
Elder Affairs Triad Grant	340				340
Library SEMLS Grant	7,505	8,282			15,788
Library State Aid Grant	296	10,666	4,964		5,999
Library Public Grant	2,111	699			2,810
Library on the Same Page Grant	0	7,500	6,788		712
Grant Totals	$145,163	$359,038	$239,286	$0	$264,914
Grand Totals	$510,574	$816,972	$636,743	-$61,645	$629,158

Last Name	First Name	Primary Department	Gross Pay
QUILL	MARY E	Board of Assessors	70,064
KRUPCZAK	DEBRA J.	Board of Assessors	49,112
WARNER	ELLEN	Board of Assessors	37,278
GRANVILLE	MARY E.	Board of Assessors	1,300
MILLER	ELSA J.	Board of Assessors	1,200
PATROLIA	MICHAEL C.	Board of Assessors	1,200
		Department Total	$160,154
TRADD	TARA	Board of Health	60,008
GOODWIN	MARY C.	Board of Health	32,085
GODZIK	JOSEPH R	Board of Health	24,039
FITZSIMMONS	JUDITH E.	Board of Health	14,222
CAHILL	CORINNE H.	Board of Health	399
		Department Total	$130,752
EGAN	ROBERT M.	Building/Land Use	80,379
PILCZAK	JOANN	Building/Land Use	47,563
HINDLEY	DIANE M.	Building/Land Use	19,602
NOONAN	NANCY ANN	Building/Land Use	42,834
		Department Total	$190,378
SESTITO	CARL A	Dept. of Public Works	76,350
SESTITO	ANTHONY C	Dept. of Public Works	75,093
LIVINGSTON	BOYD J	Dept. of Public Works	66,584
SWANSON	ANDREW W.	Dept. of Public Works	62,931
GUARENTE	CHARLES E.	Dept. of Public Works	57,126
EKBOM	LEO A.	Dept. of Public Works	55,865
BUTMAN	KENNETH BARR	Dept. of Public Works	55,236
THAYER JR	KENNETH E.	Dept. of Public Works	53,535
PIEPENBRINK	ROBERT	Dept. of Public Works	52,235
EDGETT	PHILIP L.	Dept. of Public Works	48,937
BAKER JR	GRANVILLE C	Dept. of Public Works	48,448
MARSH	HERBERT L	Dept. of Public Works	46,385
MURRAY	CHRISTOPHER	Dept. of Public Works	46,264
SNOW	MARY L.	Dept. of Public Works	39,641
BROWN	HERBERT L	Dept. of Public Works	7,686
LANZILLOTTI	AUSTEN K	Dept. of Public Works	6,515
MCCORMACK	ANDREW J	Dept. of Public Works	5,201
MACDONALD	FRANK A	Dept. of Public Works	385
ZYRKOWSKI	BRIAN	Dept. of Public Works	289
		Department Total	$804,705
ELWORTHY	LINDA A	Elder Affairs	63,073
BARRETT	CAROL A.	Elder Affairs	39,865
HORSEFIELD	MARTHA R	Elder Affairs	22,736
SALERNO	GERTRUDE	Elder Affairs	19,710
BUCKLEY	JOHN	Elder Affairs	18,349
		Department Total	$163,733
ADAMS	BRIAN	Facilities	73,211
KELLY	MARK H.	Facilities	65,527
LINCOLN	DEREK A.	Facilities	61,607
EMANUELLO	ANTHONY P.	Facilities	45,620
MACE	RICHARD	Facilities	10,328
RATTENBURY	HENRY A	Facilities	3,852
SULLIVAN	DANIEL	Facilities	3,404
		Department Total	$263,549
TRASK	MARK H.	Fire Department	112,837
BILODEAU	PAUL T.	Fire Department	110,722
SILVIA	ROBERT D.	Fire Department	103,105
MAHONEY JR.	FRANCIS X.	Fire Department	101,158
RUNEY	JAMES P.	Fire Department	100,657

Last Name	First Name	Primary Department	Gross Pay
CURLEY	JAMES F.	Fire Department	95,626
PROTULIS	ROBERT F.	Fire Department	95,458
HERNAN	JOHN M.	Fire Department	81,094
FORDE	ROBERT	Fire Department	79,643
DOCKRAY	JOHN J.	Fire Department	79,319
SMITH	DANIEL	Fire Department	79,211
MARTIN	ROBERT	Fire Department	78,745
HALL	JAMES	Fire Department	75,925
DURETTE	KEVIN J.	Fire Department	75,311
CUNNINGHAM	DANIEL	Fire Department	72,315
BELANGER	RANDY P.	Fire Department	69,738
WENZLOW	ERIC W.	Fire Department	69,541
HICKEY	JONATHAN M	Fire Department	65,507
MORRISON	LAURA CHRIS	Fire Department	61,109
FIORI	JAMES E.	Fire Department	59,701
ROSANO	RANDALL W	Fire Department	59,215
DONOVAN	KEVIN D	Fire Department	56,829
HALEY	JOHN W	Fire Department	55,958
NADEAU	ROBERT A	Fire Department	34,622
PERGOLA	JOSEPH M	Fire Department	15,989
MAYNARD	STEVEN L.	Fire Department	3,000
MCKAY	THOMAS	Fire Department	1,333
BROOKE	WILLIAM A.	Fire Department	333
MENDES	DANIEL I	Fire Department	262
NORLIN	ERIC M	Fire Department	245
DONOVAN	MARK A	Fire Department	159
HEALY	JAMES	Fire Department	96
		Department Total	$1,894,763
GIBBONS	LORREN S.	Harbormaster	50,490
MACDONALD	RYAN J	Harbormaster	8,333
O'MALLEY III	THOMAS J	Harbormaster	8,196
JOHNSON	ROBERT A.	Harbormaster	4,835
		Department Total	$71,854
RAFFERTY	JACQUELINE S	Library	71,141
MOODY	SHARON	Library	55,293
COUGHLIN	MARY E.	Library	47,207
WALSH	GAYLE	Library	44,648
GAILUNAS	PAUL J.	Library	42,845
DWYER	JANET	Library	34,395
NORTON	KRISTIN	Library	27,209
WALSH	LAURIE L.	Library	22,470
OHRENBERGER	MARJORIE	Library	22,289
LONDERGAN	MARY E.	Library	8,626
LENGYEL	BRIGID	Library	5,099
NELSON	BRONWYN	Library	3,872
ISIHARA	IKUKO	Library	3,268
LAAS	ALEXANDRA	Library	1,612
FEGREUS	ELIZABETH	Library	1,503
HILLMAN	KATHRYN M	Library	772
JENKS	KAREN A	Library	221
REEL	MICHAEL C	Library	208
BURGESS	MATTHEEW C	Library	117
KLEINZ	JACQUELINE M	Library	96
		Department Total	$392,891
COGILL	DAVID C.	Police Department	196,546
SMALL	JOHN H.	Police Department	150,533
HUSSEY	JAMES	Police Department	128,090
MCLEAN	JAMES P.	Police Department	126,783
TREANOR	JEFFREY	Police Department	125,080
QUIGLEY	WILLIAM P.	Police Department	114,544
CONTE	JOHN C.	Police Department	101,017
STEVERMAN	REGEN	Police Department	91,363
LENNON	GREGORY J.	Police Department	82,171

Last Name	First Name	Primary Department	Gross Pay
YANNIZZI	FRANCIS P.	Police Department	81,103
WILSON	PAUL M.	Police Department	80,456
HUNT	GARRET A.	Police Department	75,803
REARDON	PATRICK	Police Department	71,064
KENNEY	PATRICK	Police Department	70,711
MATOS	LISA M.	Police Department	63,437
TARANTINO	CHRISTY J.	Police Department	60,904
GRANT	CHRISTOPHER	Police Department	59,065
WIGMORE	THOMAS W.	Police Department	55,352
BAGLEY	EDWARD	Police Department	54,792
LOWERY	PATRICIA A.	Police Department	52,410
MCCARTHY	KELLI	Police Department	50,017
WILLIAMS	DANIEL	Police Department	49,180
DOUGLAS	PATRICIA A.	Police Department	48,799
DOYLE	JENIFER J.	Police Department	48,612
NOONAN	BRIAN W.	Police Department	40,029
FORD	ANDREW J.	Police Department	39,963
BROOKS	COREY	Police Department	32,798
PEEBLES	BRIAN M.	Police Department	27,860
BRIGHAM	PAUL B	Police Department	25,508
COSTA	LOUIS C.	Police Department	22,886
MALOUF	FREDERICK G	Police Department	21,550
AHLSTEDT	RICHARD	Police Department	20,536
SHEA	GREGORY M.	Police Department	19,149
SAUNDERS	SCOTT	Police Department	18,793
PETERS	SHELLEE L.	Police Department	18,489
CASAGRANDE	ROBERT C.	Police Department	18,113
MURPHY	PAUL W.	Police Department	17,283
LUCAS	MATTHEW J	Police Department	16,769
MCLAUGHLIN	JAMES	Police Department	16,602
MAHONEY	JON F.	Police Department	16,199
FARINA	COREY M.	Police Department	16,185
WHITTIER	WILLIAM F	Police Department	15,439
REARDON	TIMOTHY P	Police Department	15,376
CONNEELY	SEAN	Police Department	14,822
FIDROCKI	WILLIAM	Police Department	13,754
FICARRA	SCOTT	Police Department	13,733
GOYETTE	TIMOTHY J	Police Department	12,983
MCGEE	NANCY	Police Department	12,614
O'ROURKE	JOHN	Police Department	12,587
PERAINO	MICHAEL J.	Police Department	12,109
ACHILLE	ROBERT	Police Department	12,087
HARTNETT	GREGG T	Police Department	12,007
SWEENEY	ANDREW J	Police Department	11,623
FAHEY	SEAN M	Police Department	10,552
MCKENNA	RICHARD J.	Police Department	10,168
HANCOCK	EDWARD	Police Department	8,087
FALL	GREGORY	Police Department	7,804
NORRIS	JOHN	Police Department	7,297
CAVANAUGH	SEAN T.	Police Department	6,173
PIERCE	CHARLES J	Police Department	6,143
RICE	ROBERT	Police Department	5,918
MCADAMS	DARREN	Police Department	5,914
CADIGAN	THOMAS M.	Police Department	5,417
ADAMS	KATHLEEN M.	Police Department	5,391
SALITURI	JOEL E	Police Department	5,241
HENVEY	CAROL	Police Department	4,457
GILMARTIN	JAMES A.	Police Department	4,043
CHRISTIE	JAMES J	Police Department	3,661
FLANAGAN	JAMES P	Police Department	3,588
AIGUIER	BRIAN E.	Police Department	3,167
GREELEY	THOMAS P.	Police Department	3,091
TRACEY	PHILIP E.	Police Department	2,937
SHALNO	STEVEN	Police Department	2,826
STEVERMAN	ERIK O.	Police Department	2,667
SUTHERLAND	JAMES E.	Police Department	2,245
NOGUEIRA	FRANK	Police Department	2,212
HAMACKER	MARK	Police Department	2,163
RAPPOLD	ROBERT	Police Department	2,087

Last Name	First Name	Primary Department	Gross Pay
DUNN	DANIEL A	Police Department	1,794
LOWRANCE	RAWSON R.	Police Department	1,623
HARRISON	JEFF	Police Department	1,608
O'HARA	MICHAEL	Police Department	1,508
CANNY	DAVID	Police Department	1,439
SULLIVAN	ROBERT	Police Department	1,360
MCCRACKEN	JOSEPH H.	Police Department	1,261
BULMAN	JAMES	Police Department	1,244
BOWEN	JAMES	Police Department	1,168
CARTHAS JR	ARTHUR P	Police Department	1,113
BEST	MICHAEL A	Police Department	1,107
RICE	TAMI	Police Department	1,063
CHURCH	DANNY D	Police Department	1,008
OSHEA	AMANDA L.	Police Department	992
TALBOT	KEVIN	Police Department	832
FARRELL	THOMAS	Police Department	798
BAILEY	DOUGLAS	Police Department	731
CURRAN	JAMES P	Police Department	704
CORSON III	KENNETH R.	Police Department	687
MARCELLA	ANTHONY G	Police Department	687
GAETA SR	THOMAS P	Police Department	672
WYMAN	CHRISTOPHER	Police Department	504
COLETTI	DAVID F	Police Department	462
GUARENTE	DANIEL	Police Department	462
MCISAAC	JOHN F	Police Department	462
SWEETLAND	ROBERT T	Police Department	462
MCCUE	FRANIS X	Police Department	451
CONNOLLY	GERALD	Police Department	399
ALLISON	DONALD F	Police Department	368
ELMES	STEPHEN R	Police Department	368
SCHROUT	ERIC	Police Department	368
WALETKUS	ALAN	Police Department	368
SMITH	WILLIAM H	Police Department	359
SWEENEY	RONALD E.	Police Department	359
WYMAN JR	JOHN R	Police Department	359
MCINNIS	GERALD	Police Department	357
BUONAUGURIO	PATRICK	Police Department	336
GLENNON	SEAN M	Police Department	336
GREENWOOD	DONALD H	Police Department	336
KENNEDY	MARK P	Police Department	336
RAYNE	STEPHEN T	Police Department	336
RYAN	EDWARD T	Police Department	336
WOOD	KENNETH F	Police Department	336
BRENNAN	MICHAEL	Police Department	328
DURANT	KENNETH	Police Department	328
FELTRUP	MARK T	Police Department	328
COYLE	ALFRED	Police Department	168
MACDONALD	RICHARD	Police Department	168
O'REILLY	JOSEPH	Police Department	168
RYAN	JOHN	Police Department	168
BRENNAN	MARK F	Police Department	164
MURRAY	MICHAEL S	Police Department	164
WEEKS	DAVID	Police Department	151
		Department Total	$2,742,906
CARROLL	JAMES	Recreation	46,159
WORLEY	JOHN M.	Recreation	43,602
BARRA	MICHAEL J	Recreation	13,412
EQUI	MARTHA A.	Recreation	7,600
STEVENSON	JEREMIAH	Recreation	4,416
MCDONALD	LINDSEY L.	Recreation	3,666
BONNER	KIMBERLY	Recreation	3,282
CURTIN	MICHAEL E	Recreation	3,105
ST. PIERRE	PAUL	Recreation	2,660
CORCORAN	BLAIR	Recreation	2,369
MCDONALD	PAULINA A	Recreation	2,286
LOVALLO	ANDREW	Recreation	2,279
OCONNELL	MATT	Recreation	2,216

Last Name	First Name	Primary Department	Gross Pay
WISE	ELLEN	Recreation	2,193
BIAGINI	ANDREA L	Recreation	2,187
CONWAY	COLIN	Recreation	2,170
MCLELLAN	RYAN	Recreation	2,120
GALLAGHER	MOLLY K	Recreation	2,110
KRUPCZAK	JARED P	Recreation	1,541
BATES-MCARTHUR	REBECCA M.	Recreation	1,530
ANDERSON	GARY K	Recreation	1,470
SMITH	GORDON R	Recreation	1,361
LANDON	ELIZABETH	Recreation	1,314
LANDON	CHARLOTTE D	Recreation	1,310
HUNT	NATALIE T	Recreation	1,232
BONNER	KAREN C.	Recreation	1,218
CLOUGHERTY	FLORENCE	Recreation	1,208
MCDONALD	SARAH E.	Recreation	1,146
RICHARDSON	EVAN J	Recreation	1,060
CARBONE	WILLIAM C.	Recreation	972
CLOUGHERTY	GRACE H	Recreation	703
WALSH	ALLISON K.	Recreation	648
ETHIER	PATRICIA	Recreation	534
		Department Total	$165,076
WALSH	DENISE	School Department	154,042
CISNEROS	KENNETH R.	School Department	114,944
ANTOLINI	JOEL	School Department	110,105
GILL	MICHAEL PATR	School Department	101,438
GILL	LINDA	School Department	100,066
GALLOTTA	ALAN R.	School Department	99,240
DEGENNARO	DAVID	School Department	96,663
WANDS	JOHN	School Department	94,295
SHEEHAN	JANET	School Department	94,166
DECHIARA	JENNIFER	School Department	93,380
MRZYGLOD	NANCY	School Department	93,234
PORTER	ANNE LESLIE	School Department	93,016
HORIGAN	SUSAN M.	School Department	90,717
SWEENEY	TORIN	School Department	90,342
DUFFY	MAUREEN M	School Department	89,392
GORDON	CYNTHIA B.	School Department	88,396
THOMAE	ANN M.	School Department	87,189
KURKER	KIM M	School Department	87,053
LEE	MARGARET	School Department	86,742
FORD	RONALD J.	School Department	85,360
KENNY	LYNNE	School Department	85,016
MCGRAIL	PATRICIA	School Department	84,608
CONROY	THERESA	School Department	84,370
HENRY	DEBORAH A.	School Department	84,370
WOMERSLEY	KATHLEEN	School Department	83,774
CISNEROS	ELIZABETH A.	School Department	82,421
CORKHUM	SUZI Y.	School Department	81,912
WELCH	MICHAEL R.	School Department	81,863
SANDLER	KERRI L	School Department	81,400
GIBSON	BARBARA A	School Department	80,798
YESS	DENISE ANNE	School Department	80,679
DYKAS	KEVIN P.	School Department	80,460
BUCKLEY JR	JOHN C	School Department	80,390
SULLIVAN	VICTORIA	School Department	79,746
BRINDLEY	PENELOPE A.	School Department	79,526
MARKS	BRYAN E	School Department	78,657
JORDAN	KATHLEEN A.	School Department	78,239
JORDAN	MARGARET	School Department	77,793
COOK	LAUREN M.	School Department	77,786
BARBIERI	DIANE M	School Department	77,557
AFANASIW	PETER	School Department	76,984
LAFOUNTAIN	ALLEN W.	School Department	75,809
CRIMMINS	CAROLYN L.	School Department	75,349
GIBSON	COLLEEN E.	School Department	75,205
BEAL	DEBORAH G.	School Department	74,941
RITTS	JUDITH A	School Department	74,779

Last Name	First Name	Primary Department	Gross Pay
MAGNUSSEN	DAVID R	School Department	73,639
WOOLEY	STEPHANIE E.	School Department	73,297
BIERMAN	CAROLE L.	School Department	73,119
JONES	DANIEL C.	School Department	72,840
BERRY	MAUREEN M.	School Department	72,840
OWENS-RIGBY	ELIZABETH R	School Department	72,840
BIAGINI	STEVEN	School Department	72,467
MCGRATH	ELIZABETH M.	School Department	72,440
WINTER	LAUREN M	School Department	72,291
BERKOWITZ	NINA B.	School Department	71,898
MORRISSEY	PATRICIA A	School Department	71,687
SWARTZ	LAURA C.	School Department	71,605
DIMINNIE	LESLIE	School Department	70,718
HIGGINS	JOY L	School Department	70,040
WILLIS	JAMES	School Department	69,861
HANSON	JEANNE B.	School Department	69,316
MCNAMARA	PAMELA J.	School Department	68,778
KEATING	LAURA R.	School Department	68,557
WEYDT	MICHAEL	School Department	67,715
SULLIVAN	ALLISON B.	School Department	67,133
TUSCHER	ROBERT	School Department	66,870
ROHRER	EILEEN	School Department	66,715
JOHNSTON	KARIN	School Department	66,651
TRITTO	STEPHANIE T.	School Department	66,611
LEVY	ROBERT	School Department	65,564
THOMAS	JANE V	School Department	65,096
BLIDNER	ARON	School Department	64,356
DUGAN	MARY P.	School Department	63,955
BERMAN	ANN	School Department	63,185
DEWAAL	JULIA P.	School Department	63,038
LEONARD JR.	EDWARD J.	School Department	62,863
GIULIANO	LAURA	School Department	62,525
CLARK	JENNIFER A.	School Department	60,686
FOLEY	KERRI ANN	School Department	60,525
PALMIERI	VINCENT	School Department	60,378
MCTIGUE	JOAN	School Department	60,140
MONTEIRO	JENNIFER	School Department	59,965
FISH	WILLIAM	School Department	59,961
NELLIGAN	CATHERINE	School Department	59,556
BLUESTEIN	NANCY A	School Department	58,240
PARRELL	ERICA K	School Department	57,589
CAPOBIANCO	KRISTIE E	School Department	56,999
HOGAN	MICHAEL	School Department	56,421
WHALEN	MEREDITH	School Department	56,187
ERLANDSEN	ROBERT J.	School Department	55,999
MORIARTY	STEPHANIE C.	School Department	55,733
GIBBONS	EMILY F.	School Department	55,017
CASSIANI	JOAN M.	School Department	54,969
BERMAN	CHRISTINE J.	School Department	54,835
CALLAHAN	JEAN L.	School Department	54,627
DISABATINO	JENNIFER A	School Department	54,461
LEWIS	ARNA	School Department	54,367
GOLDSTEIN	CHERIE A	School Department	54,109
BEAUDRY	KAYNE M.	School Department	54,104
OGDEN	ELIZABETH A.	School Department	53,718
MAGNUSSEN	NANCY	School Department	53,482
FORTIN	JONATHAN T.	School Department	53,172
WELCH	SUSAN N	School Department	53,125
BOTTI	CHRISTINA A	School Department	53,106
HATHAWAY	DEBORAH M	School Department	53,056
MCALARNEY	KATE	School Department	52,529
O'HARA	MEGHAN	School Department	52,460
GITTENS-CARLE	ALEISA M.	School Department	52,124
LECOUNT JR.	ROBERT A.	School Department	52,108
NOBLE	STEPHANIE	School Department	51,921
MCCABE	JASON D	School Department	51,729
LUCKI	ROSALIE L	School Department	50,619
GIBBS	KAREN	School Department	50,476
CLAASSEN	MICHELLE	School Department	49,336

Last Name	First Name	Primary Department	Gross Pay
FLAHERTY	STEPHEN M	School Department	48,834
JONES	THOMAS W.	School Department	48,185
SULLIVAN-SANGE	KATHLEEN	School Department	47,905
HOLLAND	THEODORE L.	School Department	47,350
PESCATORE	JANE	School Department	47,165
HANNON	PETER H	School Department	47,069
QUEENAN	CAROLYN E.	School Department	46,626
KING JR	JOSEPH W	School Department	45,806
MOSHER	MICHELE S	School Department	44,696
SMITH	MARGARET L.	School Department	44,696
DANIELSON	JOHN	School Department	44,400
KOTTER	JEFFREY	School Department	44,362
GROSSMAN	CHRISTINA	School Department	44,228
HOLLAND	MARGARET	School Department	44,228
GALLAGHER	ASA	School Department	43,714
MURPHY	KAREN	School Department	42,854
MCINNIS	KAREN E	School Department	42,658
HATHON	ROSE M	School Department	42,431
LEWIS	MICHAEL A	School Department	41,929
MCPHILLIPS	JENNIFER A	School Department	41,620
DAVIS	JOSEPH G	School Department	41,412
LEAHY	DENISE M.	School Department	41,252
COLLINS	JUDITH	School Department	40,718
O'BRIEN	CASSANDRA G.	School Department	40,305
DICKSON	KELLY B.	School Department	40,062
LEWIS	MARGARET	School Department	39,700
FIGUEIREDO	JUDITH A	School Department	39,011
COSMAN	SUSAN	School Department	38,351
DONOGHUE	DONNA M	School Department	36,707
JOYCE	MICHELLE	School Department	36,624
TRASK	AMY	School Department	35,927
MEADE	JONI	School Department	35,780
WILEY	MEG	School Department	35,250
YOUNG	DAVID	School Department	35,121
WOLLAM	RACHEL N.	School Department	34,753
MARAT	MARY	School Department	34,131
RIOUX	CASSANDRA	School Department	33,466
DUNCAN	NATHANIEL	School Department	33,011
MCGOWAN	ERIN C	School Department	31,918
LAUZON	ELIZABETH L.	School Department	31,814
HILL	CHARLOTTE	School Department	31,353
MONTGOMERY	JENNY M.	School Department	31,143
GREGORY	JANE E.	School Department	31,106
DOW	DAMA E.	School Department	30,680
CROUGH	SANDRA	School Department	29,515
SIMMONS	LISA	School Department	29,042
MINGELS	BRADLEY T	School Department	28,929
PERKINS	DANIEL S	School Department	28,429
SULC	JENNIFER W	School Department	27,792
FOLEY	JOSEPH	School Department	27,602
NUTTING	JONATHAN	School Department	27,421
MARTIN	APRIL A.	School Department	26,364
CANZATER	BEATRICE	School Department	26,081
SANFORD	WILLIAM E	School Department	25,924
ZAPPOLO	SANDRA L.	School Department	25,107
SABO	JEAN	School Department	24,863
BROOKS	KATHRYN A	School Department	24,455
R.-GRIFFITHS	GRACE M.	School Department	24,448
ALBANESE	PAULA M	School Department	23,725
CLAY	VIRGINIA E.	School Department	22,213
FABIAN	KATHERINE	School Department	21,695
SADLER	SUSAN M.	School Department	21,687
KURTZ	JACQUELINE	School Department	20,266
SUGRUE	LISA V	School Department	19,644
CREIGHTON	NANCY F.	School Department	19,564
RIPATRAZONE	JOANNE M.	School Department	19,561
ANDRUS	JOAN B.	School Department	19,411
LEHR	JOANNE	School Department	19,411
SMITH	PEARL F	School Department	19,411

Last Name	First Name	Primary Department	Gross Pay
WILD	LINDA S.	School Department	19,411
AYER	ALISON G.	School Department	19,411
CLIFFORD	DIANE	School Department	19,411
SALERNO	HEIDI C.	School Department	19,411
SEPPALA	LIANE L.	School Department	19,411
SHANNON	DEBORAH M.	School Department	19,411
BARRY	MARGARITA	School Department	19,390
MCDAVITT	KAREN E	School Department	18,951
DAVIS	AMY	School Department	18,882
GRADY	BETH S	School Department	18,859
REGAN	BRENDA W.	School Department	18,755
KELLEY	JILL L	School Department	18,268
BAUM	ROBERT W.	School Department	18,138
YUROF	KELLI	School Department	17,948
STROINEY RUSSE	SALLY	School Department	17,746
PENWELL	KATHRYN R	School Department	17,691
AMERO	ERIC F	School Department	17,400
SMITH	RACHEL W	School Department	17,060
GRANDE	LUCIA G.	School Department	16,736
MCELHINNEY	COLLETTE	School Department	16,675
STRUZZIERY	LAURA A	School Department	16,650
DEGENNARO	ALLISON	School Department	16,570
DONATO	MARIA I.	School Department	16,544
HENEGHAN	BETH A	School Department	15,909
ONEIL III	THOMAS J	School Department	15,739
FARRELL	CAROLYN	School Department	15,594
KENNY	BRANDON P	School Department	15,384
DALTON	BLAKE	School Department	14,942
LILLE	REBECCA A	School Department	14,895
WILKINSON	MOLLY E	School Department	14,895
MURPHY	JUSTINE C	School Department	13,802
BORDONARO	SARAH A	School Department	13,742
RHODES	KATHLEEN E.	School Department	12,749
SHERIDAN	M. ELIZABETH	School Department	11,950
ROSS	ANITA	School Department	11,646
BRYANT	DORIAN	School Department	11,569
MALONE	EMILY	School Department	11,057
MONACO	LYNN B.	School Department	10,928
SCHWANTNER	DERRY	School Department	10,655
CALABRIA	MARIA	School Department	10,624
D'ELIA	JOANNE	School Department	10,544
RIDGE	EILEEN	School Department	10,533
MARASCIO	JOSEPHINE	School Department	10,374
RYAN	SUSAN M.	School Department	10,314
SNOW	DOROTHY B.	School Department	10,269
JACOBUCCI	EILEEN C.	School Department	10,157
VINTON	DAVID S	School Department	10,076
TRUGLIA	SILVANA	School Department	9,569
POLLARD	KIMBERLY N	School Department	9,430
HALEY	VALERIE A.	School Department	9,392
SPADEA	MARIA	School Department	9,144
O'BRIEN	TAYLOR L	School Department	9,066
RAY	THOMAS P	School Department	8,961
MAGNER	ROMINA V	School Department	8,727
LEARY	EDWARD J.	School Department	8,625
MARKS	LAURA	School Department	8,498
BROWN	PETER A	School Department	8,292
STILLMAN	MARGARET M	School Department	8,063
WILFAND	WENDY	School Department	7,990
QUINLAN-MARCEL	ERIN J	School Department	7,907
MALOUF	THERESA A	School Department	7,705
OUELLETTE	ANNE	School Department	7,229
BANAHAN	JEAN A	School Department	6,806
ASTINO	JEANNE	School Department	6,800
PORRO	COSMO	School Department	6,767
MORDE	MATTHEW R	School Department	6,693
MCELGUNN	MAUREEN G	School Department	6,550
GRAVES	JOHN	School Department	6,051
CASONI	LOURDEEN	School Department	6,000

Last Name	First Name	Primary Department	Gross Pay
LEVANGIE	JOHN A.	School Department	5,992
LEMANSKI	ALLISON M	School Department	5,626
MADGE	TRACI L.	School Department	5,377
BENNETT	PAMELA M.	School Department	5,334
O'CONNELL	BERNADETTE	School Department	5,310
WALSH	ROBERT	School Department	5,244
OFFERMAN	LISA	School Department	4,910
NEDROW	RUTH	School Department	4,830
COAKLEY	ABIGAIL	School Department	4,818
DAVIS	CRAIG	School Department	4,700
CURRAN	CHARLES	School Department	4,696
JAFFE	CHARLES A	School Department	4,696
SPOFFORD	ROBERT B	School Department	4,696
WEINTRAUB	JANE B	School Department	4,630
MAHONEY	PHILIP	School Department	4,583
PATTISON	BRIAN J.	School Department	4,583
VENTRESCA	THOMAS	School Department	4,583
MAREE	AMY	School Department	4,496
BARNARD	CLAIR J	School Department	3,885
KIDDER	IAN	School Department	3,760
LEWIS	MATTHEW	School Department	3,745
ROWAN	MEGHAN K.	School Department	3,630
CZAJAK	PATRICIA	School Department	3,590
KAMP	SUSAN	School Department	3,455
SCHMITT	JUDITH	School Department	3,268
BUCKLEY	PETER	School Department	3,255
MEEHAN	SARA G.	School Department	3,212
TOWER	CHRISTINE	School Department	3,209
DUGGAN	JOHN F	School Department	3,183
TAGGART	CHRISTINE	School Department	3,183
MCMILLAN	MATTHEW	School Department	3,090
PALMER	JENNIFER	School Department	3,090
ROMAN	ANTHONY	School Department	3,090
MORGAN	DONNA	School Department	3,050
LOMBARDI	JOHN G	School Department	3,027
LAMPI	ANDREA R	School Department	3,025
DELANEY	DARLENE M.	School Department	3,025
FLYNN	LISA	School Department	2,825
RACCUIA	KAREN A	School Department	2,760
PELLETIER	ELIZABETH	School Department	2,552
CICIOTTE	CAROL	School Department	2,545
THOMS	NORMAN	School Department	2,520
ELY	FLORENCE	School Department	2,375
JOHNSTON	HEATHER	School Department	2,150
HERNBERG	KATHLEEN	School Department	2,080
WOOD	JO-ELLEN S	School Department	2,037
RUGGIERO	BO	School Department	2,037
WALSH	ROBERT	School Department	2,007
EDWARD	WILLIAM K	School Department	1,800
SAPOSNIK	SCOTT A	School Department	1,733
MCMANUS	ERIN	School Department	1,650
COX	JUDITH L	School Department	1,613
CARROLL	PAUL	School Department	1,606
HILL	BRIAN	School Department	1,606
TARPEY	LORRAINE C	School Department	1,570
GREELEY-PICKAR	EVA MARIA	School Department	1,545
FEGREUS	JANE M.	School Department	1,238
KILPATRICK	BONNIE	School Department	1,160
O'KANE	MARGARET M	School Department	1,150
DEVIN	MAURA M	School Department	1,090
RAYMOND	JENNIFER B	School Department	1,050
BEARY	KAREN M	School Department	990
KING	DON E	School Department	990
GILDEA	KELLI A	School Department	870
GERBIS	JENNIFER F	School Department	830
BECKER	LAURE	School Department	720
BLACKINTON	MARY	School Department	680
FEENEY	JOHN M	School Department	600
O'DELL	DANIEL S	School Department	600

Last Name	First Name	Primary Department	Gross Pay
GILL	KELLY	School Department	525
BINDA	EUGENE	School Department	515
MULLEN	DOROTHY	School Department	460
WATTS	KRISTEN	School Department	413
DEWAAL	JOHN	School Department	375
MEEHAN MATTHEW	JENNIFER S	School Department	300
NOTTAGE	SARAH E	School Department	300
CROWELL	JODY BETH	School Department	239
CAYER	MICHELLE	School Department	225
DEYESO	MICHAEL	School Department	225
GENELLO	LAURA S	School Department	225
GRIP	LEAH	School Department	225
REPLOGLE	STEWART	School Department	225
HICKEY	IAN	School Department	150
HOWARD	KRISTIN	School Department	150
MASTROMARINO	MARY E.	School Department	150
MCNAMEE	FRANCIS C.	School Department	150
NOBLE	SARAH	School Department	150
PAGE	EILEEN	School Department	150
PINKUS	DANIELLE	School Department	150
DOOLEY	LISA ANN	School Department	75
MORIN	PATRICIA A.	School Department	75
MULLEN	ANN	School Department	75
		Department Total	$11,725,178
GRIFFIN	WILLIAM	Selectmen's Office	132,496
ORAM	JENNIFER B	Selectmen's Office	58,749
CARISTI-MACDON	MARIE F	Selectmen's Office	18,824
JACKSON	ROBERT W.	Selectmen's Office	1,600
CARR	EDWIN	Selectmen's Office	1,375
CARLSON	PAUL	Selectmen's Office	1,000
DORMITZER	RALPH	Selectmen's Office	1,000
KOED	FRED	Selectmen's Office	1,000
QUIGLEY	KAREN M	Selectmen's Office	667
WADSWORTH	DAVID H	Selectmen's Office	600
PATTISON	PAUL	Selectmen's Office	500
VANDERWEIL	R. GARY	Selectmen's Office	375
LEHR JR	ARTHUR L	Selectmen's Office	350
		Department Total	$218,535
BUCKLEY JR.	J. MICHAEL	Town Accountant	102,427
HENDERSON	JANE E.	Town Accountant	30,453
		Department Total	$132,880
DOUGLAS	MARION L.	Town Clerk	65,430
ST.PIERRE	CAROL L.	Town Clerk	50,352
FORD	EDYTHE	Town Clerk	326
CHARLES	MARGARET R.	Town Clerk	326
VOLUNGIS	JUDITH P.	Town Clerk	326
		Department Total	$116,760
LITCHFIELD	LINDA M.	Treasurer/Collector	66,560
MCCARTHY	KATHLEEN E	Treasurer/Collector	54,537
PARNELL	SANDRA E	Treasurer/Collector	44,234
		Department Total	$165,330

REPORT OF THE TOWN TREASURER/COLLECTOR

The following is the Annual Report for the Office of Treasurer/Collector. It contains
a Reconciliation of Town Cash Accounts, Report of the Tax Collector and a listing of
wages and salaries paid for calendar year 2008.

In Fiscal Year 2008, the Office processed approximately 11,976 Real Estate tax bills,
575 Personal Property tax bills, 9,442 Motor Vehicle Excise tax bills, 409 Boat
Excise tax bills and 10,568 Water and Sewer bills.

In addition, the Office is responsible for processing payroll for all Town employees,
issuing all accounts payable checks and maintaining custody of all Town receipts.

I would like to thank the residents of Cohasset for the opportunity to serve the Town
and thank Sandy Parnell for her efforts.

Respectfully Submitted,

Kathleen E. McCarthy

Acting Treasurer/Collector

RECONCILIATION OF TOWN CASH ACCOUNTS
June 30, 2008

Balance in Treasury July 1, 2007	$13,515,675
Receipts	85,398,989
Disbursements	(87,312,107)
Balance in Town Treasury June 30, 2008	$11,602,557
Cash on Hand	150
Bank of America	174,806
Eastern Bank	57,269
Hingham Institute For Savings	2,439,015
Hingham Institute For Savings - Trust Funds	254,203
Massachusetts Municipal Depository Trust	791,140
Mellon Bank	508,427
Pilgrim Bank	2,327,992
Pilgrim Bank - Trust Funds	1,554,473
Rockland Trust	1,312,488
Rockland Trust - Trust Funds	1,084,385
Vanguard Group - Trust Funds	1,098,209
Total Funds in Town Custody	$11,602,557

REPORT OF THE TAX COLLECTOR
FISCAL YEAR 2008

	Balance Forward	Committed	Abated	Refunds	Receipts	Liened/ Adjusted	Ending Balance	
Real Estate Taxes -								
Levy of 2008	0	25,310,920	126,343	44,297	24,686,957	-90,690	451,227	451,227
Levy of 2007	329,588		7,225	14,048	255,271	-81,140	0	-
Levy of 2006	48,227		569	569	24,409	-23,818	0	-
Levy of 2005	(342)			342			0	-
Total Real Estate Taxes	$377,473	$25,310,920	$134,137	$59,256	$24,966,637	-$195,648	$451,227	
Personal Property Taxes -								
Levy of 2008	0	162,154	487	1,454	159,843		3,278	3,278
Levy of 2007	627				324		303	303
Levy of 2006	954						954	954
Levy of 2005	542			5			547	547
Levy of 2004	586				0		586	586
Levy of 2003	682				18		664	664
Levy of 2002	781				101		680	680
Levy of 2001	916				71		845	845
Levy of 2000	2,651				1,145		1,506	1,506
Levy of 1999	2,374				1,135		1,239	1,239
Total Personal Property Taxes	$10,113	$162,154	$487	$1,459	$162,637	$0	$10,602	
Other Property Taxes -								
Deferred Property Taxes	473,527	90,901					564,428	564,428
Tax Liens / Tax Title	141,149	147,045		1,410	83,284		206,320	206,320
Tax Foreclosures / Possessions	87,317						87,317	87,317
Community Preservation Surcharge	4,061	335,180	3,906	412	329,018		6,729	6,729
Total Other Property Taxes	$706,054	$573,126	$3,906	$1,822	$412,302	$0	$864,794	
Excise Taxes -								
Motor Vehicle 2008	0	1,123,175	20,131	10,413	1,050,872		62,585	62,585
Motor Vehicle 2007	52,225	201,472	19,950	16,022	228,617		21,152	21,151
Motor Vehicle 2006	14,810	11,729	1,890	1,471	18,864		7,256	7,255
Motor Vehicle 2005	6,185	1,986	1,336	551	3,271		4,125	4,125
Motor Vehicle 2004	4,658		2,439		1,409		810	810
Motor Vehicle 2003	4,334				511		3,823	3,823
Motor Vehicle 2002	2,885				88		2,797	2,797
Motor Vehicle 2001	3,915				566		3,349	3,349
Motor Vehicle 2000	2,533				165		2,368	2,369
Motor Vehicle 1999	5,362				155		5,207	5,208
Boat Excise (All Years)	9,377	19,174	1,424	236	17,654		9,709	9,709
Total Excise Taxes	$106,284	$1,357,536	$47,170	$28,703	$1,322,172	$0	$123,181	
Departmental Charges -								
Water Use Charges	306,980	2,864,227	146,989	1,579	2,889,980	-71,403	264,414	264,414
Water Liens	8,220	72,400	910		63,365	-10,436	5,909	5,908
Sewer - Central District	111,402	717,600	6,190	342	703,197	-34,070	85,887	85,887
Sewer - North District	25,905	292,860	3,629		285,172	-8,387	21,577	21,577
Sewer Liens	8,432	36,654			41,544	-1,520	2,022	2,022
Moorings Fees	207	52,992			53,199		0	-
Ambulance Fees	356,673	404,347	1,636	3,342	374,886		387,840	387,840
Drainage Betterments	88,889				22,622		66,267	66,267
Unapportioned Betterments	5,147,325				54,622	-394,517	4,698,186	4,698,186
Apportioned Betterments	9,107	418,887	5,138		416,433		6,423	6,423
Committed Interest	2,779	52,715			51,662		3,832	3,832
Total Departmental Charges	$6,065,919	$4,912,682	$164,492	$5,263	$4,756,682	-$520,333	$5,542,357	

2008 ANNUAL REPORT OF THE BOARD OF ASSESSORS

The property tax levy is the revenue a community can raise through real and personal property taxes. The property tax levy is the largest source of revenue for the Town of Cohasset. The property tax levy for Fiscal Year 2008 was $25,473,074.16 representing 66% of the $37,676,319.16 budget. The residential share of the levy is 93%, while commercial, industrial, and personal property account for 7%.

It is the responsibility of the Assessors' Office to establish fair market value for all properties in the Town of Cohasset. During Fiscal Year 2008, the Assessors' Office conducted a full revaluation of the town. The staff conducted an analysis of all arms-length sales that occurred in the town during calendar year 2006, reported sales trends in the real estate market, and completely adjusted the land valuation tables, in preparation for certification. The Department of Revenue required land valuation methodology in accordance with newly adopted guidelines. After extensive review by the Department of Revenue the values were certified for Fiscal Year 2008. The total valuation of the town was $2,403,120,204 with a tax rate of $10.60 per thousand dollars of assessment.

In addition to the revaluation of real estate, the Assessors' Office is responsible for the assessment and commitment of motor vehicle excise and boat excise, betterment assessments, and the collection of new growth based on building construction. During 2008, the staff conducted field inspections or review of all building permits in the Town of Cohasset.

The Board of Assessors would like to thank David Wadsworth, Town Historian, for volunteering to collect property photos for the Assessors' database. David's efforts have produced several hundred digital images that were downloaded to the assessment database throughout the year. Also, the Board would like to acknowledge Deputy Assessor, Mary Quill, Assistant Assessor, Debra Krupczak and Administrative Assistant, Ellen Warner for their professionalism throughout the year.

Respectfully submitted,
Mary E. Granville, Chairperson
Michael C. Patrolia, Clerk
Elsa J. Miller, Member

2008 BOARD OF HEALTH ANNUAL REPORT

The Board re-organized in April of 2008. Peggy S. Chapman, RN remained as Chairperson, with Stephen N. Bobo assuming the Clerk position and Robin M. Lawrence, DDS as member. Joseph R. Godzik, VMD remains the Health Agent on a part-time basis and Tara N. Tradd, Health Inspector/Office Manager. Judy Fitzsimmons retired as public health nurse and now assists Mary Goodwin, RN, who serves as the Town's Public Health Nurse.

Stephen N. Bobo continued to work with other town partners resulting in the approval of the Stormwater Committee's Stormwater By-Law which was approved at the Annual Town Meeting. Stephen N. Bobo has been working tirelessly to achieve this and has been instrumental in having the By-law written.

Stephen N. Bobo also instituted the Brain Fitness Program. Brain plasticity is a new field of neuroscience. The software program offers services to improve everything from reading skills to improved driving for elders. The Paul Pratt Library, through a grant has installed the computerized brain fitness exercise software on the library's many laptops for anyone's use.

Students at the Center for Student Coastal Research (CSCR) continued to monitor water quality in Cohasset Harbor and the surrounding area. Enterococci bacteria levels continue to be high especially in the area of the so-called "Parker Avenue Cut". The US Environmental Protection Agency concluded their water quality investigation of Cohasset Harbor and rendered a report which is available in the Board of Health Office.

The Board continues to monitor water quality at the beaches around town and in Cohasset Harbor. Samples are collected weekly from mid-June to Labor Day at Bassing Beach, Cohasset Harbor at the Yacht Club, Sandy Cove, Sandy Beach, Black Rock Beach and Little Harbor near Cunningham Bridge. This year Health Inspector Tradd was assisted by CSCR Student Marcus Charles. Marcus ran split lab samples of the Beach waters all season long. Marcus's lab results were outstanding in comparison to G&L Laboratory's results. Marcus's beach water quality project report is available at the Board of Health office. A big thank you to Marcus for helping protect the Public Health. Bassing's Beach was closed for one day on three separate occasions due to high bacterial counts. All other beaches remained opened all season long.

Emergency Preparedness continued to be high on the Board's agenda. Pandemic influenza planning continues. This year's focus is on Communication the Board of Health is surveying and upgrading their communication needs to ensure continuity in a time of an emergency. The Emergency Dispensing Site (EDS) Plan is completed and is in the process of being reviewed and updated. The Board also hosted an Emergency Preparedness Starts at Home training session in May for the Medical Reserve Corps (MRC) members in Region 4B there were many who participated. The Board continues to recruit for the MRC. Persons who have no medical training are needed for support roles. Applications for both medical and support staff are available at the Board of Health Office or the town website www.townofcohasset.org.

The annual Health Fair was held at the Second Congregational Church on September 16, 2008. Over 100 residents participated. Free screenings for cholesterol (total and HDL) blood glucose, bone density, oral cancer, glaucoma, skin cancer were offered as well as nutrition, mental health evaluations and bike and car seat safety promotions. New this year was PSA testing for prostate cancer with 22 people screened.

Two Flu clinics for senior citizens and high risk adults were held at the Town Hall, as well as a town wide flu clinic including children over the age of nine. Clinics were also held at Harborview Housing and Sunrise Assisted Living Center. 840 doses of flu vaccine were administered. Many volunteers assisted with the paperwork, flow and administration of vaccine at the flu clinics.

The Board supported Jim Hamilton and the many students of Cohasset High who organized and volunteered for the annul Earth Day Cleanup. The turnout was huge success. Tara Tradd is the coordinator of the Adopt of a Street Program. Seven areas in town have been adopted by various groups. This new environmental program is a partnership between the Town of Cohasset and community minded businesses, organizations and citizens. By working together we can continue to provide a beautiful environment for all of us. This program will also educate and encourage people to stop littering and take pride in their community. To become part of this new and exciting program contact Tara Tradd at: tarat@townofcohasset.org.

The Board will be presenting in 2009 a revision to the Drinking and Irrigation Well Regulation; changes include more sampling and monitoring requirements.

The Board will continue to be responsive to issues of public health, like the windmill installation to assure that compliance with environmental and public health regulations are being met. Water quality will be the principle focus.

The Board thanks all its volunteers who assist with programs and clinics. Much is accomplished through your continuous efforts.

The Board is grateful to all who assist with programs and clinics through volunteer efforts and monetary donations throughout the year.

Nursing Services Provided in 2008

Keep Well Clinics	169
Adult Immunization	900+
Diabetic / Cholesterol Screening	62
Health Fair Participants	102+
PSA Testing	22
Communicable Disease Follow Up	16
Home Nursing Visits	192
Office Nursing Visits	1031
Total Nursing Visits	1223

The Board received the following revenue during 2008:

Licenses and Permits:	$14,210.00
Witnessing Percolation Testing	$5,722.50
Disposal System Construction Permit:	$4,325.00
Other:	$10,527.00
PHN Gift Account:	$1,997.50
Medicare Reimbursement:	$11,169.63

Respectfully Submitted:

Peggy S. Chapman, RN, CS, Chairperson
Stephen N. Bobo, Clerk
Robin M. Lawrence, DDS, MPH

2008 REPORT OF PLYMOUTH COUNTY MOSQUITO CONTROL PROJECT

The Commissioners of the Plymouth County Mosquito Control Project are pleased to submit the following report of our activities during 2008.

The Project is a special district created by the State Legislature in 1957, and is now composed of all Plymouth County towns, the City of Brockton, and the Town of Cohasset in Norfolk County. The Project is a regional response to a regional problem, and provides a way of organizing specialized equipment, specially trained employees, and mosquito control professionals into a single agency with a broad geographical area of responsibility.

The 2008 season began dry with a low water table which increased into the summer season. Efforts were directed at larval mosquitoes starting with the spring brood. Ground and aerial larviciding was accomplished using B.t.i., an environmentally selective bacterial agent. Upon emergence of the spring brood of mosquitoes, ultra-low volume adulticiding began on May 27, 2008 and ended on September 26, 2008. The Project responded to 14,346 requests for service from residents.

In response to the continued threat of mosquito borne diseases in the district, we continued our surveillance trapping, aerial and ground larviciding, and adult spray in areas of concern to protect public health.

Eastern Equine Encephalitis was first isolated from *Culiseta melanura*, a bird biting species, by the Massachusetts Department of Public Health in Carver on August 14' 2008. Of the season's total of thirteen EEE isolates, two were from Plymouth County as follows: Carver -8/14, Halifax-9/14.

Based on guidelines defined by the "Vector Control Plan to Prevent EEE" in Massachusetts, one Plymouth County town, Lakeville, was elevated from "Low Level" to "Moderate Level" of EEE Risk" effective Oct 4, 2008. All other towns in Plymouth County Mosquito Project remained in the "Low Level Risk" category. We are pleased to report that in 2008 there were no human or horse EEE cases in Plymouth County.

West Nile Virus was also found within the district. A total of 6 birds tested positive for WNV in the following six towns: Halifax, Hingham, Scituate, Kingston, Whitman and Plymouth. Approximately fifteen birds were handled through this Project as a dead bird repository. A total of seven isolations of WNV in mosquitoes were found in the following towns: Abington - 7/29, Brockton - 8/12, Kingston – 9/5, Mattapoisett – 8/7 and Whitman – 8/26, 9/3. We are also pleased to report that in 2008 that there were no human or horse West Nile Virus cases in Plymouth County. As part of our West Nile Virus control strategy a total of 59,047 catch basins were treated with larvicide in all of our towns to prevent WNV.

The remaining problem of EEE and WNV continues to ensure cooperation between the Plymouth County Mosquito Control Project, local Boards of Health and the Massachusetts Department of Public Health. In an effort to keep the public informed, EEE and WNV activity updates are regularly posted on Massachusetts Department of Public Health website at www.state.ma.us/dph/wnv/wnv1.htm.

The figures specific to the Cohasset are given below. While mosquitoes do not respect town lines the information given below does provide a tally of the activities which have had the greatest impact on the health and comfort of Cohasset residents.

Insecticide Application. 1,049 acres were treated using truck mounted sprayers for control of adult mosquitoes. More than one application was made to the same site if mosquitoes reinvaded the area. The first treatments were made in May and the last in September.

During the summer 1,150 catch basins were treated to prevent the emergence of *Culex pipiens*, a known mosquito vector in West Nile Virus transmission.

Our greatest effort has been targeted at mosquitoes in the larval stage, which can be found in woodland pools, swamps, marshes and other standing water areas. Inspectors

The figures specific to the Cohasset are given below. While mosquitoes do not respect town lines the information given below does provide a tally of the activities which have had the greatest impact on the health and comfort of Cohasset residents.

Insecticide Application. 1,049 acres were treated using truck mounted sprayers for control of adult mosquitoes. More than one application was made to the same site if mosquitoes reinvaded the area. The first treatments were made in May and the last in September.

During the summer 1,150 catch basins were treated to prevent the emergence of *Culex pipiens,* a known mosquito vector in West Nile Virus transmission.

Our greatest effort has been targeted at mosquitoes in the larval stage, which can be found in woodland pools, swamps, marshes and other standing water areas. Inspectors

continually gather data on these sites and treat with highly specific larvicides when immature mosquitoes are present.

Finally, we have been tracking response time, which is the time between notice of a mosquito problem and response by one of our inspectors. The complaint response time in the Town of Cohasset was less than two days with more than 119 complaints answered.

Mosquito Survey. A systematic sampling for the mosquitoes in Cohasset indicates that *Ae. vexans* was the most abundant species. Other important species collected include *Cx. species* and *Cq. perturbans.*

We encourage citizens or municipal officials to visit our website at www.plymouthmosquito.com or call our office for information about mosquitoes, mosquito-borne diseases, control practices, or any other matters of concern.

Anthony Texeira
Superintendent

Commissioners:
Carolyn Brennan, Chairman
Leighton F. Peck, Vice-Chairman/Secretary
Kimberly King
William J. Mara
John Kenney

Director's Report
December 30, 2008

The Mission of Cohasset Elder Affairs is to offer outstanding
Programs and Services that provide for the physical, social and
emotional needs of our older adults by assisting them to lead
independent, stimulating and self-reliant lives as members of
the Town of Cohasset.

The Goals of Cohasset Elder Affairs:
1. To provide Educational Programs for older adults and families on critical
   current senior issues.
2. To provide Outreach Assistance for seniors unable to come to the Senior Center.
3. To provide Transportation Services, (utilizing paid and volunteer drivers), that will
   assist seniors to get to medical appointments, food shopping and other essential
   places that will assist the senior to "age in place".
4. To provide programs that promote healthy life style choices, stimulate the mind,
   and increase laughter.
5. To foster intergenerational programs (with other Community Agencies) that will
   enrich the lives of older adults, families and children.

   Revised by CEA Board of Directors 10/16/2006

The guiding force of Cohasset Elder Affairs is its Board of Directors whose
challenge is to assure that the Mission is being carried out in a fiscally
responsible manner by the Director of Elder Affairs and the Senior Center
Staff.

PROGRAMS AND SERVICES OFFERED THOUGH CEA FY 2008

TRANSPORTATION:

The greatest growth in service requests in 2008 were for Medical Transportation
and for Escort Food Shopping Transportation. FY 2008 we provided 4721 units
of transportation service. 34 percent of all trips were for Medical Appointments
and Escort Food Shopping. The Escort Food Shopping Program is a great one and
two devoted drivers go with 10-12 seniors each week to local markets. The
drivers assist people with poor vision to pick out foods, they lift bundles from
the van into the home and also assist the senior to put away groceries.

OUTREACH/ADVOCACY:

Our Outreach Worker/Shine Councilor, Carol Barrett, provided 4012 units of service
to Cohasset's seniors. These services include assisting seniors to choose the Medicare
D Plan that best fits their needs, individual counseling, home visits to the frailer
senior, assisting with applications for fuel assistance and other programs. Carol also
assigns the Respite Care providers, the Friendly Visitors and monitors the Telephone Reassurance program...
Carol also has worked closely with other providers to offer
a Lunch-time Lecture series on Wednesdays that keeps seniors aware of Health,
Insurance, Medication, Housing options and other pertinent topics.

VOLUNTEER COORDINATION:

Our Volunteer Coordinator, Martha Horsefield, recruited, trained and placed 20
new volunteers, so that we have 157volunteers who donate between 40 hours-150 hours per year. An
additional 100 volunteers took part in the Cohasset PTO Annual
"Make A Difference Day". Thanks to these wonderful volunteers, (from
toddlers to grand-parents), 24 senior homes had leaves raked and homes winterized.
. The Volunteers donated 7304.5 hours of service at an estimated value
(using Points of Light Foundation recommended numbers) that exceeds
$112,197.00.

FY 2008 Cohasset Elder Affairs also hosted many fun social activities including the End
of Year Summer Picnic, a Valentine's Tea, Mother's Day Brunch. The Cohasset Patrolmen's Association also
sponsored the Second Annual Father's Day Cookout and the
Roy Family, Joe Campbell, the Staff of Atlantica Restaurant and volunteers served a
Delicious Thanksgiving Feast to 150 seniors. FY 2008 CEA was involved in some
wonderful intergenerational programs including the Thanksgiving Feast at Atlantica where all were entertained
by the High School Jazz Quintet and some of the members of the West Side Story. Halloween with the preschool classes at SSCC, "One Town One Book Poetry Bash" with the fourth grade students at the Deer Hill
School which was
followed up by "Lets Fly A Kite Day" and a picnic on the Common

Our exercise programs continue to grow and this year thanks to the owners and
therapists from Nantasket Therapeutic Massage we offer, once a month, Reflexology
and Chair Massage for seniors at the Senior Center., as well as Tai Chi, Senior Aerobics,
Line Dancing, a monthly Health Clinic with the Town Nurse and bi-monthly Podiatry.

FISCAL 2008 OPERATING BUDGET DETAIL

Municipal $ 193,978 (154,578 Salaries, 39,400 Operating)

State F. Grant $ 9172.00 (Used to partially fund Coordinator of Volunteer Services)

Title III E. $ 2395.00 (Respite Care Giver Program Grant)

In-Kind Donations: Use of Church Halls and Custodial Services, Cohasset
Sailing Club, Atlantica Restaurant, Gourmet Club Meals and Volunteer
Services and Elder Affair Gift Donations = $ 150,000.00

CONCLUSION:

FYI 2008, the Social Service League of Cohasset presented
CEA with a check for $5000.00 which was used to begin a NEW SENIOR
CENTER BUILDING FUND, two additional families donated another
$2000.00 to the Fund. Currently there are 1640 residents in Cohasset 60
years of age and older out of a total population of 7705 residents. The seniors
deserve their own dedicated space with adequate and safe parking. Currently CEA is
renting a small amount of space from the South Shore Community Center that
does not allow us to expand Programs and Services to meet current and future needs.

I would like to offer my deepest thanks to the CEA Board of Directors,
the Board of Selectman, The Town Manager, and Finance Director, the
Advisory Committee, the Friends of the CEA, the CEA Staff and Volunteers,
And all of the Community Agencies who have been so supportive of the
programs and services we offer to Cohasset's seniors.

Respectfully submitted,

Linda Elworthy
Director of Cohasset Elder Affairs

2008 ANNUAL REPORT OF THE COHASSET HOUSING AUTHORITY

The Cohasset Housing Authority is a public agency with a five member Board of Commissioners, four of whom stand for town election and the Governor appoints the remaining Commissioner.

Commissioner	Term Expires
Helen C. Nothnagle, Chairman	Governor's Appointee
Christopher Allen, Vice Chairman	2010
Ann C. Barrett, Treasurer	2009
Ralph Perroncello, Asst. Treasurer	2012
Susan Sardina	2011

The Cohasset Housing Authority has a staff of two:

Catherine M. Luna, Execu-Tech Consultant
Jill Rosano, Maintenance Supervisor

According to their bylaws, the Board of Commissioners meets on the fourth Wednesday of each month and holds its annual meeting in June.

Cohasset's subsidized housing inventory includes 64 state units of Chapter 667 Elderly/Disabled housing located at Harborview, 60 Elm Street and 12 units of Chapter 689 Special Needs housing located at 72, 74 and 76 Elm Street. The Department of Housing and Community Development subsidizes these 76 state units. Our annual subsidies are granted upon successful annual, semi-annual, and quarterly reviews of management and regulatory compliance.

Eligibility standards for Harborview include a maximum allowable income of $46,300 for one person and the age for admission is 60. At the present time there is a waiting list of 109 people, many of whom are Cohasset residents. Local residents under state law have a preference on our Wait List. "Local Preference" as defined by state law is "any applicant living and/or working in the Town". The Board of Commissioners recommends that application for subsidized housing at Harborview be made before the need becomes critical. There is approximately a one-year wait for an apartment for a local resident and longer for a non-resident.

Modernization grants for capital improvements are awarded by our funding source, the Department of Housing & Community Development. A bond issue is expected to be introduced by the Department to fund projects in the pipeline.

In past years, the Community Preservation Committee has given unprecedented consideration to the capital improvement needs of the Cohasset Housing Authority. Money from the CPC has funded new intercom/secure door system, refrigerators, stoves, lever door handles, water- saver commodes, water-saver showerheads and a number of water heaters, and three washers and dryers for use of the residents.

In 2005 we requested funds for the replacement of the building envelope and upon the recommendation of the CPC; we were awarded $400,000 in CPC funds towards this project. Our deepest gratitude to the CPC for their thoughtful and generous consideration of our needs; to the Selectmen and the Advisory Committee for their encouraging support in placing this issue on the Town Meeting warrant; and to the citizens attending Town Meeting. Their support in approving the requests honors our senior citizens and enhances their quality of life here at Harborview.

In 2006 we submitted a Condition Assessment Report (our primary vehicle for grants awarded for Capital Improvements) requesting siding, windows and doors for the building envelope and it was approved. At that time it was also discovered that we needed new roofs and gutters. The Department of Housing and Community Development
approved the funding of $ 1,000,000.+ for these improvements along with the $400,000 in CPC funds awarded the Authority. This work is complete and we are eternally grateful to DHCD and the CPC for a practically new development.

In 2007 we were awarded funding from the DHCD to improve the drainage, walkways, roadway and parking in the amount of $548,384.00. This work will be complete in the fall of 2009.

The State's budget this year allowed for a 0% increase. We continue to request emergency funding for our complex, as weather and time take their toll.

Our continued gratitude to the Norfolk County Sheriffs Department for always being there when we need assistance. To the Public Works, Police and Fire Departments for their continued generosity, insuring the safety of our residents; to the students from Notre Dame Academy, the Girl Scout Troup 4870 for always remembering us. We thank you.

The Board of Commissioners continues to pursue its mandate of providing affordable, safe, and secure housing and of reviewing and updating regulatory policies/procedures. It remains diligent in the research of opportunities to create affordable housing for those with the greatest need.

Respectfully submitted,
Helen Nothnagle, Chairman
Susan Sardina, Vice-Chairman
Ann C. Barrett, Treasurer
Ralph Perroncello, Member
Christopher Allen, Member

BUILDING DEPARTMENT ~~ 2008 ANNUAL REPORT

In 2008, the Building Department issued 335 building permits for $26,976,963 worth of construction value.

3 permits were issued for 3 new residential structures on previously undeveloped land. 1 permit was issued for a new transit-oriented development mixed-use structure with commercial use on the first level and 16 apartments on the second level. In addition, 7 permits were issued for the demolition and reconstruction of existing homes. Hundreds more were issued for repairs, additions and substantial renovations.

In addition to permitting, inspections and zoning enforcement, the Building Commissioner inspects and certifies the safety of all public buildings and places of assembly and seals all measuring devices as the Sealer of Weights and Measures.

Building Department Issuances & Activity for 2008

Issuances/Activity	Number	Fees Collected	Total Construction Value
Building Permits	335	$ 271,117	$ 26,976,963
Certificates of Inspection	47	$ 1,475	-
Certificates of Occupancy	14	$ 355	-
Plumbing Permits	220	$ 12,957	-
Gas Permits	174	$ 7,122	-
Weights & Measures Sealing	22	$ 3,380	-
Totals	*812*	*$ 296,406*	*$26,976,963*

As always, I would like to thank all departments, boards and commissions for their continued assistance, cooperation and support.

Respectfully submitted,

Robert M. Egan
Building Commissioner
Zoning Enforcement Officer
Sealer of Weights and Measures

PLANNING BOARD ~~ 2008 ANNUAL REPORT

The Cohasset Planning Board, under the authority granted by Massachusetts General Law, Chapter 41, Section 81A-GG (Planning and Subdivision Control Law), and Chapter 40A (the Zoning Act) is charged with the review of large homes, subdivisions and site plan review of various development projects. In addition to these duties the Board completed a number of additional planning tasks in 2008.

The Board conducted public hearings on a number of Zoning Bylaw Amendment articles:
- For the March 29, 2008 Annual Town Meeting, the Planning Board conducted public hearings for four (4) zoning bylaws amendment warrant articles:
  Article 14: Zoning Bylaw Amendment: Wind Energy Conversion Facility Bylaw
  Article 15: Zoning Bylaw Amendment: Section 4.2 Permitted Uses – Table of Use Regulations
  Article 16: Zoning Bylaw Amendment: Amendment to Section 8
  Article 20: Zoning Bylaw Amendment: Inclusionary Zoning
          (This article was withdrawn by the Housing Partnership Committee.)
- For the November 17, 2008 Special Town Meeting, the Planning Board conducted public hearings for one (1) zoning bylaws amendment warrant articles:
  Article 10: Zoning Bylaw Reconciliation

The Planning Board oversaw the updating of the Cohasset Zoning Bylaws (last updated in March, 2004). Printed and available for sale, the newly updated bylaws were also posted on the Town's webpage.

A significant accomplishment of the Planning Board in 2008 was the establishment of draft "Village Design Guidelines" for the new Section 18 of the Zoning Bylaws: "Special Permits in the Village Business (VB) District" which was adopted at the November, 2007 STM. Spearheading this effort, the Planning Board worked closely with Concord Square Development consultants to create an enforceable regulatory document to be used in the permitting process for the basis of conditional approval or denial of an application for a special permit in the Village Business District. The purpose of the Design Guidelines is to provide: guiding principles that are vision statements of public policy objectives such as sustainability, affordability etc. in the Village Business District; guideline subsections based on geographical location within the Village recognizing that there are sections of the Village that are not the same and should be treated more specifically; and, principles that are more significant regulatory components relating to building design and site design in the Village.   These guidelines will remain in draft form for the first few Village Business District site plan review and special permit applications expected in early 2009 before being voted on for full adoption by the Planning Board.

Additional attention was focused on the Village Business District in terms of parking and pedestrian circulation. Concord Square Development, the Planning Board and owners of businesses in the Village met several times to review, discuss and design parking management in the Village and the municipal parking lots. In addition, discussion focused on a unified sidewalk layout on the Parkingway for continuous pedestrian circulation via sidewalk from Depot Court, through the Parkingway, to South Main Street. The goal is to provide not only a safe, continuous pedestrian passage through the Parkingway but to encourage and enhance a strolling circuit through the existing Village shops and future shops that are expected to be developed on the Parkingway (rear of So. Main St.).

The Board reviewed and approved with conditions two (2) Site Plan Review Applications for the following locations:

- 166 King Street: This application was for the construction of a new 20' X 52', one story building to be used for indoor boat repair/winter storage building. The proposed building, located behind the existing 166 King Street commercial building, would replace an existing 18' x 45' canvas on metal frame structure.
- 20 Parkingway (Rear of 55 So. Main St.): This application was for the construction of a new 2,000 SF, one story medical office building.

The Board also reviewed two (2) Definitive Residential Subdivision Plans:

- Quonahassit Trail: 3 residential lots with buildings at 209, 217 and 219 No. Main St. on 5.5+ acres are to be combined into one subdivision of land with seven proposed lots. The existing structures at 217 and 219 are to be razed or relocated. The structure at 209 is to remain intact and occupy one lot of the proposed subdivision. Six new residences are to be built on the remaining proposed six lots. The Planning Board approved this Subdivision Application with conditions.
- 29 Cedar St./Forest Ave.: This filing involved an approx. 6.27 parcel of land owned by the applicant. The applicant proposed to subdivide the lot into two lots – of 1.828 acres and 4.455 acres. The applicant's existing home is on this 4.455 acre lot, with frontage and access off Cedar Street. The second newly created lot would have frontage on Forest Avenue. The only way to access the new lot was to build a subdivision road from Forest Avenue. This application was withdrawn by the applicant when Conservation Commission review revealed that a vernal pool existed where the proposed subdivision road was to have been located thereby prohibiting construction of the road.

Two Large Home Review applications were filed and reviewed:

- 449 Jerusalem Road: This application was for the demolition of an existing 6,477 SF residential structure and the construction of a new 6,086 SF single family residential structure. After thorough review of the plans, the Planning Board voted unanimously to recommend the issuance of building permits for this construction.
- 26 Deep Run: This application was for the demolition of an existing 2,200 SF single family residential structure and the construction of a new 4,069 SF single family residential structure. After thorough review of the plans, the Planning Board voted unanimously to recommend the issuance of building permits for this construction.

A significant amount of review was focused on one large Special Permit and Site Plan Review filing for two proposed wind turbines at 215 CJC Hwy, the site of the former Cohasset Landfill. Since the filing in August of this year, several public hearings were conducted and countless hours spent on painstaking review of data and documents relative to this specific filing and to wind turbine technology in general. Public hearing and review of this application will continue into 2009.

Substantial attention was focused on the continued review of the status of conditions and progress of projects approved in the previous year(s) including: Cedarmere, Joseph's Hardware new construction, Manor Way Circle Subdivision, the Old Colony Square Transit Oriented Development and, 16-22 Depot Court. Many informal discussions were held at Planning Board Meetings for upcoming applications including residential and/or mixed use construction at 8 James Lane and 2 Smith Place as well as potential renovations at the Templar House on Jerusalem Road. The Planning Board also interacted with other Committees, Boards and Departments on issues of mutual interest and/or concern including the Economic Development Committee, the Housing Partnership, the Community Preservation Committee, the Zoning Board of Appeals, the Stormwater Committee, the Fire Department and the Alternative Energy Committee.

In this very busy year, the Board also conducted the following regular business:
- Held 22 meetings
- Reviewed fourteen (14) Subdivision Approval Not Required (ANR) applications or "Form A – Approval Not Required." After thorough review, all of the ANR applications were endorsed.
- The Planning Board regularly reviews applications filed with the Zoning Board of Appeals. After review and discussion, the Planning Board offers a recommendation to the ZBA to either approve or deny an application as well as the reason(s) for the recommendation. In 2008, the Planning Board reviewed and offered recommendations on twelve (12) ZBA special permit or variance applications.

After a combined 45+ years of service, veteran Planning Board Members Robert Sturdy and Bill Good, did not seek re-election and retired from the Board. The Board welcomed newly elected members Clark Brewer and Charles Samuelson.

Respectfully submitted,

Alfred S. Moore, Jr., Chairperson
Stuart W. Ivimey, Vice Chairperson
Charles A. Samuelson, Clerk
Michael R. Westcott
Clark H. Brewer

Norfolk County Registry of Deeds
2008 Annual Report to the Town of Cohasset
William P. O'Donnell, Register
649 High Street, Dedham, Massachusetts

The Registry of Deeds is the principal office for real property records in Norfolk County. The Registry receives and records hundreds of thousands of documents each year, and is a basic resource for title examiners, mortgage lenders, municipalities, homeowners, and others with a need for land record information. The Registry of Deeds has been a vital component of Norfolk County government since 1793, the year Governor John Hancock signed legislation creating Norfolk County, also known as the County of Presidents - the home or birthplace of John Adams, John Quincy Adams, John F. Kennedy and George H.W. Bush. The Registry operates under the supervision of the elected Register, William P. O'Donnell. In over two hundred years of continuous operation, the Registry has progressed from the days of scriveners with quill pens to computers, scanned documents and off-site access. However, in all that time our objectives have remained the same: accuracy, reliability and accessibility for the residents of the twenty eight communities that comprise Norfolk County.

Improved technology and management of records and increased levels of customer service remain areas of major focus for the Registry of Deeds. Initiatives include:

• A community outreach office hours program that brought Register Bill O'Donnell and the mobile Registry of Deeds to Cohasset on June 18, 2008.
• Free public viewing access for every document including land plans recorded by the Registry since its inception in 1793 via the internet at www.norfolkdeeds.org. The Registry regularly updates and enhances the site to include recent news, trends, press information, and answers to frequently asked questions.
• An ability for those who such as attorneys, title examiners, realtors, lenders, surveyors and civil engineers who establish an account with the Registry to print documents directly from their offices for $1.00 per page.
• A continuing technology fund investment in computer hardware in the Registry itself to insure that anyone wanting to access the records can do so.
• The expansion of the internet accessible indexing system back to 1955.
• A full service telephone and walk-in customer service center and the addition of closing rooms and tables to encourage the citizens of Norfolk County to feel comfortable in using their Registry.

Cohasset was typical of the rest of Norfolk County showing decreased real estate activity in 2008 recording a total of 213 deeds, 22% fewer than in 2007. The average price of a Cohasset real estate sale (greater than $1,000 - residential and commercial properties combined) fell 10.8% and at the end of 2008 stood at $810,988. The ongoing desirability of Cohasset real estate continues to contrast favorably with the rest of Norfolk County where the average price was $537,913. The total dollar volume of real estate sales in Cohasset for 2008 settled at $103 million, a 33% decrease from 2007. There were 525 mortgages recorded in Cohasset in 2008 which translates to 16.8% fewer than in 2007. March was the busiest 2008 month for Cohasset real estate activity accounting for 11.1% of the town's total recordings.

2008 ANNUAL REPORT OF THE CONSERVATION COMMISSION

The Cohasset Conservation Commission's bi-monthly meetings were generally scheduled to capacity to review a number of applications, including 49 Notices of Intent (NOI) and 18 Requests for Determination of Applicability (RDA) and 2 Stormwater Permits. The Cohasset Conservation Commission also conducted a large number of site visits throughout the town.

In addition to our regular proceedings, several members attended multiple meetings regarding the ongoing issues of Treat's Pond, the Harbor Health Committee and the Stormwater Management Committee.

Last year, the Commission received a $20,000 grant from the Community Preservation Act for design of the culvert at Border Street which had collapsed. Those designs were completed and went through the environmental permitting process in 2008. With the assistance of the Conservation Law Foundation, Coastal Zone Management (CZM), National Atmospheric and Oceanographic (NOAA), and the Massachusetts Department of Environmental Protection (DEP) we leveraged various grants to fund the construction of that project. However, the bid went out and came in higher than the available funds from the grants. Minor changes were made and the bid will be resubmitted in 2009 for construction.

The Commission also applied for Grants through CZM for Rain Gardens in the downtown village area. These rain gardens were designed and implemented in various locations. Their purpose is to reduce if not eliminate containments and pollution that make its way into the stormwater system and eventually empty into Cohasset Harbor. Additionally, a few years ago the Cohasset Water Commission re-opened one of the areas for the town's water supply. By implementing these rain gardens the town is protecting the harbor and water supply from pollution that would otherwise flow through these areas.

As Town Meeting passed the Stormwater Management Bylaw, the Commission held public hearings and meetings organizing and creating the regulations to that By-law. A Stormwater Agent was also selected from an RFP process. (5) Five different Engineering Firms applied. All submitted packages for review and were interviewed by the Commission. After said process, Norfolk Ram Engineers of Plymouth, MA were selected as the town's first Stormwater Agent.

Stormwater is rainwater and snowmelt that runs off lawns and streets and picks up bacteria, fertilizers, pesticides, oil and grease and other pollutants on the way to our brooks, rivers, ponds, meadows, harbors and beaches. Cohasset has a significant stormwater problem with flooding throughout town and contaminated water bodies impaired from stormwater pollution. While the bylaw does not necessarily have to prevent future development but rather ensures stormwater controls are designed for each project to prevent additional stormwater flooding and pollution leaving each site.

Projects increasing net impervious area by 500 sf will require Administrative Approval and projects altering 5,000 sf will require a Stormwater Permit from the Conservation Commission. Application and Review fees cover the cost of the Stormwater Agent.

Additionally, the Commission has been involved with requiring that (BMP's) Best Management Practices were employed on the Little Harbor Project to assist in alleviating flooding and contamination where possible.

The Commission also appropriated funds toward the Cohasset Water Commission's purchase of land for the purposes of protecting the towns watershed.

We would like to thank Alix White for her service to the Commission and congratulate Doug Wilson on becoming a voting member and Jack Creighton on becoming an Associate Member.

If you have any questions, comments or suggestions, we may reached at 781-383-4119 and have handouts regarding all bylaws and regulations of the Commission.

We would also like to thank our agent Paul Shea our Administrative Assistant Nancy Noonan for all their guidance during this busy year. We feel very privileged to have their knowledge and support.

David H. Farrag, Chairman
Richard M. Karoff, Vice-Chairman
Deborah S. Cook
Venata P. Roebuck
Sarah E. Charron
Edward S. Graham, Jr.
Douglas B. Wilson
Richard C. Perkinson (Associate)
Jack Creighton (Associate)

SOUTH SHORE
RECYCLING
COOPERATIVE
ssrc.info

The South Shore Recycling Cooperative (SSRC) is a voluntary association of sixteen South Shore towns established by Intermunicipal Agreement and Special Legislation in 1998. It was established to help member towns improve their recycling programs, and reduce the amount, toxicity and cost of disposal.

Members of the SSRC are: **Abington, Cohasset, Duxbury, Hanover, Hanson, Hingham, Holbrook, Hull, Kingston, Marshfield, Norwell, Plymouth, Rockland, Scituate, Weymouth, and Whitman.** Representatives from each member town are appointed by the chief Elected Official(s) *(list attached).*

Since its inception ten years ago, disposed tons of trash-per-household has dropped by nearly 25%, and the recycling rate for paper, cardboard, bottles and cans has risen from 16% to 22%.

In FY09, the SSRC raised its annual dues for the first time in ten years, from $4,000 to $4,500 per town. In 2008, the SSRC raised **$72,000** through these fees, and **$6,000** in outreach sponsorships from Covanta SEMASS. Those funds pay for the services of the Executive Director and for waste reduction and recycling activities that benefit member towns. The SSRC estimates that in 2008 these activities **saved Member Towns at least $151,000** (Not all figures are in at the time of publication. Highlighted numbers are from 2007).

MATERIALS MANAGEMENT

Household Hazardous Product Collections

The SSRC extended its contract for the collection and disposal of **household hazardous products** with Clean Harbors. By using the SSRC contract, Member Towns avoided a setup fee, paid about 12% less than the per-car State contract rates, **saving our towns about $38,000.** They also avoided the administrative time to bid, schedule and publicize them.

2,661 residents attended the fifteen collections held in 2008. The contract also enabled **125 residents and businesses** to attend other Member Towns' collections using the **reciprocal arrangement.**

The SSRC advertised the events with several thousand **flyers** delivered to town halls and libraries, and ongoing press releases in all **local papers and cable** TV. The Executive Director helped run twelve of the collections, handed out relevant information, provided signs, calculated the **proper billing** for the vendor to ensure that discounts and allowances were credited and visitors billed properly, and assisted with billing issues.

Construction and Bulky Waste

Through an arrangement facilitated by the SSRC with the **Bourne ISWMF**, Member Towns enjoyed a disposal rate of $75/ton for construction **and bulky waste**, which is **$12.50/ton** less **than the ga**te fee. With generation of **4,799 tons**, eight Member Towns saved **$60,000.**

Cohasset, Hanover, Kingston and Scituate save on mattress recycling by using an SSRC arranged program with Miller Recycling in Plainville to store, transport and process mattresses for $14/each. This saved the participating towns approximately **$14,600** on the **2,091 mattresses** they collected.

Compost and Brush

The SSRC extended the contracts with no pricing increases for **brush grinding and compost screening,** which had been awarded to Letourneau Corp. and Lion's Head Organics. The grinding contract was used by three of our towns for 9 days. Data on screening contract usage was unavailable.

Mercury Bearing Waste

The SSRC helped its Member towns, even Hull **and Marshfield**, which don't contract with SEMASS for disposal, to maximize their benefits from the **Material** Separation **Plan (MSP)**, including the provision by SEMASS of digital thermometers and thermostats for exchange, reimbursement for mercury disposal costs, and a Universal Waste Shed for Abington.

Paper

The SSRC has facilitated the siting of dozens of Abitibi Paper Retriever containers in all of our communities. In 2008, they captured an additional **1,013** tons of paper from the waste stream, and returned over **$6,000** to the municipalities and local organizations.

Textiles

The SSRC introduced Bay State Textiles, which pays $50/ton for used clothing and textiles, to the managers. 2008 figures are not yet available, but in 2007, eight towns recycled **280** tons of material through them, for which they were paid **$14,017**.

Books

The SSRC introduced GotBooks, which pays $100/ton for used books and other media, to SSRC members. 2008 figures are not yet available, but in 2007, thirteen SSRC towns set up twenty book collection sites through them, and repurposed 218.3 tons of material, earning $19,421.

PUBLIC OUTREACH:

Mass Recycles Paper

This statewide Campaign grew out of a 2006 SSRC pilot project. It is run by MassRecycle, and chaired by the SSRC Executive Director. The goal is to recover an additional million tons of paper each year from the Mass. trash. The Campaign has broad support from MassDEP, US EPA and the recycling industry.

Most of our towns, and half across the State, have signed the Mass Recycles Paper resolution and receive supporting outreach materials, including thousands of bill inserts. SSRC communities stand to gain about $500K/year in avoided disposal cost and revenue from the sale of waste paper.

Press Contacts

The SSRC releases articles and is a resource to the local press about waste reduction, recycling, and the proper disposal of hazardous waste. The following articles and op-eds were released to and published by the local and regional newspapers in 2008:

Don't trash your recycling efforts Dec. 19

SSRC to host **10th** Anniversary **"Shredabrations"** November

South Shore towns recycling more, wasting less August 26

Hull **Re**-joins the SSRC August 13

Al Gore commends SSRC efforts, **E**arth Day Celebration April 17

Legislators talk trash with Municipal Managers; Rep. Hynes receives award April 1

A real paper chase: Too good for the trash   Patriot Ledger, Jan. 31

Resident Contacts

The Executive Director fielded **129** calls and emails from Member Towns' residents in CY08 to answer questions, mostly about hazardous and difficult to manage product disposal.

Website

ssrc.info provides town-specific recycling information, household hazardous product collection information, SSRC meeting minutes and annual reports, press releases, a quarterly newsletter, and links to other sites. It was overhauled this past fall, and logged 3,745 visitors in 2008.

Marshfield Fair Recycling

With assistance from MassDEP and the Town of Marshfield, the SSRC supported recycling at the Marshfield Fair for the fifth year. While public education was the main benefit, seven tons of material was also recycled and composted.

Recycling containers from a previous grant were loaned out for use at Hanover Day, and are available for other area events.

ADVICE, ASSISTANCE AND NETWORKING.

The Executive Director's help is frequently sought by the solid waste managers. She maintains regular contact with them, updates them on current trends, and advises on specific needs each town has.

A sample of the assistance she provided and problems she helped solve in 2008 included:

- evaluation of Covanta SEMASS' extension proposal and alternatives for our four Tier One towns
- collaborating with Cape Cod communities on a regional disposal contract negotiation
- attendance at Board/ committee meetings in Hanson, Kingston, Marshfield, Plymouth and Weymouth
- evaluation of electronics and scrap metal processors' pricing and practices
- identifying and correcting errors on Data Sheets submitted to MassDEP
- collection, evaluation and sharing of recycling and disposal cost and tonnage data
- guidance on PAYT bag vendors
- research on outlets for expanded polystyrene for Marshfield
- sharing State Contract information on bins and carts upon request by Plymouth and Scituate
- provision of recycling stickers for barrels and bins
- delivery of free rechargeable battery collection boxes to municipal collection locations
- publicity for Marshfield & Weymouth recycling contests and Abington's Universal Waste Shed
- distribution of a ten page directory of service providers.

Paper pricing

The SSRC subscribes to *Official Board Markets* on which most towns' paper rebates are based, calculates rebates that should be paid to the municipalities by their recyclers and updates the managers each month.

Quarterly Newsletter

The SSRC publishes a quarterly newsletter filled with information of immediate interest to the South Shore solid waste community. The newsletter is circulated to over 350 town officials, legislators, regulators and volunteers, and is posted online at http://ssrc.info/newsletters/newsletters.htm.

Monthly Meetings

The SSRC provides networking opportunities and information sharing at our well-attended monthly meetings. Each meeting features a guest speaker. Solid waste collection, disposal, recycling service, outreach, pricing and proposed laws and regulations are discussed.

ADVOCACY

The Executive Director attends policy meetings, forums and conferences hosted by MassDEP, Solid Waste Association of North America, the Council of SEMASS Communities, MassRecycle, and the Northeast Resource Recovery Association. She shares what she learns with the Managers, and relays the Managers' concerns to the professional and State organizations and regulators.

The SSRC held a Legislative Breakfast in May at which Rep. Frank Hynes (D-Marshfield) was recognized with our "Recycling Hero" award for his sponsorship and support of bills and budget items that promote waste reduction. Sen. Robert Creedon also spoke at the event.

The SSRC exists to serve its member towns by facilitating their solid waste disposal and recycling functions. It always welcomes suggestions on how it can better serve its Members.

Respectfully submitted,

Claire Sullivan, Executive Director, South Shore Recycling Cooperative

2008 REPORT OF THE HOUSING PARTNERSHIP COMMITTEE

The Cohasset Housing Partnership had an active 2008 working towards the goal of providing more affordable housing options for Cohasset. With the much appreciated support of the Board of Selectmen and Town Meeting, a Housing Trust was created that will eventually assume the duties of the partnership and will provide a vehicle through which funds for affordable housing development can be raised and distributed. The Partnership also continued to investigate a number of other possibilities of creating affordable options from existing housing stock. We are grateful for the support of our efforts by the Board of Selectmen and the community at large.

Clark Brewer, co-chair	Tom Callahan, co-chair
Margy Charles	Jim Hamilton
Jim Lagroterria	Taffy Nothnagle
Steve Lucitt	Mary Grayken
Judi Barrett, consultant	

2008 ANNUAL REPORT OF THE FIRE, RESCUE AND EMERGENCY MEDICAL SERVICES DEPARTMENT

I hereby submit the Annual Report for the year ending December 31, 2008
The Fire, Rescue and Emergency Medical Services Department responded to 2515 calls for service this year.

The Department responded to **1548** fire related incidents:

Building / Structure Fires	48
Outdoor Fires / Illegal Burning	27
Motor Vehicle Crashes	97
Motor Vehicle Fires	3
Hazardous Materials Responses	14
Automatic Fire Alarm Responses	208
Investigations	273
Inspections	387
Downed Power Lines	39
Lockout / Lock-in	24
Assistance	30
Mutual Aid Fire Responses	26
Miscellaneous Responses	372

The Department responded to **967** medical emergencies **and** transported **766** patients to hospitals.

Basic Life Support (BLS) Transports	250
Advanced Life Support (ALS) Transports	424
Mutual Aid Ambulance BLS Transports	37
Mutual Aid Ambulance ALS Transports	51
Med Flight Helicopter Transports	~

The following fees were returned to the **General** Fund:

Ambulance Transport Fees	$366,500.00
10A Permit Fees	$4,559.00
Burning Permit Fees	$1,210.00
TOTAL	$372,269.00

APPARATUS

The Fire Department is currently operating with the following apparatus:

Engine 1 - 1994 Pierce - 1,750 Gallons per Minute (G.P.M.) Pumping Engine

Engine 2 - 1987 Pierce - 1,250 G.P.M. Pumping Engine

Engine 3 - 2001 HME/Central States - 1,250 G.P.M. Pumping Engine

Ladder 1 - 2004 Pierce - 105 Foot Aerial Ladder Truck

Squad 1 - 2000 Ford - 4 wheel drive - 500 G.P.M. pump

Rescue 3 - 2001 Ford - E-450 - Ambulance

Car 20 - 1995 Ford - 4 wheel drive - Incident Command Vehicle

Rescue Craft - 1993 Avon - 14ft, Inflatable Boat with Trailer

In the past year two members of the Department retired.

Acting Lieutenant Randall W. Rosano was appointed on August 11, 1977 and retired on July 1, 2008. Acting Lieutenant Rosano served the Cohasset Fire Department and the citizens of Cohasset with honor and dedication for over thirty years.

Firefighter James E. Fiori was appointed on August 11, 1977 and retired on June 30, 2008. Firefighter Fiori served the Cohasset Fire Department and the citizens of Cohasset with honor and dedication for over thirty years.

In conclusion, I would like to extend to the Citizens of Cohasset, Board of Selectmen, Town Manager, Department Heads, Members of Town Departments and all Town Committees my gratitude and appreciation for their support and assistance.

To the Officers and Firefighters of the Cohasset Fire Department my sincere thanks for your dedication and consummate professionalism while serving the Town of Cohasset.

Respectfully Submitted,

Robert D. Silvia
Chief of Department

UNIFORM CRIME REPORT   2008 STATISTICS

Offense	Reported
Robbery	1
Assaults	26
Breaking and Entering	63
Larceny	70
Larceny of Motor Vehicle	2
Vandalism	56
Criminal Complaints Sought	93
Motor Vehicle Accidents Investigated	133
Motor Vehicle Citations Issued	768
Parking Tickets Issued	680
Residential & Business Alarms answered	444
Stolen Motor Vehicles Recovered	6
Emergency and other calls for service	12,928
Department Vehicle Mileage	201,481
Special Details	2,533
Domestic Violence Cases Investigated	25
FID Cards Issued	15
LTC Issued/Renewed	38

RECORD OF ARRESTS 2008

Offense	Male	Female	Juvenile
Robbery	2		
Burglary	1		
Breaking and Entering	5		
Assault and Battery	7	4	
Assault to Murder	1		
Assault and Battery with a Dangerous Weapon		1	
Operating Under the Influence of Liquor	8	9	
Violation of Drug Laws	16	2	
Warrants	14	1	
Larceny	2		
Larceny of Motor Vehicle	1		
Minor in Possession of Alcohol	10	2	
Sell/Deliver Alcohol to Minors		1	
Receiving Stolen Property			
Motor Vehicle Violation	7		
Protective Custody	23	5	
Malicious Destruction of Property	2		
Violation of Protective Order	1		
Courtesy Booking	1	1	
Disorderly Conduct	2	1	

Record of Arrests 2008 Continued	Male	Female	Juvenile

Utter False Checks/Note	2			
Trespass	1			
Trespass on Railroad	2			
Resist Arrest	1			
Chins Runaway				
Failure to Stop for Police				
Public Drinking	-			
	110	28		6

TOTAL **144**

FEES RETURNED TO GENERAL FUND

Court Fines & Assessments	$3,200.00
Parking Violations	$18,435.00
Paid Detail Surcharge	$21,914.86
License Fees	$950.00
Request for Police Reports	$871.00
False Alarms/Billing	$400.00

TOTAL **$45,770.86**

Respectfully submitted,
James M. Hussey, Chief of Police

2008 REPORT OF THE OFFICE OF EMERGENCY MANAGEMENT

During 2008 the Office of Emergency Management continued to enhance Cohasset's ability to respond and deal with various situations, threats and disasters.

Here are some of our accomplishments:

- The Board of Health continued to train and expand their Volunteer Medical Reserve Corps.

- Our Local Emergency Planning Committee (LEPC) met quarterly to assess, develop and refine Emergency Response plans and procedures.

- We continued to develop plans for continuance of government operations should a disaster take Town Hall out of service.

- In conjunction with the School Departments Safety Plan, we have put Public Safety Radios in the schools.

- An Incident Support Trailer was added to the Fire Department fleet.

- In conjunction with MEMA we began to develop plans for a Training Exercise to be held in 2009.

We appreciate your support of our work and would like to thank all the Town Departments for their participation with us during the year.

Respectfully Submitted,

Arthur L. Lehr, Director of Emergency Management
Glenn A. Pratt, Deputy Director
James M. Hussey, Police Chief
Robert D. Silva, Fire Chief
Dr. Joseph Godzik, Health Agent

GENERAL:

The Department of Public Works is a town service organization responsible for providing essential services for the citizens of Cohasset. Services provided by this department include construction, maintenance and repair of streets, sidewalks and storm drainage systems; maintenance and repair of vehicles and equipment; maintenance of parks, cemeteries, athletic fields and off-street parking facilities; the transfer of public refuse and recyclables; snow removal and ice control; maintenance and/or removal of town owned trees; filling and maintenance of the fuel tanks.

In addition to providing routine maintenance throughout the year, the following projects were completed by or under the direction of the DPW during the last year:

Rebuilt or repaired 15 catch basins.

Cleaned 440 catch basins with the truck basin cleaner and another 44 by hand.

Dug out the flapper on Atlantic Avenue 21 times to alleviate flooding.

Rebuilt or replaced 300' of fences.

Replaced or repaired 44 traffic and street signs and devices.

In an effort to control algae in Little Harbor, we opened and closed the cat dam gates each month from April to December.

Transferred 1,621 tons of solid waste and 708 tons of C&D. Recycled 733 tons of mixed paper products, 133 tons of scrap metals and cans, 64 tons of plastics, 142 tons of glass and 1,675 gallons of waste oil. Over 300 ton of leaves and brush were processed. The amount of solid waste that is transported to the Semass Facility decreased by 134 ton from the previous year and saved the town approximately $11,000.00 Most recyclable totals increased with the exceptions of metal and paper products. Overall the town's recycling rate is among the highest in the state. This is something all residents can be proud of due to their recycling habits.

Cleaned and adjusted the self-regulating tidal gate twice a year as required.

Plowed and/or sanded 62 times.

Removed various dead or diseased trees and planted new trees and shrubs throughout the town.

Resurfaced 270 feet of sidewalk at various locations.

Oversaw construction of 120' of sidewalk on Border Street.

Conducted and recorded 31 internments at the various town owned cemeteries.

Held 7 brush days for residential brush chipping.

Rebuilt the benches at the Duck Pond.

Installed benches at the Beechwood Ballpark.

Prepared $1.404 million Annual Operating Budget and $110,000 Capital Improvement Program for Fiscal Year 2010.

The Department of Public Works would like to extend our appreciation to all town employees, boards and committees for their continued assistance and support during the past year.

Respectfully submitted,

Carl A. Sestito
D.P.W. Superintendent

2008 ANNUAL REPORT OF THE BOARD OF WATER COMMISSIONERS

In 2008, The Water Department had many significant accomplishments, including:

- Substantially completed the 1.97 miles of water main replacements in the Little Harbor area, in the cooperative project with the Sewer Department.
- Won the national PISCES Award from the Environmental Protection Agency for our raingarden project, which preliminary testing showed is dramatically effective in removing nutrients and pollutants from stormwater going into Lily Pond, and constructed an additional 4 rain gardens in the Lily Pond Watershed.
- Town Meeting voted to designate 313 acres of land now owned for a conservation restriction, completing the Water Commissions aggressive 5-year land acquisition program in the Lily Pond watershed.

WATER COMMISSIONERS. At the April 5, 2008 Town Election, Water Commissioner Glenn Pratt was reelected to another 3-year term. At the Board's reorganization meeting, Commissioner Pratt was re-elected as Chairman, Commissioner Nathaniel Palmer was elected Vice-Chairman, and Commissioner John McNabb was elected Clerk.

THE COHASSET WATER DEPARTMENT provides water for domestic consumption and fire protection to about 90% of the Town of Cohasset. Our service area does not include the North Cohasset area, which is serviced by the Aquarion Water Company of Massachusetts (formerly known as the Hingham Mass-American Water Company). The Cohasset Water Department system encompasses about 36 miles of water mains, 2,431 service connections, and 376 fire hydrants, and 564 valves. The American Water Company, under contract to the Board of Water Commissioners, operates and maintains the Water Department under the control of the Water Commission.

During 2008, a total of 305,991,942 gallons of water were produced and pumped to the distribution system from the Lily Pond Treatment Plant and the Ellms Meadow Wellfield. The minimum demand for the year was 483,850 gallons on February 27, 2008, and the maximum demand was 1,963,980 gallons pumped on July 16, 2008. An additional 35,016,056 gallons was pumped to Hingham and sold to Linden Ponds.

FINANCIAL MANAGEMENT. The Water Department is entirely self-supporting (as an Enterprise Fund) from user fees and other fees and charges (which does not impact non-customers living in North Cohasset who are served by the Aquarion Water Company in Hingham). We do not receive any property tax revenue from the Town of Cohasset. In 2008, we received over $240,000 from the sale of 35,016,056 gallons of water to the Linden Ponds development in Hingham, which commenced on November 17, 2005 when the Route 3A pump station went online.

DISTRIBUTION SYSTEM IMPROVEMENTS. In the 14 years since the water emergency in 1994, caused because of deferred maintenance in the distribution system, we have replaced or rehabilitated about 20.5 miles or about 57% of the 36 miles of water mains in the distribution, which has improved water service throughout Cohasset and has resulted in major measurable improvements in public safety by increasing fire flows in fire hydrants.

In 2008, continuing our long range water distribution system capital improvements plan first prepared by Tutela Engineering in 1996, we installed a total of 10,400 feet (1.97 miles) of water mains, many in a the Little Harbor Project conducted joint with the Sewer Department:

- Nichols Road, Smalzel Way, Carvel Cove and Orchard Cove- 4,040 feet to replace undersized water mains and new services
- Highland Avenue and North Main Street- 3,310 feet to replace undersized 120 year old water mains and new services to improve water quality and supply
- Jerusalem Road- 1,100 feet of new water main from Atlantic Avenue to Jerusalem Road Drive to replace 100+year old pipe and to allow for the planned drainage improvements, also provide new water services
- Keene Way – 890 feet (off of Beach St) to replace undersized water mains and new services.

- Little Harbor Road – 820 feet to replace undersized water mains and new services.
- Rust Way – 270 feet to replace undersized water mains and new service in coordination with new sewer line.
- Steeps Rocks Way and Jerusalem Road – upgraded water mains and valve configuration at the intersection to improve separation with sewer and other utilities
- Golf Course Road – 1,400 feet of new water main as part of a master planning effort to eliminate the dead and create a Cedar Street water main loop.
- Stanton Road- 750 feet of new main to replace the old main that was prone to breaks (3 breaks/leaks in the previous year)
- Construction oversight on various private developments such as Manor Way, Old Colony Development on Route 3A, and the Scituate Hill Industrial site project.

LITTLE HARBOR PROJECT. The Little Harbor Project is one of the largest public works projects ever conducted by the Town of Cohasset. The expansion of the sewer collection system was required by a regulatory administration consent order and took several years of planning and design. The Water Department, during this period, adjusted the scheduling of planned improvements to replace water mains in streets in the Little Harbor area. This scheduling was done to limit the planned water and sewer line construction in the streets to only one disruption to the residents. The Water and Sewer Commission met prior to the selection of a contractor to assess the advantages and disadvantages of conducting the work as two separate projects or as one joint project between the two Commissions. A joint project was determined to be the best approach for the Town.

The contractors' bids were received at the end of June 2007, and construction began in September 2007 with a completion date of August 2009. The Water Department is furnishing the material for the project and the contractor (L.M. Holdings, LLC) is installing the water mains, gate valves, hydrants and service connections (from the main to the property line). While all streets in the Little Harbor area will have a new low pressure sewer installed, only select streets are having water main improvements. Based on master planning, as well as operation conditions, water main improvements were made on Deep Run, Keene Way, Little Harbor Road, Nichols Road, Orchard Cove, Smalzel Way, Caravel Cove, North Main Street (Green St. to Depot Court), Highland Avenue (North Main to Robert Jason), White Head Road, Jerusalem Road (Atlantic to Jerusalem Road Drive). This represents approximately 14,700 linear feet of new main, and 150 new service connections. In addition to these planned water improvements, several services and pipes were repaired during the construction of the sewer mains.

Conducting such a large scale project has included input from several Town Departments. The Police and Fire departments have been involved in traffic related issues. The Special Assistants to the Town Manager have been involved in coordinating and mitigating the construction related impacts on various activities associated with the Little Harbor area and the Town Common such as the weekly Farmers Market, Senior Center events, nursery school activities and various charity events/road races. The Special Assistants have also supported the Department of Public Works involvement in the project. The Department of Public Works is involved in matters related to paving and drainage. Having all the various departments involved in the project has allowed decisions to be made that are best for the Town. Such decisions have included traffic management, repairs to the existing drainage system as encountered during construction, and repairs to the Jerusalem Road retaining wall after the sewer main was constructed. Decisions were also made based on input from residents. Input from residents was received at the staging, by telephone and at "neighborhood meetings." The neighborhood meetings were held before construction began in certain areas to explain the sequence of the construction activities and their day to day impacts to residents.

By the end of 2008, the majority of the water improvements have been completed and approximately 30-40% of the streets remain to be sewered. The majority of the Water Department's work expected to be conducted in 2009 is related to restoration of roadway shoulders and pavement. The Water and Sewer Departments utilized pavement pricing and services available to the Department of Public Works through the South Shore Consortium (provided by the Metro Area Planning Council) to control the paving work and costs. Note: The contractor is still responsible for patching the trench while the Town is responsible for preparing and overlaying the street with either the binder (bottom) or finish (top) course of pavement.

WATER MAIN BREAKS. In 2008 the Water Department responded to and repaired over 60 water main breaks. Many were the result of work being conducted to install sewer in the Little Harbor are, while others included leaks in service lines, broken services, and breaks for other reasons.

LEAD TESTING. In June the required tests of water sampled at the tap resulted in 5 sites out of 40 over the "Action Level" of 15 parts per billion which, because more than 90% of sampled sites exceeded that level, required the Water Department to issue public notices to customers and residents. The required public education materials were mailed to residents on October 15, 2008. In November we conducted another round of testing which resulted in only 4 sites out of 40 exceeding the Action Level, so no further public education efforts were required. In 2008 the Water Department offered free lead tests to customers; 46 residents requested testing and out of those 46 only 4 exceeded the action level.

LILY POND WATER TREATMENT PLANT IMPROVEMENTS. In 2008, the Water Commission: repaired the concrete base structure in the Sludge Lagoons, installed an underdrain system in Lagoons, installed a filter air scour system, installed new Rapid Mix Tank motors and propellers, and replaced the Raw Water flow meter with new Magnetic Meter.

WATER STORAGE TANKS. The Bear Hill tank was drained, about 2" of sludge was removed. The tank inspector was called in and the tank was inspected and then refilled. Both of the tanks have RFP's for the installation of antennas for cell phones. Scituate Hill tank is in the process of being evaluated for a different access to it due to Avalon project. Scituate Hill is due to be cleaned and inspected spring of 2009. Both of the tank mixers appear to be doing a very good job.

GATE EXERCISING. In 2008, the department performed its Gate Exercising program. Every gate in the distribution system, with the exception of streets that were under construction from the Little Harbor Water/Sewer project, were located in the GPS (Geographic Positioning System), cleaned out, and exercised. An inventory list of all gates was developed from this program. This process was performed systematically, street by street. The total number of gates exercised was 523. There are a 8 gates that need to be repaired, which will be scheduled to be completed in the next few years.

WATER METER & AUTOMATIC METER READING SYSTEM. In 2008 we evaluated various options to replace the individual water meters installed at each of our customers throughout our service area. We last replaced meters on a town wide basis in 1995. Industry standards suggest meters be replaced about every 7 - 15 years to assist in equitably distributing the cost of providing water to all customers. In 2008 we solicited bids to supply (1) residential water meters and (2) a fixed network automatic meter reading system. We are presently evaluating this issue.

FIRE HYDRANTS & VALVES. In 2007 we replaced 27 fire hydrants and installed 10 new hydrants. We have also replaced 20 gate valves and installed 4 new gate valves as part of the Little Harbor water-sewer project. All fire hydrants and gate valves have been identified and listed in a database that is used to track their condition and maintenance.

WELLFIELDS. The Sohier Street Wells have been abandoned because of the proximity to the Greenbush right of way. With mitigation funding from the MBTA, we have conducted exploratory well work by drilling a 4-inch exploratory bedrock to depth of 400 vertical feet well to investigate the water quantity and quality at potential new sources located near Mill Lane. Unfortunately the investigation has only encountered a 30-35 gpm supply source. Due to the limited quantity of water this location was abandoned as a source of supply.

The Ellms Meadow Wells produced 4,748,140 gallons before they went off-line on August 12th. They were taken off-line because testing showed 9 colonies of total coliform in the raw water, but zero colonies in the finished water. Further testing weeks later confirmed the presence of coliform in raw water but at a much smaller level. There was zero algae or e-coli. We kept it off line for the rest of the year to do more testing and confirm that that there was no threat to the water quality.

GEOGRAPHIC INFORMATION SYSTEMS (GIS). During 2008 the Water Department continued their ongoing program of developing their Geographic Information System (GIS) capabilities and mapping. In the first phases of this effort all of the available mapping for the Town was compiled into a comprehensive, Town-wide map. Over the last year the Water Department acquired Geographic Positioning System (GPS) equipment and collected location data on various features of our water infrastructure including pipes, valves and hydrants. Using this data, a new atlas of the water system was prepared by Environmental Partners Group that is current and accurate. This atlas is available to the staff as a hard-copy map and can also be accessed electronically through the web via the internet.

Because the Water Department staff continues to actively use this GPS equipment, the water atlas will be able to be easily updated as modifications or expansions to the system are made. In addition, this GIS information and GPS equipment can be used by the Water Department staff to field locate a valve, hydrant or other piece of the water system that needs repair or maintenance.

The Water Department has also integrated their GIS mapping with information on each service account using a new program called WaterTracker. This program allows the Department to catalogue and readily access information for each property such as their water service (tie card) information, water meter information and billing histories.

WATERSHED PROTECTION. The Water Commission employs Norfolk Ram Group to conduct watershed protection work for the Water Department. In 2008 this work included:

- Review of Watershed Threats. This work has included ongoing review of activities at the former Norfolk Conveyor, which is a state 21E hazardous waste site, and near the site of the Avalon development. The adequacy, completeness and progress of the site assessment and proposed waste site clean-up at Norfolk Conveyor continues to be reviewed, and our consultants have provided additional comments to DEP and the property owner concerning the 21E submittals of record (site assessments and remediation plans). In addition, because this site is proposed for residential redevelopment with an on-site wastewater treatment plant, our consultants have been reviewing the project application for a Groundwater Discharge Permit (a GWDP), which is required from DEP prior to discharge of treated wastewater). The Water Commission had appealed the GWDP which was issued by the DEP July 20, 2007, but in 2008 withdrew the appeal as part of a settlement with Avalon which allows the development to go forward.
- Surface Water Supply Protection Plan (SWSPP) update – as part of on-going watershed management, which is based on the SWSPP, Norfolk Ram Group continued to consult with the Water Commission on the status of progress in implementing the SWSPP, and assisted with planning of future issues. Stormwater treatment (Rain Garden Projects) and Land Acquisition (via grant applications), have been the two most important proactive elements of the SWSPP that are currently underway.
- Stream Gauging –Monitoring continued for the four stream gauge locations that track hydrologic conditions and tributary flow contributions within the watershed. Norfolk Ram Group has coordinated with American Water to visit all of the monitoring gauges on a monthly basis to download stream depth and temperature data that is collected hourly by the automated field devices. Norfolk Ram Group has been compiling and interpreting this watershed data, and data is shared and stored on American Water computers as well.

LAND ACQUISITION and Open Space Designation. In 2008 the Commission continued with land acquisitions, culminating in Town Meeting action to designate 313 acres of land under a conservation restriction. The acquired land that has been funded through numerous grant applications under the Drinking Water Supply Protection Grant / Land Purchase Grant Program that has provided 50% EOEEA grant funds for land purchases application require a conservation restriction as a condition of the grant.

NOVEMBER 13 SPECIAL TOWN MEETING. At the Special Town Meeting, the Town adopted two articles proposed by the Water Commissioners:

Article 5. RELEASE OF EASEMENTS. Passage of this Article allows the Water Department to abandon two easements for Water Department access on Nichols Road and Pleasant Street which are no longer needed. The easement on Nichols Road is no longer needed because the water main has already been relocated from private property to a roadway during the Little Harbor area water and sewer improvements program. The easement located off 100 Pleasant Street now is used for both a water main from the Bear Hill tank to Pleasant Street and for vehicular access from Pleasant Street to the tank. That easement is being moved because of the development for two house lots adjacent to the easement which would result in putting the easement very close to two front yards. The water main connecting the Bear Hill Tank to Pleasant Street will be relocated, at the developers expense, to connect the Tank to Bancroft Road, which will improve the water flow in the Hillside Area. The vehicular access will be moved to an already existing Water Department easement from the tank which connects the tank to Reservoir Road above the top of Pleasant Street.

Article 6 .CONSERVATION RESTRICTIONS FOR WATERSHED PROTECTION. Passage of this Article starts the process to place a Conservation Restriction on 313 acres of land, in the "Brass Kettle Brook Conservation Area," which is land owned by the Water Commission and the Town located in the Lily Pond Watershed. This land acquisition program, and this final step of placing the Conservation Restriction, is a significant accomplishment of the Water Commission and the Town in their ongoing program for protection of the Town's public drinking water supply. Studies show that acquisition of watershed land, especially in large contiguous parcels such as been done here, is a proven means to protect drinking water quality from contamination and to reduce treatment plant costs.

Passage of the Article authorized the Board of Selectmen and Board of Water Commissioners to petition the Legislature to pass a Special Act authorizing them to impose a Conservation Restriction on this land restricting its use to conservation, open space, and water protection purposes. Once the Special Act has been passed by the Legislature, the Board of Selectmen and Board of Water Commissioners will be able to grant the Conservation Restriction to the Trustees of Reservations.

Of the total 313 acres, 191 acres have been acquired over the last five years by the Board of Water Commissioners for a total of about $3,000,000 with funds from the Water Department, the Cohasset Community Preservation Fund , the Cohasset Conservation Trust, the Massachusetts Executive Office of Environmental Affairs Land Acquisition Grants, the Cohasset Conservation Commission, Trustees of Reservations, and private donations. The state grants require the placement of a Conservation Restriction as a condition of receiving the grants. The other 122 acres is land already owned by the Town or the Water Department in the area.

PISCES AWARD FOR THE RAIN GARDEN PROJECT. The Town of Cohasset has been awarded the prestigious PISCES award by the Environmental Protection Agency for the raingarden project, because of the innovative funding method that was used for the project.

In calendar year 2008 a total of 4 additional rain gardens were constructed. In addition to the completed work, also during this year, 7 other rain gardens were completed with plantings along Route 3A. There are 2 rain gardens being planned for construction in 2009. These proposed gardens along with those already competed, result in a total of 35 rain gardens along with 2 bioretention swales and the Rte 3A oil/water separator.

The Board of Water Commissioners continues to implement a program of improving water quality in the Town. A key piece of this initiative is to treat the pollution at its source. In order to accomplish this goal, rain gardens are being installed within the Town's right-of-ways, drainage easements and on Town property. Rain gardens are depressed planting beds, constructed with special soil mix and plantings, which collect "first flush" stormwater flowing along the edge of roads and allow it to infiltrate into the soil, where natural biological and chemical processes reduce the level of pollutants and nutrients in the run-off. Stormwater which has passed through the rain gardens is returned to the existing drainage ways. Norfolk Ram Group, on behalf of the Water Commission, worked closely with the Cohasset Garden Club to determine appropriate plantings.

This stormwater improvement project was extended one year and is entering its final year (completion and close-out due in June 2009), utilizing funds from our Section 319 Grant ($255,000) and the 2% low interest loans ($497,500) from the Clean Water SRF (CWSRF) program. Over the first half of calendar year 2009 we will continue to implement both structural and non-structural solutions for eliminating and/or reducing nonpoint source pollution in the watershed for Lily Pond and the Aaron River Watershed. The s.319 grant was awarded in 2003; we submitted the formal loan application for the CWSRF loans on October 15, 2004.

Thirty-two (32) rain gardens have been constructed to date in areas that are tributary to Peppermint Brook and Lily Pond, such as areas around the Clay Spring Road development, Pond Street, Route 3A, and King Street; and areas tributary to Aaron River Reservoir. There is also a demonstration rain garden at the Lily Pond Water Treatment Plant and a bio-swale constructed along the Plant's driveway, which were the first constructed in Town.

In the summer of 2008 we completed construction under the final two contracts for the construction of 4 additional rain gardens; and 7 other rain gardens were completed with plantings along Route 3A. Only two (2) remain to be constructed in the Spring of 2009. When fully completed, a total of thirty six (36) stormwater capture locations will be addressed. This Project utilizes structural best management practice (BMP) solutions and incorporates low impact development (LID) strategies wherever possible to contain and minimize off-site flows and pollutant loading in these areas. Structural BMPs being implemented include hooded catch basins, bioretention facilities (a.k.a. rain gardens), roadside swales with biofilters and spill containment oil/water separator facilities.

NHESP Surface Water Monitoring Program- In May, July and October 2008, biological surface water sampling was conducted as part of the Lily Pond Attenuated Bluet Monitoring Plan required by the Natural Heritage and Endangered Species Program of the Commonwealth of Massachusetts, Division of Fisheries & Wildlife. This trophic state monitoring program included sample collection at three locations within Lily Pond to enable NHESP to assess potential impacts from the installation of the in-Pond aeration system.

RAIN GARDENS AT ELLMS MEADOW. In calendar year 2008 the Water Department cooperated with the Town on an additional stormwater improvement project that benefits the Ellms Meadow Wellfield. The Town completed installation of one (1) rain garden and two (2) constructed wetlands at the intersection of Norfolk and Cushing Roads. The one rain garden will intercept and treat stormwater at a final catch basin in Norfolk Road near the intersection with Cushing Road; and the two constructed wetlands, located on the north side of Cushing Road at this intersection, will intercept "first flush" stormwater from two (one 10-inch and one 12-inch diameter) drainage outfall pipes that exist in that area and that discharge toward the Zone 1 for the wellfield. These new stormwater BMPs were part of a larger project that was designed by Norfolk Ram and funded in part by a state CZM grant plus Cohasset matching funds which included Cohasset Preservation Committee funds.

LILY POND AERATION SYSTEM. The in-pond aeration system consists of a pilot-program of five aeration disks that have been installed in the deeper sections of Lily Pond. These low-disturbance aeration disks will help to increase the dissolved oxygen levels in the deeper sections of Lily Pond, helping to prevent manganese from being solubilized and entering the treatment plant. The heavy vegetation in Lily Pond may limit the aeration system's ability to disperse dissolved oxygen. The pilot program for the operation of the in-pond aeration system went into operation at the end of December 2007 and ran until December 2008.

In December the Water Commission voted to allow skating on Lily Pond and turn the aeration system off for the Winter. The aeration system has not shown conclusive results one way or the other as to its effectiveness. There are too many seasonal variable to know if the changes in raw water quality are due to the aeration system or normal seasonal fluctuation.

To be clear, with these matters (such as the specific impact of the aeration system) there is no empirical measurement since that would require eliminating everything else in effect and just measuring the impact of aeration within a controlled environment. It does appear there has been a positive effect on manganese removal due to the aeration system, and indeed there are many other benefits to the pond in water quality and its overall ecosystem.

The greatest impact on manganese removal comes from optimized plant operations. The team at the plant has done an extraordinary job at manganese removal, which is measurable in testing and visible in the distribution system. This is a function of both the treatment process and externalities such as aeration. Last year, in its first year of operation, we needed to run the aeration system continuously for a period of time which overlapped with Winter. It would not have been possible to measure any result had we not run it continuously, nor would the necessary cumulative affect been possible if we had started then stopped.

Now that we are beyond the initial start-up phase and the aeration system has been in operation for over a year, we are able to shut it down for a limited period of time. The Water Commission voted unanimously to shut it down for the winter in the hopes of allowing skating on the pond this year. We take to heart

to desire to have recreational access to the pond and do everything we can to help accommodate this.

MANGANESE REMOVAL. The Water Commissions on-going plant process optimization has resulted in major improvements in the removal of manganese from raw water, which reduces the incidences of discolored water experienced by customers. These improvements included: switching from Potassium Permanganate to Sodium Permanganate, dosing Sodium Permanganate based on the residual in the flocculation basins, increased air flow from the aeration system compressor, and a variety of dosing changes for pH and Permanganate based on changes in raw water conditions – to more finely tune the chemical additions to reduce manganese and improve water quality.

NEWWA CONFERENCES. At the September 26 Fall Conference of the New England Water Works Association (NEWWA), Commissioner McNabb presented a paper, *"Analysis of the Massachusetts Drinking Water Infrastructure."* In the paper, McNabb described the $8.5 billion shortfall in funding needed over the next 20 years to adequately maintain and upgrade the Massachusetts drinking water infrastructure. The presentation was based on a report that Commissioner McNabb prepared for Clean Water Action, was released in January, 2008, received extensive press coverage, and helped promote a bill at the State House to create a Massachusetts Special Commission on Water Infrastructure Funding.

Commissioner McNabb has also been selected to present a paper at the American Water Works (AWWA) April 8-10, 2009 national Water Security Congress in Washington, DC on a potential security vulnerability in the national drinking water infrastructure, and to present a paper on the Cohasset Water Departments successful watershed protection program at the NEWWA Annual Meeting April 1-2, 2009 in Worcester, Mass.

SOURCE WATER ASSESSMENT & PROTECTION (SWAP) REPORT. On January 16, 2004 the Massachusetts Department of Environmental Protection (DEP) issued the final SWAP Report for the Cohasset Water Department. The SWAP report identifies the sources of Cohasset public drinking water supply, the protection areas around those supplies, inventories the potential sources of contamination, and makes a number of recommendations to improve protection of our water supplies. The Cohasset Water Commission, in its ongoing watershed protection program, following the 2002 *Surface Water Supply Protection Plan*, is planning on implementing the recommendations of the SWAP along with the many other water supply protection measures already underway. A copy of the SWAP Report is available at the Lily Pond Water Treatment Plant and on the Water Department web site, www.cohassetwater.org.

ENERGY SAVINGS. The Water Department has taken the following steps in 2008 and in the previous two years to increase energy efficiency and reduce electrical use:

- Installed new doors with R-value of 40 on garage. Old doors had no insulation 6-06
- Ten motors replaced to new high efficiency plus VFD rated motors. Savings 12 to 15%.
- Edison 13KV transformer replaced. New one has no PCB's and is 10% more efficient.
- Replaced 480/120-208 volt dry transformer to a high efficiency one. 35% savings.
- Replaced old boiler. The new boilers are 33% more efficient than old boiler.
- Replaced eight fan coil unit heaters. Old ones were plugged. New ones estimated 50% more efficient.
- All plant lighting was replaced with new ballast and bulbs. 8% more efficient.
- Replaced meter readers truck with new small efficient 5 cylinder vehicle. The motor is 50% more efficient.
- Implemented a new method of cleaning sludge lagoons. 50% more efficient.
- Replaced of de-humidifier. 60% more efficient.
- Currently looking into MASS HEFA contract for non-profits, savings on electric, gas contracts.

COOPERATION WITH OTHER TOWN DEPARTMENTS: The Cohasset Water Department cooperated with many other Town of Cohasset departments during 2007 including:

- The water department provided significant improvements to Town roadways, working cooperatively with the DPW and Sewer Commission as part of the Little Harbor Project.
- Provided a water supply for the veterans memorial and other parks at Lyons Memorial Park (North Main St and Joy Place) and various location along the Town Common.
- Assistance was provided to the DPW for a sidewalk/drainage improvement project on Forest Ave.
- Assisted DPW in locating buried pipes and manholes of a 90+ year old drainage system located on Jerusalem Road.
- The Water Department does billing for the Sewer Department.
- Quarterly Collaboration with Sewer Department for Billing
- Worked with DPW on multiple paving jobs, including South Main Street, Beechwood Street, Church Street, and Doane Street
- Assisted DPW in obtaining video camera equipment to inspect and document drainage pipe conditions
- Coordinated construction activities with various parties regarding road races, walks and other charity events

CONCLUSION: The strength and successes of today's Water Department have been possible because of the vision and extraordinary efforts of the Water Commission and staff in the 1970's, to conceptualize, design, permit, and build the Aaron River Reservoir and the Lily Pond Treatment Plant which turned Cohasset from a water-poor town to a water-rich town.

During 2008, the Cohasset Water Commission has implemented many major infrastructure investments, operational initiatives, land acquisition and landscaping projects which significantly enhance our ability to protect our water supply, treat, pump and deliver excellent drinking water and reliable water service for domestic and firefighting use for our customers - our ratepayers in Cohasset. We have accomplished these important achievements within our current rate structure, since our financial position remains excellent.

The Board of Water Commissioners and the Water Department would like to thank all the Town officials, boards, citizens, and committees who have supported and assisted us throughout 2008. We will continue to improve the water system in the coming years for the benefit of all customers and the Town of Cohasset.

Respectfully submitted,

BOARD OF WATER COMMISSIONERS

Glenn A. Pratt, Chairman
Nathaniel Palmer, Vice-Chairman
John K. McNabb, Jr., Clerk

2008 SEWER COMMISSION ANNUAL REPORT

2008 was a busy year for the Sewer Commission. The expansion of the town sewers to the Little Harbor/Atlantic Avenue area and expansion of the treatment plant by 50% to accommodate the additional flow from the new services. Work on these two construction projects was active throughout the year in combination with drainage and water system improvements. The treatment plant modifications were 90% complete by years end and the sewer collection system about 65% complete. The Deep Run/Rust Way portion of the North Cohasset Sewer District expansion was about 95% complete.

It is anticipated that the North Cohasset expansion will consume the remaining capacity allowed in the Town's Inter-Municipal Agreement (IMA) with the Town of Hull. The remaining work in North Cohasset is the construction of a flow metering manhole to better measure flows. It is anticipated that this expansion area will be given authorization to activate their services in early 2009. Information packages will be mailed to home owners describing connection procedures.

The portion of the collection system expansion which will flow to the Central Treatment Plant has progressed on or ahead of schedule and a concerted effort has been made to work around special Town events and to not significantly compromise traffic in the area. It is anticipated that connections to this system will be authorized during the summer of 2009 after a few additional months of operation with the new Wastewater Treatment Plant membranes.

The Sewer Commission has been preparing a Grinder Pump Solicitation which will maximize warranty, quality and performance, while reducing initial and long term costs for residents using the new low pressure sewer system. To further simplify the sewer connection process, the Commission has recently proposed the use of a Project-Wide Conservation Commission filing for sewer connections. This process will integrate the local regulatory responsibilities of the Sewer Commission, the Board of Health and the Conservation Commission to facilitate and expedite the connection process. It will also reduce user costs and insure local regulation compliance. Specifics regarding the integrated process should be finalized in early 2009.

The wastewater treatment plant (WWTP) upgrades and expansion continued throughout the year while still ensuring suitable operation of the existing processes to allow full compliance with all permits. Among other upgrades, new membranes were installed to allow the expansion of the plant's capacity from 300,000 to 450,000 gallons per day. The new membranes have been performing quite well and operational processes and procedures are being thoroughly tested prior to the connection of the new districts. The system will be operational for at least six months prior to connection authorization.

In past years peak flows (caused by severe rain fall and groundwater leakage into the old collection system piping) at the treatment plant had occasionally resulted in tank overflows. One of the steps taken to prevent or mitigate overflows is an extreme flow handling system. This system was installed at the facility and is in place to help prevent these occurrences in the future. Since the new membranes have been in place, at least two severe storm events, which resulted in very high flows, have been accommodated without any threat of overflow. The extreme flow handling system has not been called into play, but is available should it ever be needed.

An objection was raised about the location of the Little Harbor/Atlantic Avenue Sewer expansion project staging area on Jerusalem Road. This objection resulted in an appeal to the ZBA of a decision by the Town's Building Inspector which allowed the location of the staging area. The appeal was denied by the ZBA. The project staging area was screened and site trailers were painted to make the temporary structure less obtrusive. The central location of the staging area has provided significant benefit to the project and to expediting construction work.

Inflow and infiltration (I/I) flow monitoring work in prior years was expanded upon during 2008. Evidence of peak flows to the treatment plant during 2007 flood events in Jacob's Meadow provided direct evidence of freshwater influences to the proximate sewer system. Since prior mainline sewer restoration work has enhanced pipe integrity, service rehabilitation was targeted as the next step to help reduce I/I influences. The Commission has worked with Town Counsel to formulate a temporary license procedure to allow the Town to upgrade such services which are on private property. The Commission anticipates working with a few select sites in this area to act as service upgrade demonstration projects. These demonstration sites are anticipated to be implemented in early 2009 with wide-spread upgrade procedures being applied there-after. Other flood prone areas will be addressed after the Jacob's Meadow area is complete.

At the direction of the Sewer Commission, an analysis of historical flows and loadings by the consulting engineer, Coughlin Environmental Services, concluded in December that capacity existed for an additional 56 EDU's (Equivalent Dwelling Units) to be connected to the Central Sewer District. The Commission had been maintaining a "waiting list" for additional connections and will be contacting listed entities in early 2009 for allocation of these additional EDU's. Many of these additional EDU's are anticipated to help enhance re-development and new development activities within the Town Center.

John Beck, Chairman
Sean Cunning, Vice Chairman
Wayne Sawchuk, Clerk

2008 REPORT OF THE COHASSET HISTORICAL COMMISSION

The Cohasset Historical Commission submits with pleasure the annual report of projects worked on during 2008 for the Town of Cohasset.

According to the by-laws of the Commonwealth, "Local Historical Commissions are an important part of municipal government in Massachusetts. They are responsible for community-wide historic preservation planning. Historical Commissions advise elected officials and other boards on historic preservation issues, including zoning changes, the re-use of municipally owned historic buildings, and master planning or preservations of historic landscapes." (Taken from Massachusetts Historical Commission summary sheet)

Inventory Forms- Over 2000 historical properties in Cohasset have been inventoried and forms placed on file with the Massachusetts Historical Commission. All inventory listings can be accessed on-line by going to the Massachusetts Historical Commission website and going to "Search the MACRIS Database." Copies of the inventory forms are also available at the Paul Pratt Library and at the Historical Society's Pratt Building. This past year, MHC developed the policy that the photos for the inventory can be digitally transmitted to the State. This has helped to cut our expenses. Also, as a result of this change, we have been able to help the Assessor's office update their computerized property file.

National Register of Historic Places - The following properties and districts in Cohasset are listed on the National Register of Historic Places.

> Caleb Lothrop House, Summer Street (1976)
> Government Island Historic District, Lighthouse Lane (1994)
> Cohasset Common Historic District (1978, 1996)
> Josephine M Hagerty House, Atlantic Avenue (1997)
> Central Cemetery, Joy Place (2003)
> Bates Ship Chandlery/Maritime Museum, Elm Street (2003)
> Captain John Wilson House, Elm Street (2003)
> Pratt Building, South Main Street (2006)

Many other properties in town are eligible to be listed on the National Register. There was an inquiry about the historical significance of Woodside Cemetery. Upon further research, it was determined not to be eligible.

"State or federally involved" projects - We received communication concerning a marine archaeological survey for the Hull Offshore Wind Power Project in Hull. We also received communication on the documentation to be submitted to MHC to be used to determine the possible historical impact of the installation of the wind turbines at Crocker Lane.

2008 Report of the Cohasset Historical Commission Continued

Local Involvement –

   1. Government Island National Register site. The Historical Commission has a vested interest in this site and wants to keep this property historically correct. Thanks to the DPW, the area is cleared of weeds and mowed. We are working on the final phase at the Minot's Ledge Light Replica, which includes signage. In January, the New England Lighthouse Lovers (NELL) visited the site. People   from all over New England were able to tour the Replica and visit the Light Keeper's House. We all learned more about the workings of the lighthouse from Doug Bingham of the American Lighthouse Foundation. Next year (2010) celebrates the 150th anniversary of the lighting of Minot's Ledge Lighthouse.

   2. A member of the Historical Commission has been serving on the Town Hall Restoration Committee. David Farrag, chairman of the Town Hall Committee, presented the various plans for the Town Hall at our September meeting. We voted to send a letter of support to the MHC concerning funding through the Massachusetts Historic Tax Credit Project.

   3. We were advised of the plans for the 40B housing project at 25 Ripley Road. This property is on the State inventory listing.

   4. In conjunction with the Cohasset Historical Society, we reviewed Cohasset's connection to Abraham Lincoln with a representative from the Boston Globe in preparation for Lincoln's 200th birthday celebration in 2009.

   5. During the Cohasset Art Festival, we sold "1-4-3" Minot Light T-shirts, sweatshirts, license plates and tote bags. We have inventory in both youth and adult sizes. The proceeds from these sales are used towards work on the Replica.

As the town goes forward, Cohasset Historical Commission feels strongly that we need to be involved with the long-range planning of our very historic and picturesque town. In order to look and plan for the future it is necessary to study the past.

We thank the various town departments and committees that have helped and supported our goals. The Commission meets each month except during July and August. Meeting schedules are posted on at Town Clerk's office at Town Hall.

Respectfully Submitted,
Rebecca Bates-McArthur, Chairman
David Wadsworth, Secretary
Marilyn Morrison
Nathaniel Palmer
Hamilton Tewksbury

2008 REPORT FOR THE COMMITTEE ON TOWN HISTORY

This December just in time for Christmas sales, Cohasset's sixth history book was published, *Exploring Historic Cohasset* by Jacqueline Dormitzer. It is an eighty-page guidebook, printed four-color process throughout on coated paper with a mechanical wire-o binding which allows the book to lie flat for easy reference. It features ten walking and driving tours around Cohasset with brief descriptions about the historical sites on the tours. There is a brief Cohasset history at the end of the book. Kimberlee Alemian designed the guide. The price is an affordable $15.

All funding was provided by our book account. Sales outlets are primarily Buttonwood Books and the Cohasset Historical Society with books available from the Town Clerk's Office.

The Cohasset Mariner, as in the past, helped in promoting this new publication by running several articles about the new publication including a retrospective of the Town's history publications produced by the Committee on Town History. All the history books produced by the committee with the Town of Cohasset as publisher are the three companion narratives by E. Victor Bigelow, Bert Pratt and Jackie Dormitzer and the two anthologies edited by Jackie Dormitzer. All these books are registered with the Library of Congress and have been assigned ISBN numbers so that they can be identified on the web. The books have been designed so that they make a compatible set on a bookshelf.

The Committee on Town History will continue to remain active helping with the marketing of our books at the Village Fair and Art Show. There has been some discussion about publishing a history of the Native Americans in Cohasset.

Respectfully submitted,

Jim Hamilton, Chairman

2008 ANNUAL REPORT FOR THE PAUL PRATT MEMORIAL LIBRARY

The use of the Paul Pratt Memorial Library continued to grow and change with the times in FY2008. Checkouts of books, DVDs, new audio book formats and other materials increased by 7% from FY2007. We have expanded our resources to include more access to electronic sources, many of which are available from our web site. Our public computer terminals are more popular than ever, and the hits on our website (cohassetlibrary.org) reached 1.57 million, up 43% in the past year. The website is constantly being enriched, and a committee of staff and trustees succeeded in making it even more user-friendly than before.

The Children's Program, under the leadership of Children's Librarian Sharon Moody, continues to attract large numbers of children and their parents; attendance at the 135 story hours, summer programs and reading groups was up 18% from last year. For adults, we sponsored 69 events, administered by Reference Librarian Gayle Walsh, including films, author talks and book discussion groups. The Friends of the Cohasset Library funded and assisted in staffing most of these efforts. Our second town wide reading program, "Cohasset Reads Together," also was sponsored and funded by The Friends, and a third program is in the works for FY2009. The Friends, collaborating with the staff, expanded the outreach effort, with Melody Maurer joining Marjie Murphy to read and deliver books at Sunrise and Golden Living. Carolyn Coffey was elected the new chair of the Friends when Gail Flynn chose to step down after many years of service.

The Cohasset Library Trust, Inc., established in 2006 to manage and help grow the library's endowment, received a $100,000 gift from the South Shore Music Circus. To honor this generous donation, the Trust will invite an eminent author to lecture for the benefit of the entire Town. This year, endowment income contributed $32,748 to the operating budget.

The library was pleased to receive three more grants this year. The Net Lender grant was one again awarded to our library, because we loaned more materials than we borrowed. A second South Shore Music Circus grant of $10,000 helped us buy a self-checkout station to let patrons check out materials independently, and a $2500 grant from the LSTA is funding a preservation survey of our historic materials.

We chose to install a RFID (Radio Frequency Identification) system for all our library materials that will automate both check-out and inventory, saving valuable staff time and providing security as our circulation, services and number of visitors expand.

Our Director and our staff continue to provide an environment that promotes reading, learning and community activities seven days a week. We thank the town government and our loyal patrons for their support.

Respectfully submitted,

Stacey Weaver, Chair	Rodney Hobson	Sarah Pease
Elizabeth Baker	Marylou Lawrence	Barbara Power
Sheila Evans	Agnes McCann	Patience Towle

2008 REPORT OF THE RECREATION COMMISSION

It gives us great pleasure to report to residents, the activities of their Recreation Commission for 2008:

2008 marked a major transition for the Recreation Department. John (Jack) M. Worley retired after 32 years as Cohasset's first Recreation Director.

To put into words what Jack has meant to the town for over 32 years would not do him justice. His work started in a tiny office in the old wing of Town Hall in 1976 taking over a few programs that were run by volunteers to where it stands today as a model of efficiency admired by other communities.

His work attributes are too numerous to mention although his dedication and his kindness to others are unsurpassed. His fight to keep this 'non-essential' service alive in Cohasset through tough fiscal times inspired all those who knew him and worked for him. He has left his mark on all the programs he had his hand on from the summer program to the youth soccer and basketball programs.

His insight and input were invaluable over the years on all aspects of recreation in Cohasset. He championed the efforts to transform the old highway garage into a teen center for middle school students.

It is to this extent that not only Cohasset is indebted to his lifelong passion but the entire recreation world should applaud him for his efforts. If a man's life can be measured by the number of people he has an influence on, then Jack has no equal.

It is also with distinct pleasure that we are able to report that James (Ted) E. Carroll, Jr. was engaged May 1, 2008 as Director of Recreation.

Ted has been associated with the Cohasset, Hingham and Hanover Recreation Departments during the past 26 years. As a resident of Cohasset, Ted began working for Cohasset Recreation part time, while still in High School. Ted's involvement with the Cohasset Recreation has ranged from Sports Coordinator, Summer Playground Director, to elected Commissioner.

Having spent 13 years with Hingham Recreation Department, he most recently was the Recreation Administrator for the town of Hanover. As our newly appointed Director, Ted brings with him years of experience in other communities, coupled with a firm grasps and understanding of Cohasset's Recreation operations.

Several new initiatives the Department has taken on include a new website www.cohassetrec.com. This website and the online registration tool will make us more efficient and streamline registrations.

During the past few months we have also increased our efforts to transform the Teen Center/Garage into a full time Recreation Center. With this endeavor, will be our ability to offer a variety of programs and services at the facility, while also functioning as a teen center for Cohasset youngsters.

During the year, approximately 4,000 individuals of all ages participated in a variety of structured programs, activities and events. While budget restrictions persist, our latitude of use of the Revolving Account Fund for 100% Self-Supporting Programs are continuing under this financial mechanism causing no impact upon taxpayers. In fact, via the Recreation Commission's policy to charge an Administrative Service Fee charge to all R.A.F. sponsored programs, taxpayers are reimbursed for the cost of the recreation budget. That is, revenues produced via Administrative Service Fee's, coupled with budget sponsored program fees, service fees and charges helps reimburse taxpayers for the budget of their Recreation Commission. Only revenue on deposit in the General Fund can be considered recapitalization revenue.

During Fiscal Year 2008, ending June 30, 2008 the Recreation Commission produced for the General Fund $98,385.62. Over $5,000.00 was produced for use by the Commission via grants and matching grant funds and donations. Concurrently, $31,926.96 was transacted via Revolving Account Funds for 100% Self-Supporting programs via fees charged participants for a variety of services. Approximately another $300,000.00 was transacted via other and direct self-supporting financial systems during F.Y. 2008, manifesting over $435,000.00 of recreational services to residents. These figures do not include the thousands of man-hours that are annually donated by hundreds of residents, in support of a variety of program operations.

Due to the financial difficulties town government faces during Fiscal Year 2008/2009, the Recreation Commission continues to stay about 75% self-supporting via revenue dedicated to the General Fund of the Town only. Via fee charges and administrative service fees to contractors to the Commission our intent will be to recapitulate about 75% of our budget costs back to taxpayers. It is our intent to do this with as little financial impact upon users of our services as possible.

Municipal recreation is for the benefit of all residents and we continue to direct our efforts towards assurance of equal access and opportunity to the entire community. To this end, a specific and calculated portion of revenue was not collected this year from residents who were temporarily unable to pay full fee charges for services. In many instances time was volunteered in lieu of full fee payments, benefiting the department and participants of programs.

We continue our effort to increase the number and types of programs offered. Many of the programs will be made available via contracted services thru our Revolving Account Fund for 100% Self –Supporting Services. Via this method, the per capita fee collected will be collectively utilized to operate the programs financially, while 15% of the gross revenue collected will be deposited back to the General Fund of the Town, hence, back to tax payers.

Programming represents only one aspect of the responsibilities, duties, and functions as prescribed and conferred upon the Recreation Commission by both Massachusetts General Laws and By-Laws of the Town. Continuing efforts are focused upon upgrading and renovating existing outdoor recreational facilities under jurisdiction of the Commission. Often times these undertakings are coordinated via a lending of both public and privately solicited resources and efforts, easing taxpayers' burden.

Numerous town departments and officials have continued to support our effort in this area for which we remain enormously grateful. Further, we remain indebted to many private and civic groups for their magnanimous efforts and resources. Via the efforts of the Cohasset Basketball Boosters Club and Cohasset Soccer Club, the community is well served beyond the operations of sports programs only.

The seven member, elected board of the Recreation Commissioner's, volunteer their services to the Town and department meeting regularly in order to discuss a wide-spectrum of topics relative to the leisure needs and pursuits of all residents. Further, the Commissioner's establish policy, and provide departmental direction, support, and assistance. Each meeting is publicly posted at least one week prior to date and residents are cordially invited to attend and participate in any meeting. Essential to our proper function, and absolutely vital towards success, is the ability to remain responsive to the dynamic Community needs. We consider your input and feedback our most important source of guidance.

Degree of community interest and support for recreational and leisure-time services can directly be measured by two essential factors. First and most logically, interest is measured by the level of participation by residents in various services. Secondly and perhaps as important, interest and support is readily recognizable by the extraordinary numbers of volunteers who donate their time, effort and expertise in conduct with a number of our programs, events and activities. Cohasset is indeed very fortunate to have many extremely talented residents willing to lend a hand and share their particular expertise.

The Recreation Commission wishes to acknowledge gratitude to the many individuals, civic and business organizations, school and sport's groups, Town boards, committees and departments who have lent their support and assistance in our efforts to best serve the recreational and leisure needs of residents of all ages. While too numerous to mention each by name, none are forgotten and all are sincerely appreciated and thanked.

Respectfully yours,

James H. Richardson, Chairman
Lillian M. Curley, Vice-Chairperson
Lisa L. Lojacono, Secretary
Abigail H. Alves
Anthony J. Carbone
Daniel J. Martin
Roseanne M. McMorris

James E. Carroll, Jr., Director

GOVERNMENT ISLAND ADVISORY COMMITTEE – 2008 ANNUAL REPORT

The Island's 62nd birthday – 2008. The Town through the Board of Selectmen bought the Island – 7.4 acres – from the Government for $29,000.00 or about, $3,900.00 per acre. The area consists of ledge woods, shoreline and graded areas to be used by the fisherman, sailing club members, townspeople (YOU) and visitors to the Town.

Our activities throughout the year call for sporadic meetings to discuss/solve a current question. This meeting schedule may change.

The normal maintenance of the Island goes on with good cooperation between Carl Sestito, DPW Superintendant, his crew and the GIAC.

Please, as we have said many times, take some time to visit the area with your family. Enjoy it, absorb it, and drink in some history that is right here in your harbor – your backyard.

Respectively submitted,

Hamilton T. Tewksbury, Chairman
Constance M. Ashfar
Lorren S. Gibbons, Harbormaster
Rebecca Bates-McArthur

2008 COHASSET TOWN HALL RESTORATION AND RENOVATION COMMITTEE

The committee had a busy year in 2008. The committee completed and presented the feasibility study that was procured by the town with funds from the Community Preservation Committee. The feasibility study included a historic, building code, electrical, structural analysis of the old portion of the town hall. The committee also sent out a questionnaire to the town hall employees who work in the old section. After interviews and investigations, plans were created to update, restore, and renovate the town hall. The current hall suffers from extreme distress due to deferred maintenance. Bathrooms are not functional, windows are broken, most all systems are past their useful life, the hall has no sprinkler system, and there is little use of the auditorium which used to be used for banquets, meetings, and other uses in the past.

The committee with the assistance of the Architect Carr, Lynch and Sandell created two different plans for design to restore and renovate the town hall. Plan A was to keep the hall generally the same but due to the current configuration. Due to the tresses on the 2nd floor the it severely limited functionality of space and does not solve handicap access issues. Plan B was to put the town offices on the 1st floor and Auditorium on the 2nd floor. This would allow for increased and functional office space, bathrooms the addition of a much needed meeting room. The auditorium would be easier to install cable television cameras and a studio. A small kitchen would be placed in the basement and an extra room for town hall record storage would be created. Copies and plans of the feasibility study are available in the Library, Town Clerk's Office, Selectman's office and the Cohasset Historical Society for the public to review. The Town Hall Restoration and Renovation Committee voted unanimously for Plan B. The Selectman also voted 4-0 with one abstention for Plan B as well.

The Committee in the Spring of 2008 applied and received $300,000 in funds from the Community Preservation Committee to begin restoration and renovation for the outside of the Hall. This is subject but not limited to the windows, gutters, chimney, pilasters and drainage. These were immediate needs that will not interfere with any future construction inside the hall. It was learned through the feasibility process that the gutters were undersized (they were residential size being used for commercial) and emptied pushing water into the foundation and the basement when flooding occurs. Plans for these restorations were created especially for the windows in which a full restoration will occur. Due to their historic nature, the windows were schematically designed so that the winning bidder would have a specific set of plans for restoration that would be performance based (meaning the windows will be able to last for decades). A set of those plans are at the Selectman's office and the Cohasset Historical Society (for future generations when updating needs to occur). The winning bidder for this project was Campbell Construction which had previously completed historic renovation projects on the Martha's Vineyard Edgartown Lighthouse as well as other historic properties.

As a part of this process, history regarding the hall has been uncovered. All the windows have been dated as to their installation. All are either the originals from 1857 or from the 1928 renovation. Additionally, different architectural features were discovered as well as a digested report from the town hall reports for every which is listed in the historical section of the study.

In the Special Town Meeting in November, a resolution was presented to allow the Selectman to accept grants, tax credits and monies for the furtherance of this project. The resolution was passed unanimously. While only a resolution it was important to get approval from the town for the grant process. While the financial world has changed due to the world economic crisis in the Fall, there are still funding authorities that the committee will continue to apply to in 2009.

For 2009 the committee will see through the restoration and renovation of the outside which is continuing through Spring of 2009 and will file the necessary paperwork with Federal, Commonwealth and Non-Profits for grants, tax credits and monies to see the project through.

David H. Farrag, Chairman
Werner Diekman
Donna McGee
Lisa Pratt
David Wadsorth

SOUTH SHORE REGIONAL VOCATIONAL TECHNICAL SCHOOL DISTRICT
2008 COHASSET TOWN REPORT

On Wednesday, September 4th, 2008, Charles D. Homer began his first full year as Superintendent-Director, welcoming 587 students including 165 for the class of 2012. South Shore continues to offer quality vocational technical education to the Towns of Cohasset, Scituate, Norwell, Hanson, Hanover, Whitman, Rockland and Abington for the past four decades.

This year South Shore had 27 seniors qualify for the John and Abigail Adams Scholarships for scoring in the top 25% of their class. As educational demands continue to soar, so do the program offerings to keep in line with economic trends. South Shore students continue to excel in meeting state and national vocational and academic standards before them. As technology continues to change, so must the technical offerings in order to better prepare students to become successful in their communities.

Extracurricular activities continue to expand each year. Approximately 50% of the student population participates in an athletic or extracurricular activity each year. Our Drama Club continues to offer a Dinner Theater presentation each spring with sellout seating. As well, out athletic teams continue to compete at state level competitions in various sports each season.

The Commonwealth's School Building Assistance is continuing to work with us in order to replace our roof and windows. The estimated cost of this project is projected to be $2.5 million dollars for a building that opened in 1962. As we become more involved in this construction project, we will be meeting with local officials in or eight member communities.

The South Shore School District is represented by eight appointed School Committee members from each town's Selectmen's Office:

Robert Heywood, Chairman – Hanover
Gerald Blake, Vice Chairman – Rockland
John Manning – Scituate
Daniel Salvucci – Whitman

Robert Molla – Norwell
James Rodick – Hanson
Kenneth Thayer – Cohasset
Lenwood Thompson – Abington

Currently 2 students from the Town of Cohasset will graduate this June 5th:
John Emanuello
Nicholas Silvia

South Shore would like to thank our eight member towns for their continued support over the years. Our goal will be to continue to train students to be life-long career technical students who in turn will be successful back in their own communities. We understand the importance of fiscal responsibility in our district, especially in tough economic times and we will work with our member communities and continue to offer the best vocational opportunities possible.

Respectfully submitted,
Kenneth E. Thayer
Town Representative
South Shore Regional School District Committee

"Where the mission is to continue the commitment to excellence"

Teaching and learning are what great schools are all about. The focus of the Cohasset Public Schools continues to be on the classroom and maximizing student performance. The goal is to maintain the overall strength of the school system while recognizing continued local and general economic challenges.

Despite these difficult fiscal times, our students are doing very well by a wide variety of quantitative measures. Indicators of progress this past year include:

- SAT (mean increases) over 1 year
  Verbal scores from 549 to 557
  Math scores from 562 to 581
  Writing scores from 560 to 566

- District AYP ELA
  From 94.4 (2007) to 94.3 (2008)
  District AYP MATH
  From 89.8 (2007) to 90.5 (2008)

We are very proud of all of our students and their outstanding academic accomplishments. We appreciate a hard working student body, supportive parents, a dedicated faculty and staff and a School Committee committed to maintaining high standards. Together we can:

- Challenge all students to Proficiency and Beyond
- Close Achievement Gaps Where They Exist and
- Function as a Professional Learning Community

In the Fall, many members of the class of 2008 found themselves heading to some of the most prestigious colleges and universities in the country. They are a credit to the Cohasset community.

The school department is most appreciative of the continued fiscal support of the Cohasset community. The community support is needed more than ever if we are to reduce class size, remain current in the curriculum, and prepare students with 21st century skills. A special note of thanks to the Cohasset Education Foundation, the Parent Student Organization and the various Booster clubs, who supported our budget in so many ways this past year. You provided the support and the resources that enabled us to meet or surpass the high expectations we set in 2008.

We recognize this year a number of retirees from the Cohasset Public Schools who have moved on to the next phase of their lives. Retiring after 35 years of service in education, with 6 years to the children of Cohasset, as an English teacher and Spinnaker Advisor is Ms. Christine Berman. Also retiring after 24 years of service as a guidance counselor at the elementary and high school level is Mr. Edward Leonard. After 26 years of service as a High School Science teacher and Department Head is Mr. David Magnussen. Joining him in retirement after 19 years of service as an English Language Arts teacher at the Deer Hill and Middle Schools is Mrs. Nancy Magnussen. And finally, after 37 years of service at Deer Hill is Joan Cassiani. We congratulate them all and wish them well.

Our children are the future of our community. We hope to continue to partner with the Cohasset community to meet the educational needs of all of our children as together we accomplish our mission to "continue the commitment to excellence."

Respectfully submitted
Denise M. Walsh, Ed.D.
Superintendent of Schools

Individual building reports for 2008 will follow from the principal of Osgood, Deer Hill, and Cohasset Middle-High School.

As the year 2009 begins, the Deer Hill School Community looks forward to continuing toward achievement of our goals in the Cohasset Public Schools 2004-2009 Strategic Plan. The spring and fall of 2008 were very exciting times for us at Deer Hill. As of October 1, 2008, enrollment at Deer Hill School was 356 students, an increase of 6 students from the same date in the previous year. Class sizes ranged from 19 to 25 in sixteen classrooms, grades three, four, and five. Teaching and support staff remained consistent with the prior year with two notable exceptions: Mrs. Joan Cassiani retired in June, 2008 after thirty-seven years of dedicated service and Mrs. Katherine Penwell joined our fifth grade team. Mrs. Kathryn Brooks was hired for the role of Math Specialist for both Deer Hill and Osgood Schools.

We join the district in promoting our commitment to excellence in all aspects of teaching and learning. Our faculty has enjoyed extensive professional development in inquiry-based science education, writing instruction, elementary level mathematics instruction, and interactive white board ("Promethean Board") technology. We have strengthened our literacy program by organizing all resources available to our students and teachers in one central location under the supervision of our Literacy Specialist. Materials are now available to fit a number of literacy functions in an easily accessed format, and our collection of mentor texts and leveled classroom sets continues to grow.

In the spring of 2008 Deer Hill School was a recipient of a competitive grant from the Massachusetts Department of Education to promote instruction for students who are Gifted and Talented. We were able to send a team of teachers and one administrator to the University of Massachusetts in Boston to study Gifted and Talented Education in a graduate level course. One outcome of that training was a plan for an objective, multi-facted system of identification of students who would benefit from specialized instruction. Another outcome was the expansion of our schoolwide enrichment program, EMC^3, to promote pedagogy consistent with Gifted and Talented Education. Many new programs have been designed to continue from fall to spring, allowing students the opportunity to delve deeply into an area of strong interest. Our enrichment programs fall within three broad areas of learning standards from the Massachusetts Curriculum Frameworks: Science, Technology, Engineering and Mathematics (STEM), Humanities (including literature and visual arts), and Civics and Government (including Student Leadership and Community Service). Favorites from prior years, such as Great Books and Studio Art, are still available. Others, including Chemical Reactions, School Newspaper, and Drama, have become new student favorites.

We continue to enjoy tremendous support from the Deer Hill School community and the Cohasset community at large. In the spring we received extensive funding from the Cohasset Education Foundation for a Science, Technology, Engineering, and Mathematics (STEM) lab. This exciting learning environment – complete with laboratory furniture, inquiry based science kits, scientific equipment, and state of the art technology – has kindled a passion for science in our students that textbook-based instruction can't match. Our teachers enjoy using the digital presenters purchased for us by the CEF every day in a wide variety of ways. Our generous PSO has sponsored outstanding enrichment programs for our students, including multicultural musical presentations, scientific exploration, and historical re-enactments. We are continuously grateful to our Deer Hill PSO for their sponsorship of so many enrichment programs, fundraising, teacher grants, volunteer coordination, and staff recognition. Our parents and guardians have come out in droves to support our students' academic, artistic, musical, and dramatic efforts.

In order to inform our instructional practices and programming decisions, we continue to implement a comprehensive assessment system. We assess our students in major subject areas using formal and informal measures regularly throughout the year in order to be current in our understanding of student learning needs. We also participate with districts across the state in the Massachusetts Comprehensive Assessment System (MCAS). In 2008, Deer Hill MCAS scores were once again above the state average in all three grade levels in all subject areas and the district once again made Adequate Yearly Progress (AYP) as defined by the Department of Elementary and Secondary Education (DESE, formerly DOE). In grade three, 2008 scores reported *75%* in *Above Proficient* or *Proficient* in Reading and in Mathematics, *68%* were either *Above Proficient* or *Proficient*. In grade four, *73%* of students scored in the *Advanced* or *Proficient* category in English Language Arts (ELA) and *65%* of the students scored in either *Advanced* or *Proficient* in Mathematics. In grade five, *80%* of students scored in the *Advanced* or *Proficient* category in ELA, *77%* in mathematics, and *80%* in Science and Technology. Overall, these scores represent the steady progress Deer Hill students are making as they achieve the rigorous learning standards of the Massachusetts State Curriculum Frameworks.

As we move forward, we are mindful of our responsibility to promote in our students those skills necessary for success in the twenty-first century. Among the most important of these are communication, creativity, critical thinking, problem solving, self-direction, and information skills. We look forward to a renewal of our History and Social Sciences Curriculum and the examination of updated textbooks. We will revise our report card to reflect the performance criteria and learning standards that form the heart of our instruction. In the spirit of continuous improvement, we are reframing our academic program planning to reflect levels of rigor and relevance found in world-class elementary level programs. Our students and staff will continue to work together in an environment that exemplifies respect for one another in a professional learning community. Under the leadership of our Superintendent and School Committee, and with the strong support of our Curriculum and Instruction Director, Student Services Director, Business Manager, Facilities Director, Technology Coordinator and our parent and community groups, we will continue our commitment to excellence at the Deer Hill School.

Respectfully submitted,
Jennifer deChiara, Ph.D.
Principal, Deer Hill School

ANNUAL TOWN REPORT
2008
JOSEPH OSGOOD SCHOOL

The Joseph Osgood School celebrated the 10th anniversary of its opening in September! A festive Open House for parents was planned with a video of 420 children singing and celebrating in their party hats! We have much to celebrate at the Osgood—a beautiful facility, up-to-date curriculum and instructional materials, a highly qualified staff, and supportive parents.

Our school community successfully worked together in 2008 to achieve the goals of our School Improvement Plan. Efforts to improve communication led to an increased number of informational programs for parents in the areas of curriculum and assessment, student behavior, and district policies. In collaboration with the Deer Hill School, our reading specialist and members of the faculty presented a program to inform parents about assessments and how they are used to plan instruction. District school psychologists presented a program for parents to promote positive student behaviors, and adjustment counselors planned an additional evening event with the Character Education Committee to discuss the new district Bullying Policy. Parent forums and coffees on other topics of interest were also held during the school year to discuss curriculum and student support services.

Our goal to promote high expectations for all was met through initiatives to meet the individual needs of students. An assessment plan was implemented that assisted in identifying needs and in planning programs to challenge each student to work according to his/her potential. Osgood faculty enthusiastically implemented a revised Everyday Math program and new science and social studies curricula. Teachers also participated in professional development activities that supported new programs, writing, and technology. Additional professional development activities included a focus on how to prepare students for the 21st century.

The importance of 21st century skills will continue to be our focus as Massachusetts looks at new education reform strategies in a plan developed by educators, business leaders, and civic leaders to prepare students for a world economy and global society. We are working to provide STEM (Science, Technology, Engineering, Math) opportunities in the early years that will create excitement and interest for future generations. Achieve Now is a new interactive technology tool that is being utilized to create that excitement and interest. It is a hand-held, mobile instructional program that provides enrichment and extends learning. The generosity of the Cohasset Education Foundation (CEF) has assisted us in providing additional learning opportunities. Osgood students and staff are greatly benefiting from the donation of a new computer lab and LCD monitors for classroom computers. We are also enjoying the benefits of curriculum enrichment and supplemental instructional materials provided through Parent School Organization (PSO) donations.

Progress towards school and district safety goals were met in 2008 with the continued support of the Cohasset Police in the practice of safety drills. The Department assisted us in planning and following guidelines for preparedness in the School Safety Plan. Playground safety and student supervision were additional focus areas along with increased paraprofessional staff training.

Our goal to meet present and future needs identified by our School Council presented many challenges as we developed a school budget to maintain services. Tuition funding along with state grant funding have allowed us to continue to provide a high quality full-day kindergarten program with optimal class size and excellent instructional materials. Our integrated preschool program for three and four-year-olds continues to be a great success, and we have developed a Primary Learning Center program for our Cohasset children with severe special needs. Another program about which we are very excited is the COMPASS Program. We have reorganized our before and after school program and have increased learning opportunities for participating children through integrated thematic activities and technology.

We are very proud of our accomplishments and thankful for the support of the community as we celebrate the first decade in the "new" Osgood School. The Osgood faculty and staff look forward to preparing our children for the revolutionary changes that will occur in the next decade!

Respectfully submitted
Janet Sheehan, Principal
Joseph Osgood School

The year 2008 was a year of reflection on essential needs for student success for the Cohasset Middle-High School community, with a "Breaking Ranks II" focus on Middle and High School reform by all staff, a focus on operational efficiencies and on curriculum review and renewal. In the process, the school saw a number of accomplishments in 2008, including more academic success for our students, restructuring of the Middle School, and continued high levels of participation and achievement in co-curricular activities.

The Class of 2008 produced 79 graduates, 100% of whom earned competency determinations according to Department of Education standards. Eighteen members of the class were recognized as members of the National Honor Society, twenty-three graduates earned eligibility for the John and Abigail Adams Scholarship Award. Sixty-five students also earned Stanley Z. Koplik Certificates of Mastery by the Massachusetts Department of Education for scoring advanced on at least one of their grade 10 MCAS tests and at least proficient in the other. Further, 91% of the graduating class enrolled in various public and private four-year colleges and another 4% plan to attend two-year college or preparatory school for a total of 95% of the Class of 2008 continuing to further their education in some capacity.

Cohasset High School continues to exceed expectations for adequate yearly progress, as defined by the Massachusetts Department of Education and the federal No Child Left Behind legislation. Our SAT scores remain highly competitive when compared to surrounding communities, showing gains in overall scores from previous years. The school offers credit in nine different Advanced Placement electives with our total student enrollment up 21% from the previous year of 194 students enrolled to 235. Results on AP exams demonstrate the preparation and success of the 118 students who participated in 194 exams, on which 148 (approximately 76%) were graded to be eligible for college credit. Four students received National Merit Scholarship commendations in recognition of their performance on the PSAT.

Our students distinguish themselves as they participate in a number of our extra-curricular and co-curricular activities as well, including athletics, band, chorus, drama, journalism, student council, and community service. Our programs continue to excel because of the commitment, dedication, and hard work of our students and staff. Some examples of this include Luke Brewer's participation in the Massachusetts Art All-State program, Sarah Trahon's participation in the South Shore Arts Festival, and numerous pieces of student art from both the middle and high school for consideration in the prestigious Boston Globe Scholastic Art awards program. The 7th Annual "Eat Your Art" exhibit was a giant success featuring edible art from grades K-12, and adults from the community. On the musical side of the arts William Choi was selected for Senior District and SEMSBA Orchestra along with Lauren Mack and Elizabeth Crawford for SEMSBA Chorus. The band and chorus also received top honors at the Creative Arts Workshop (CAWS) in New York. The student body, under the direction of Bryan Marks and Stephanie Moriarty, performed "West Side Story" in the fall, featuring Jennifer Magruder, Ian Porter, Ellie Baumgarten, August Oddleifson, and Andrew Bell. Additionally, both the Cohasset Middle School and High School participated in the Massachusetts Theater Guild's one act play competitions for middle and high schools throughout Massachusetts. The Middle School performed "The Ever After" by Nathan Hartswick, and earned a silver medal. Individual outstanding performance awards were awarded to Trevor Schramm, Isabelle Robinson, and Robert Nahill. The high school's production of Alan Haehnel's "A Whole New You" earned State Semi-finalist status with three awards for excellence in acting to Sally Meehan, Ellie Baumgarten, and Tara Goodwin.

Athletically, Cohasset High School ice hockey and girl's basketball teams qualified for post season tournament play. The wrestling and swim teams had a number of individuals qualify for state tournament action with wrestler Steve Hurlbut earning South Sectional finalist and Jack Murphy winning a South Sectional championship. The boys swim and dive team won the Patriot League. The winter season was highlighted by the girl's basketball team winning the South Shore League, South Sectional, and State Championship. Captain Sammi Lehr was recognized by Fox 25 News as Player of the Year, and Coach John Levangie earned Coach of the Year recognition from the Massachusetts Basketball Coaches Association. In the spring, Cohasset High School's lacrosse teams qualified for the state tournament, with the boy's team advancing to state finalists. The team received numerous individual awards and two young men, Charles Czerkawski and Mark Flibbotte earned High School All-American honors from USA Lacrosse. The boy's baseball team won the South Shore League title for the first time in 49 years. In addition, the boy's and girl's tennis teams qualified for post season play, with the girl's team winning the South Sectional title and coach Gigi Meehan being recognized as the Boston Globe Coach of the Year.

This past fall, the Cohasset High School girl's soccer team qualified for the state tournament and enjoyed its best postseason ever, as they finished as Division 3 South Sectional champions. Coach Deb Beal was recognized as the Boston Globe Division II Coach of the Year, and Maggie McGoldrick earned Boston Globe and Boston Herald All-Scholastic recognition. Maggie, along with Sarah Coggins and Torey Hart were recognized as Eastern Massachusetts All-Stars. Throughout the year a number of students earned league all-star recognition and others were recognized as Patriot Ledger All-Scholastic (4 this past fall alone) for their sport. The Athletic Program distinguished itself by finishing 7th in the Boston Globe All Scholastics Award for Division 4 with a 60% overall winning percentage in all of our varsity sports.

The school bell rang for the last time for science department head and teacher Dave Magnussen, middle school English teacher Nancy Magnussen, high school English teacher Christine Berman, and high school guidance counselor Ed Leonard, who after many years of distinguished service to the Cohasset community, chose to retire. We wish them well and appreciate their service. A number of staffing changes were made throughout the summer in preparation for the new school year. We welcomed in 2008, 5 new teachers at the middle school as well as 3 new teachers and a guidance counselor at the high school who come to us with outstanding skills. These new staff members join a faculty that numbers 69 to serve the student population at the Middle-High School where there are currently 310 students in the Middle School and 382 at Cohasset High School.

Staff members have taken on initiatives for school improvement such as curriculum review and renewal, differentiated instruction, bully prevention education, and student performance analysis. Dr. John Wands, joins Ms. Stephanie Wooley by volunteering to assist in the development of future MCAS English Language Arts and Mathematics tests by the Massachusetts Department of Education, while another staff member, Mrs. Peg Jordan continues to serve, along with Dr. Wands, as a reader for the AP Spanish and AP English tests respectively. The school community has further benefited from additional financial support provided by the Parent School Organization and the Cohasset Education Foundation, whose efforts have enabled the purchase and expansion of the middle school technology with ActivBoard and ActivStudio hardware and software for a number of classrooms and continued opportunities for distance learning through Virtual High School. These initiatives, coupled with the dedicated staff and motivated student body have combined to better prepare our students with the 21st century skills they will need after they graduate from Cohasset High School.

Respectfully submitted,
Joel Antolini, Principal
Cohasset Middle-High School

CPSIA information can be obtained
at www.ICGtesting.com
Printed in the USA
BVHW04*0746280818
525723BV00019B/106/P